MW01616303

See the Good/God in Everything

VOL. 1

See the Good/God in Everything

VOL. 1

The Secret to Inspire
Gratitude, Build Hope and
Find Joy in Every Day

BY REGINA CLIFFORD

First published in Australia by Lightning Strikes Press in 2024.
Lightning Strikes PO Box 133 Mosman Park, WA, 6912, Australia.

The events and conversations in this book have been set down to the best of
the author's ability, although some names and details have been changed to protect
the privacy of individuals.

For more information, address: info@reginaclifford.com.

First paperback edition: April 2024

Editor: Jason Pettus / Cover Design: Ian Koviak
Interior Design: Morgane Leoni / Author Photo: Deanne Whyte
Illustrations: shabanashoukat49 - Adobe Stock

ISBN 978-0-9756636-1-5 (paperback)
ISBN 978-0-9756636-3-9 (hardback)
ISBN 978-0-9756636-2-2 (ebook)
ISBN 978-0-9756636-0-8 (audio)

A catalogue record for this book is available from the National Library of Australia.

www.reginaclifford.com

**All Bible quotes in this book are from the New King James Version
unless otherwise stated.**

To the One with whom all
things are possible.

To John, Victoria, and Charlotte—
you are my greatest joys.

To my parents and brothers—
for your constant love and support.

Table of Contents

PREFACE

NEW MOM

WIFE

MARRIAGE

FORGIVENESS

FAMILY

BEING A WOMAN

INFERTILITY

BLENDED FAMILIES

FRIENDS

GROWING UP

Preface

It was February 2020 and my daughter was two months old. Being a parent was so different to anything I had ever done before. No amount of education, travel, or experience could prepare me for it. I was an extremely anxious first-time mom. I was nervous to take her outside, or nervous if my husband wasn't around, or nervous if I was doing things right. I had this ridiculous baby bag that, I kid you not, was the size of carry-on luggage. I filled it up with as many things as I could possibly think of for every short outing we took. I remember we went to a café once and this bag was an embarrassment. I was embarrassed to have it. It was so big and bulky to handle, and so full of baby stuff that it would take me ages to find what I was looking for. These were the days I used to travel with a thermometer and baby medicine...you know, just in case. Honestly, if something had happened, we could just drive straight home; we never went far from our house in those first few months anyways. But alas, I was paranoid. I remember shortly after that café incident that I thought, why didn't someone tell me I don't need a huge baby bag! I barely needed a specialised baby bag in the first place, let alone a huge one.

That was when I started writing this book. I could see in my parenting life, in my marriage and with my extended family, there were so many incidents (present and in hindsight) in which there were life lessons. In thinking and writing about these lessons, I could also see that the goodness of God was in my life constantly, and if I just changed my view on my situations and was aware of how good things actually were, my whole spirit would change. There is good/God in your story too.

NEW MOM

Days of Fulfilment, and Not

There are days when life with your new baby seems amazing. You're so filled with love and joy, and all the mess and work of a new baby seems worth it. And then there are days when it's just plain hard. Your baby isn't sleeping, you've got more vomit on you than you've ever had at any other time in your life, you haven't showered in days, and you're living off of carbs and whatever junk food you can grab when you have a free moment. Even saying there are days of fulfilment is incorrect; moments of fulfilment is more like it. There are moments of fulfilment when your baby smiles at you or falls asleep so peacefully in your arms; and then there are hard moments, such as trying to stop a crying baby in the middle of the night, or wondering how in the world you have your child's vomit all over your face. It happens. The way I see it, a baby can be considered either a blessing or a burden. If I'm convinced my baby is a blessing, then those hard hours, days, and moments will be slightly easier to deal with, and I have hope for better things to come.

Lord, help me to love more. Help me to see that my child is a gift from You, even in the hard moments. Help me in my weaknesses and especially during times that seem difficult and I feel like I'm running on empty. Help me to put things in perspective, and to choose to see the good things in my life.

> *'So do not fear, for I am with you; do not be dismayed,*
> *for I am your God. I will strengthen you and help you;*
> *I will uphold you with my righteous right hand.'*
> —ISAIAH 41:10 (NIV)

Fed Is Best

I was raised being taught that 'breast is best' for goodness knows how long, so obviously I had planned on breastfeeding my daughter when she was born. I was well-educated on the pros and cons of breastmilk and formula, and I took online lactation classes. Even my midwife/doula was there to support me. What I didn't read about was that I may need to supplement my baby with formula in the early newborn days, and as well that I may feel bad about it. And I did. My milk didn't come in until close to the ninth day after birth, and it was a long nine days with a newborn. I can't tell you the torture, pain, and guilt I went through (not to mention the latching issues, the blistered and bleeding nipples, and the almost non-stop baby crying). It was when we were at home and the baby was barely having any wet diapers that we made the ultimate decision to supplement her ASAP. Luckily the hospital gave us premixed formula to take home, which we did. No matter if I wanted to feed my daughter breast milk, she needed food, and she needed food now! Breastfeeding can be extremely hard, but feeding my baby is more important than the means in which she's fed.

Lord, help me be the best mother I can be to my child. Guide me by Your Holy Spirit, and even when things don't go as I had planned, help me to be flexible and not to get worried or anxious, knowing that You know all the details of my life as a mother.

> *'And we know that all things work together for good to those who love God, to those who are the called according to His purpose.'*
> —ROMANS 8:28

See the Good/God in Everything

I Never Paid Much Attention to Moms Before...

Being a mother changes your view on other mothers. Honestly, I had never really paid attention to mothers before. I was a single lady for a very long time; and while, yes, I had some friends who were mothers, I just assumed mothers were like single ladies but slightly different because they had a baby. But when I had my daughter, I just saw mothers in a whole new light. After I had my daughter, whenever I saw another mother, I would have such an extreme and heartfelt respect for them being a mother. I mean, first there's pregnancy, then labour and delivery, and then the job of raising a child. It blows my mind how irrevocably having a child changes you. I salute all you mothers out there.

Lord, thank You for mothers and fathers. Give them Your wisdom in raising their children in Your ways. Lord, help us to remember that children are Your inheritance, and help us to raise them in ways that give You the glory.

> *'Behold, children are a heritage from the Lord, the fruit of the womb is a reward. Like arrows in the hand of a warrior, so are the children of one's youth. Happy is the man who has his quiver full of them; they shall not be ashamed, but shall speak with their enemies in the gate.'*
> —PSALM 127:3–5

Everything Changes

The minute a baby is born, everything changes. You've dramatically shifted from a couple to a family with Mommy, Daddy, and little baby. This affects everything, from no longer being able to eat together without one of you holding a baby, to having to schedule in quality time with your spouse when the baby is asleep. Everything changes in an instant. It's amazing how everything about your life shifts, once a baby arrives on the scene. I was lucky the first few weeks after my child was born, as I had my parents and husband to help out, cook, clean, do laundry, hold the baby, and even feed her at times. But when my parents left and my husband went back to work, around the time my baby was one month old things got super tough. I was so used to being a lone housewife, and suddenly I was a full-time mom as well. I remember those first few months; getting myself fed and changed, getting dinner ready, and maybe doing a load of laundry, as well as looking after the needs of my little one, was more than enough. It was actually too much while feeding a baby every few hours. Having a new baby is all-encompassing and requires a lot of grace and patience. Your life will never be the same, now that you have a little one.

Lord, thank You for giving us enough grace for each and every day. Thank You for Your wisdom and guidance as we raise up Your inheritance.

'And God is able to make all grace abound toward you, that you, always having all sufficiency in all things, may have an abundance for every good work.'
—2 CORINTHIANS 9:8

See the Good/God in Everything

A Mom is Born

When a baby is born, a new mom is born too, and things will never be the same again. Unlike driving a car, you don't need a license to have a baby. It's crazy—they should probably start doing that! When my beautiful daughter was laid on my chest after she was born, I had no idea the magnitude in which my life would change. I had read the books, I had done the courses, and I had scoured the internet for information on having a new baby and parenting. What they all failed to mention is the weight of responsibility you'll feel to keep a tiny human alive, and to grow them into a decent human being. When a baby is born a new mom is born too, so go easy on yourself, and know that God gently leads those who are with young.

Lord, thank you for Your wisdom. Guide me, Holy Spirit, every day, hour, and minute, and especially in raising my children. Amen.

'He will feed His flock like a shepherd; he will gather the lambs with His arm, and carry them in His bosom, and gently lead those who are with young.'
—ISAIAH 40:1

The Same Me

I thought perhaps that when I became a mother, I would transform into a totally different person. There was this thought that with the birth of my child, everything about me would change, and I would become like a magical new creature called Mommy. I was a new mom; I had no idea what to expect! The reality is that I'm the same me, but with a new facet. Yes, I now have a small human who depends on me for all her needs, but actually I'm still very much the same. I'm constantly changing, growing, and learning now. I've got a new job, and I'm learning the ropes; however, becoming a mother hasn't changed me the way the Holy Spirit does. When we choose to do the right things and follow the leading of the Holy Spirit, we become more sensitive to Him. The more sensitive and obedient we become to Him, the more our character resembles Jesus. Jesus said He only does what the Father tells Him (John 5:19). What obedience! Being a mother is such a magnificent privilege the Lord has given us. But to be the mothers of God we're called to be, we should be close and sensitive to the Holy Spirit, and let Him do a mighty work in us so that we can raise up the inheritance of God, His way. We really are merely stewarding His inheritance. And Lord, help us to steward well!

Thank you, Lord, that You make us mothers. Help us to steward Your inheritance. Give us Your wisdom, fill us with Your love and understanding, and help us to raise up our children in Your ways.

'But we all, with unveiled face, beholding as in a mirror the glory of the Lord, are being transformed into the same image from glory to glory, just as by the Spirit of the Lord.'
—2 CORINTHIANS 3:1

See the Good/God in Everything

The Ever-Important Vagina
(Warning: Graphic Descriptions)

It sounds crass, but it's true: I never realized it until I pushed a baby out of there how my one seemingly least honourable body part would play such an important role in my family. When my daughter was born, there were a lot more people in the room than I thought there would be. I distinctly remember my husband, my mother, my midwife, my OB-GYN, and three nurses. Don't get me wrong; I'm so thankful for all the people involved in the labour and delivery of my child, and I'm not complaining about the number of people there providing support and doing their very integral jobs. But they were all there and taking part in an event that isn't the most polished, yet so integral to life and family. In my relationship with my husband, my vagina brings pleasure to us both. As my husband says, 'It's the glue to a marriage'. It's a normally hidden body part, yet absolutely indispensable in my family. And it's my body part. It's a part of the female body, the part of a wife and mother that brings forth both pleasure to her husband and life from her body. What a miraculous design!

Thank You, Lord, that I am fearfully and wonderfully made! Help me to look after my body and to glorify You in my body and spirit.

'And those members of the body which we think to be less honourable, on these we bestow greater honour.'
—1 CORINTHIANS 12:23

Babies Do Weird Things

One thing I've found very interesting about babies are some of the weird things they do. When my baby was no longer a newborn but a bit older, she did the weirdest thing when I was about to nurse her. She would stare at my shirt, as if she could see the nipple underneath, and make the weirdest faces and noises. When she was a bit older than that, she would even paw at my chest. I knew she was doing so because I was her food supply, but I kind of felt like an object, the 'Mommy Milk Machine'. I think it's pretty amazing how the female body works and provides, and I'm thankful for the time I had nursing her. But it's so odd, the things a baby knows instinctively. It's so amazing how even at such a young age, she knew where her milk supply was coming from, and she had a way to communicate that with me.

Lord, thank You for my beautiful child. Thank You that You are faithful to Your promise. Lord, help me to raise up my child in Your ways, so when she is older she will not depart from it.

'For You formed my inward parts; You covered me in my mother's womb.'
—PSALM 139:13

Babies Pick Up on Your Vibe

I like to think that I'm a pretty temperate person. I don't experience extremely high or low emotions generally. I mean, I do have off-days, such as when my blood sugar is particularly low or I'm exhausted, but other than that I'm pretty chill. But there was one time when my baby girl was only a few months old, and my husband did something that

See the Good/God in Everything

just made me throw a fit. I was so angry with him that when I went out to reach for my baby, she just started crying uncontrollably, as if I had bad juju. I knew instantly that what had set her off was my anger at my husband. So, I had to go away, collect myself, and forgive my husband. And I had to remember that my emotions affect her as well, and will either bring peace or disunity.

Lord, help me to be aware that I affect my baby in so many ways. Help me to keep my heart clean and keep the peace in my home.

'Create in me a clean heart, O God, and
renew a steadfast spirit within me.'
—PSALM 51:10

R.E.S.P.E.C.T.

I know the song 'R.E.S.P.E.C.T.' and I know the definition, and I believe I treat people with respect. But I think after becoming a mom, respect moved the 15 inches from my head to my heart (my husband's line—I'm borrowing it). My respect and admiration for mothers and others raising children has increased a thousand-fold. To raise a child every day, for them to be healthy and well, and for them to become a well-rounded, competent member of society after a few dozen years is amazing. It takes an obscene amount of patience, love, sacrifice, commitment, and hard work every day to look after a child, and I salute all those who have done it before me.

Thank you, Lord, for those who have put in the time, effort, and love to raise your inheritance. Help us to raise our children in Your ways, for Your glory.

*'Train up a child in the way he should go, and
when he is old he will not depart from it.'*
—PROVERBS 22:6

Be Happy for Your Baby

As a normal hormonal woman, I have off-days. But as much as possible, I try to be happy for my baby. We know that babies won't remember details about the first few years of their life, but they'll remember if Mommy was generally happy or not. And I don't mean you have to be laughing all day long, but keep your heart clean. If things are bothering you or stressing you out, pray about it, call a friend, or have a heart-to-heart with your spouse. Don't just bottle up issues but deal with them, and have a chat with Daddy God. Don't get me wrong, you need to put baby down to get some stuff done! When my baby got older and started to entertain herself, for example, I would regularly put her down in her playpen and put away the dishes or fold laundry. But, a few times a day I would put everything else aside and focus on just her. We would play together, read, have a chat or a tickle or a cuddle, without any distractions. I wouldn't worry about the rest of my busy life but instead focus on the growing beautiful baby in front of me. Happy mommy, happy baby.

Lord, help me to thrive in Your joy. Help me to deal with issues in my life that boggle me down, and help me to be joyful, even in tribulation. Lord, surround me with supportive and loving friends and family.

'Do not sorrow, for the joy of the Lord is your strength.'
—NEHEMIAH 8:10B

See the Good/God in Everything

The Lord Gently Leads Those with Young Children

Isaiah 40:11 is a scripture about God gently leading those who are with young. This scripture has been so comforting to me during the past few months as a new mother. Becoming a new mom and getting used to the shift of life with a new baby is a challenge. I always want to do what's right for my child, and to be the best mother I can be, but sometimes I still make mistakes along the way. To be honest, I think the reason the Lord gently leads those with young children is because our own guilt, regret, or remorse from the mistakes we make in parenting is more than enough of a burden, without even considering God's opinion on it. When my baby girl was about three months old, I decided to go on our first solo outing (without her daddy) to the shops near our house. I was in a bit of a rush because of the time, and so was going hurriedly down the stairs with my baby in my arms. My husband had instilled a new rule too, that when going up and down the stairs we should hold onto the railing, since we were both new to this parenting thing. Well, I slipped on a stair tile and my three-month-old baby rolled out of my arms and onto a few steps below me. She was thankfully okay, and we did get her checked out at the doctor's, but no one could make me feel guiltier than I already felt. And God didn't rebuke me or discipline me, but gently loved on me and comforted me in my blunder. He encouragingly told me that even though I made this mistake and felt terrible, I would be able to continue on, with His help.

Lord, thank You that You are with us and never leave us. Help us in our weaknesses, and when we fail as parents. Help us to rely on Your Holy Spirit for all aspects of our lives.

*'He will feed His flock like a shepherd; He will gather
the lambs with His arm, and carry them in His bosom,
and gently lead those who are with young.'*

—ISAIAH 40:11

Learning Curve

I warn you now, when your child is born (especially your first child), the learning curve is steep. I had read the books and blogs, I had talked to friends, and I had taken the courses online and in person. Yet that first day with my new baby was terrifying. I've never had a human, just born, to look after before, without any supervision. What do I know about having a baby?! I remember in those first few hours, my husband wanted to go down to the café to buy a coffee. I was paralysed. He was going to leave me alone with this new little human?! I had no experience. For a second it was like all the preparation I had done was just gone! But, I put on a brave face and told him to make sure his phone was on, in case the baby cried and I didn't know what to do! I was scared out of my mind. I had many instances like that in the first few months. I used to pray that I would just get through the day. But soon the days added up to weeks, which added up to months, and here I am ten months later, and so thankful to have made it this far. I still Google every little thing, I still ask my doctor seemingly silly first-time-mom questions, and I still pray really hard not to mess things up. Momma, the learning curve is steep, but God is with you and He will guide you. Your hours will turn into days, then into weeks, then into months too.

Lord, we thank You that there is nothing we face that we cannot overcome with Your help. Thank You for Your Holy Spirit who guides us in all things.

See the Good/God in Everything

'Trust in the Lord with all your heart, and lean not on your own understanding; in all your ways acknowledge Him, and He shall direct your paths.'
—PROVERBS 3:5–6

It Can Be Very Disgusting

When my daughter was young and her digestive system was still very immature (as is normal with all babies), there were a lot of spit-ups and vomits. There were days I would easily have to change my clothes three or four times a day. There was even a time when she was around six months old that, due to the position I was holding her in, she ended up vomiting on my face. Yes, I even got some vomit in my mouth. It was disgusting, but you learn to roll with it. Things have improved the last few months as my daughter has gotten older, but instead of vomits and spit-ups it's usually half-eaten smears of food that get all over me. Why does no one tell you that being a mom can be a pretty disgusting and ungracious job? My daughter is at the stage of eating finger foods, and there are days when she'll swipe all the food I've painstakingly made for her onto the floor. At these times, one comfort for me is that God sees me, and He knows everything I go through. He sees the things that no one else sees—the long hours, the mess, the work, the patience upon patience, and then putting it all aside to be fully attentive, engaged, and happy for my baby. I'm reminded that Jesus didn't come to be served, but to serve and be a ransom for many. Part of being a mother is learning to serve, and to be sacrificial. Some of the most loving, gracious, and hard-working people I've met are mothers. In learning to serve our families and others, we're learning how to be more like Jesus every day. It isn't an easy walk, but you're strengthening your arms and building strength, courage, patience, perseverance, and love.

Thank you, Lord, for our families. Help us to be serving mothers and wives. Help us to be more like You and to be the mothers and wives that You called us to be.

'Just as the Son of Man did not come to be served, but to serve, and to give His life a ransom for many.'
—MATTHEW 20:28

Playing Defence

I've never really played any sports that require defence. I used to swim, run, and do dragon boat, but nothing that required preventing the other team from scoring. So, I didn't really get the concept; that is, until I had a baby who became obsessed with crawling into my dishwasher. You may laugh, but it's true. Of all the drawers and cupboards in my kitchen, my talented and agile little toddler is enthralled with my dishwasher the most. It must be the sliding racks, and the fact that it opens up so wide and close to the floor, that causes her to beeline straight for it when she sees it being opened. You wouldn't believe the speed in which my little crawler/walker can get to it! So now strategy plays into the kitchen-child dynamics. Before opening my dishwasher, I gauge my opponent. I see if she's distracted enough, then quickly pull it open. I place my body between the dishwasher and said toddler and have her in the corner of my eye to see if she'll dart towards the open door. If she's headed towards it, I open into a wider stance and go into a slight squat, sticking my bottom in her direction to fend her off and try to delay the inevitable. My arms go wide to ensure no little appendages make their way past me, and I close it as soon as I can! Sometimes I'm not successful and my little opponent gets past me and starts climbing onto the rack, pulling utensils out of the basket and grabbing plates and bowls with speed. As a last resort I tackle my opponent, grabbing her around the waist and swinging her flailing body around. I ignore the squeals and cries and place her back down a few feet away. I have overcome my opponent... until next time.

Thank You, Lord, for teaching us something new, each and every day. Thank You for the fun and joy that children bring. Help us to always see the good, and to cherish the everyday little things, as children grow up so fast.

'A merry heart makes a cheerful countenance, but by sorrow of the heart the spirit is broken.'
—PROVERBS 15:13

New Levels of Patience

So, my little daughter isn't so little anymore. She's also definitely not a baby. She's 13 months old and a full-blown toddler. She doesn't toddle anymore, she's now a proper walker, and has started to run too! She runs away from me! But, with this new age of development has come some new and interesting aspects. My little girl has become vocal and opinionated. She points at every little thing, and if she doesn't get the thing she wants, she'll vocalize her opinion with groaning, huffs, puffs, and shrieks. Also, with her new vocalized opinion comes her physical response, arching her back, hitting and flailing. I used to think I was generally a patient person. I was very low-key and easygoing. But even my patience has gotten used up more times than I like to think about, especially since she got opinionated. So, I'm praying for more patience. I can see that my patience and tolerance need to level up! I personally don't know how people with more than one child can tolerate it—they are my heroes.

Thank You, Lord, that there is nothing we will face in our lives that You do not equip us for. Thank you for Your Holy Spirit and for empowering me every day. Help me to have more patience and wisdom, especially when dealing with my child. Help me to keep the peace and to raise my child in Your ways.

'Always be humble and gentle. Be patient with each other, making allowance for each other's faults because of your love.'
—EPHESIANS 4:2 (NLT)

More Wisdom

The learning curve doesn't stop. My 14-month-old is going through new things. I think she's wanting to go down to one nap a day. She generally sleeps like a champ for 11 hours straight at night, but recently she's been waking at night and taking hours to go back to sleep, especially if she's had two really good naps earlier that day. She was taking two naps up to a few weeks ago, but now she's been refusing her second nap altogether. She'll lie in bed and talk to herself but not sleep at all. She can also easily go five hours without getting cranky. According to the internet, these are possible signs that she's ready to go down to one nap a day. However, most kids go down to one nap a day between 15 to 18 months old, and my little one is at the 14-month mark. So, what to do? I spent all last night scouring the internet for information, visiting different health sites and sleep blogs, reading about the different signs of a child wanting to go down to one nap, and the ways to go about initiating the change; and I prayed for more wisdom in raising my child. I feel like every time I start

　　　　　　　　See the Good/God in Everything

to get the hang of this parenting thing, something changes, or she learns a new skill, or she changes her sleep schedule, or she starts teething again. Sometimes I feel like I can't keep up. So, I look to Daddy God to guide me, the one who knows my daughter even better than I do. The one who knew her when she was still inside my womb. I look to Daddy God to guide me and give me wisdom. To give me peace, patience, and understanding on this parenting journey.

Thank You, Daddy God, that You know my child better than I do. Lord, give me more wisdom. Guide me, Holy Spirit, in raising my child. Help me to find good correct information, and to know which bit of it applies to my child. Help us to have a good, knowledgeable, and patient doctor. Help me to have a good support system and receive wise advice from those who have gone before me. Help me to reach out to others when necessary. Help me to be teachable and adaptable in my parenting. Thank you, God, that You don't leave me alone on this journey, and that You are with me through it all.

'Your ears shall hear a word behind you, saying,
"This is the way, walk in it," whenever you turn to
the right hand or whenever you turn to the left.'
—ISAIAH 30:21

I Can't Wear Nice Things

No one told me that my clothes would be ruined as a mother. Woe is me! First, we go through pregnancy and the multitude of clothes in different sizes and with different functionalities (hello nursing tops!). Then we go through the vomit stages and the explosive poo stages. Then comes the baby food. (Actually, when our little one started on purees, things were really good. It was when she started eating food full-time and wanted to feed herself that everything got really messy.) So, after 13 months of almost no new clothes, I went shopping one day. I got a bunch of cute new joggers. I was wearing them at home when my little girl had just finished eating her garlic butter shrimp pasta dinner and a plum for dessert, when she incessantly made it known that she didn't want to remain in her high chair. So, I took her out straight and put her on the ground. She immediately wrapped her oily buttery greasy hands all over my new joggers, to my annoyance. I'm the rookie parent who didn't clean her child's hands before taking her out of her highchair! An unbelievable beginner's mistake, but one I'll definitely not be making again. To you it may sound like the stupidest thing, but it mattered to me. To finally have new clothes that fit, then have them ruined the first day of wear, wasn't nice. But, I take it in stride. Life is really not that bad, and clothes are only clothes. My mother gently reminds me that this time in my child's life is just a season; that I should take the good with the bad, because it won't be like this forever.

Thank You, Lord, that life is not that bad. Thank You for Your inheritance, and the beautiful gift of our wonderful child. Help me to see the good in life, and not focus on the inconsequential. Help me to always be gracious and grateful. Thank You for Your constant love and provision in my life.

See the Good/God in Everything

*'To everything there is a season, a time
for every purpose under heaven.'*
—ECCLESIASTES 3:1

The Learning Curve Continues

Our daughter is now 14 months old. She is a walking, running, noisy, messy, and easily distracted child. She loves to get into our cupboards, and can find interest in the most random items around our house. Everything is new and fun, and needs to be touched or eaten. She's started to climb. *Don't get me started.* Things have changed a lot over the last 14 months. My big issue with her now is eating. It was so much easier when she was feeding from a bottle 24/7; I knew how many ounces to feed her, and how often. Even when she stared eating purees, it was easy for me to quantify how much food she was getting. But when she went onto finger foods full-time, things got difficult for me. She can now control how much food she wants to eat, if she wants to play with her food, or if she wants to dump it all on the ground. Apparently this is normal, that children will wax and wane in the amount of food they eat. Also, due to their slightly slowing rate of growth, their appetite will reduce. Other things that impact this are changes to naps, teething, distractions, independence, etc. There's also the issue of milk and iron. Drinking too much cow's milk inhibits the absorption of iron, which can lead to anaemia. But is she getting enough iron from red meat, which is the easiest form of iron to be absorbed in the body? As you can see, the amount of information I'm dealing with these days with regards to her eating and nutrition is endless. It's like every new month there are more milestones, more development, and so much more information for me to master. My daily prayer is to be a fast learner, to have grace for myself in the process, and to make the right decisions for my daughter.

Thank You, Lord, for Your inheritance. Thank You for the beautiful gift You have bestowed on us. Never let us take her for granted that she is from You, and is Your gift to us. Holy Spirit, guide me in all things, and help me have wisdom in every area of my parenting. Help me have grace for myself in my parenting, and to be the mother You have called me to be.

> *'Behold, children are a heritage and gift from the LORD, the fruit of the womb a reward.'*
> —PSALM 127:3 (AMP)

I Wish People Would Give Easy Answers

There have been a few times in our young daughter's life where I had a slight concern about my child, and sought advice from other parents. This turned out to be only marginally helpful, mainly because I wish people would just give succinct and clear answers, and that their responses would be exactly the answer I was looking for. This is wishful thinking, however. My first concern was when my daughter transitioned to cow's milk from baby formula. She was drinking a lot of it, and I was concerned that she wasn't getting enough iron, as too much cow's milk can inhibit iron absorption. She was also not taking in a good amount of solid food, and I worried that maybe too much cow's milk was causing this as well. The answers I got from friends were helpful, though not exactly what I needed to know for our situation; that babies don't starve themselves, and that as long as she regularly eats red meat, she'll get the form of iron most easily absorbable for her body. This is all part of the learning curve of being a parent. The answers are good, and helpful, and correct. But sometimes I just wish people would give me the exact answer I need for my situation instead of having to figure it out myself.

See the Good/God in Everything

The answers I really needed (which I figured out myself eventually) were: reduce her cow's milk intake a bit and she'll eat more food; and if iron is a concern, give her iron-fortified cereals or children's multivitamins with iron. Done!

Lord, we thank You that You are always guiding, leading, and teaching us in our parenting. Help us to be humble and teachable, and to be good examples for our children. Lord, we pray for more wisdom and discernment in every aspect of our lives.

> *'Give instruction to a wise man, and he will be still*
> *wiser; teach a righteous man, and he will increase in*
> *learning. The fear of the LORD is the beginning of*
> *wisdom, and the knowledge of the Holy One is insight.'*
> —PROVERBS 9:9–10 (ESV)

Waxing and Waning

One thing I find difficult as a new mom is the waxing and waning of my little toddler's sleep patterns. It seems every few months in their first year, there's a sleep regression of some sort, due to one developmental milestone or another. And if it's not that, it's teething, which is random and almost unending. And if it's neither of the two, it could be because she's trying to tell you that she wants to go down to one nap a day. My once extremely good sleeper and napper will go through times of very little sleep, where my patience is stretched to the breaking point and I feel all hope is lost. I am humbled once again, and through tears, I pray for wisdom to know how to handle the situation at hand. There is a waxing and waning with many aspects of parenting that I'm still coming to grips with. My former outgoing and social daughter is now clingy to bits! I love my daughter, but sometimes it feels like a little too much for me to handle.

Thank You, Lord, that You are with me through the highs and lows, the learning curves, and the humbling and stumbling of being a parent. Lord, I need Your wisdom above all else! Guide me, Holy Spirit, with how to parent my child. Lord, give me more grace. Thank you, Lord. Amen.

'But He gives more grace. Therefore He says: "God resists the proud, but gives grace to the humble."'
—JAMES 4:6

Be Flexible

I'm a person of structure and routine. I like to know what I'm doing, where I'm doing it, who's going to be there, and what the program will be like. I don't particularly like it when I need to be flexible, and if I'm doing a new thing, I like to know as much information as possible. It's just the weird way I am. So, when we had a baby—boy, was that a shock to the system! Things constantly changing, sometimes overnight. So, when my baby was old enough to be on a structured day with her naps and feeding, Mommy was a happy camper! But with babies and kids, even if they are on a routine, things can change up so easily. We went on a holiday, for example, and things definitely changed; and when my daughter started a new gym class, things changed again, because she was so tuckered out! I don't personally like to be flexible, but I see the necessity of it with having a child. It's so important because kids are constantly changing, growing, learning, and developing. It's also good to learn to be more flexible, because God works both in our routine and

See the Good/God in Everything

in our flexibility. Part of hearing from the Holy Spirit is being flexible and adaptable to His schedule and timing, and not our own.

Thank You, Lord, that Your Holy Spirit guides us and teaches us. Help us not to be so conformed to our ways and routine. Help us to be flexible to Your leading. Help us to be sensitive to the Holy Spirit.

'Not that I speak in regard to need, for I have learned in whatever state I am, to be content.'
—PHILIPPIANS 4:11

Your Holiday Will Revolve Around Naps and Bedtimes

We went on our first holiday when our daughter was 17 months old. The first three days were so difficult sleep-wise that I told my husband if our daughter didn't start sleeping regularly and through the night, we were going home early, end of story. My husband could stay, but our daughter and I would go back home to where sleeping was easy, back to our own beds and everything familiar. I knew getting our daughter to sleep in a new place would be hard, but I wasn't prepared for the absolute sheer sleeplessness onslaught. Our holiday actually revolved around her sleeps. She would only nap after lying reclined in her stroller for half an hour, then being put directly from there into the car. We tried to get her sleeping in the stroller, but it didn't work. We tried to go straight to getting her to sleep in the car—it also didn't work. We figured out that only that routine worked for her, so we replicated it every day just so she could take a nap. We scheduled all appointments around her naps. Our holiday revolved around our daughter's naps. It wasn't ideal, but it was necessary. It took about four days, but by that fifth day I was able to put her down in her travel crib and she would just lie down and sleep like she normally does. No crying, no wailing, no co-sleeping, no rocking, just sleeping.

Thank You, Lord, that You give us more grace. Help us to have grace, an abundance of patience, and Your wisdom when we are on vacation. Help us to have Your strategies and to help our children through changes.

'All your children shall be taught by the Lord, and great shall be the peace of your children.'
—ISAIAH 54:13

My Vagina Is No Longer the Same (Warning: Graphic Descriptions)

Sorry for the graphic details, but no one told me that my vagina wouldn't be the same as it had been pre-vaginal delivery. The first time I even heard a hint of this news was when my obstetrician asked me if I wanted an episiotomy during delivery. I knew what an episiotomy is, of course—it's when they cut the perineum a bit to make the opening wider for birth. But I couldn't understand why a woman would choose to have one voluntarily, so I asked the doctor. She said that some women choose to have an elective episiotomy because they believe it will 'make things tighter' post-vaginal delivery, after stitches. What?! My vagina was going to change?! Hasn't enough of my body changed already from carrying this baby? Now my vagina too?! Of course, you don't notice it immediately, but pushing a baby out of there will definitely change

See the Good/God in Everything

things. It was when my husband and I started having intercourse again that the difference was noticeable. It got slightly better with time and Kegel exercises, but 18 months post-delivery and it's still noticeably different. I guess this is what it's like to be a mother...?

Thank You, Lord, that You give us children as an inheritance. Help me to not see my bodily changes as negative, but as marks of a warrior, and the stamps of motherhood. Help me to love the body You've given me, in whatever form it may take, and to deal with any body image issues I may have. Help me to be a good example to my children and to love my body and look after it well.

> *'Can a mother forget her nursing child? Can she feel no love for the child she has borne? But even if that were possible, I would not forget you!'*
> —ISAIAH 49:15B (NLT)

Be Kind to Yourself

Maybe it's because I lean towards being an introvert, but I find it hard to be engaged and present with my child every minute of the day, especially now that she's older and active. Pre-child, when my husband and I would be in each other's company all day long, we would have our moments of alone time, moments when we would zone out and do our own thing. I may play the piano, or go do some housework, and my husband might watch a bit of YouTube, or tinker around with something. But those days are long gone. With my daughter around, I feel the mom guilt of zoning out. When she's playing around the house, I feel bad when I'm busy doing other things, or when I need a moment to myself to decompress or just have some quiet time. But I realize this is necessary for my own mental health and, as well, to get things done around the house. So, I try to manage this the best I can by allowing myself time to empty the dishwasher or cook dinner, or just to have some quiet time while my husband looks after her; but following that, I make sure I spend time with her, playing or doing an activity together. It's a fine balance between looking after a household, looking after yourself, and being engaged with your child. And let's be honest; as women and mothers, looking after ourselves tends to be the bottom item of our to-do list.

Thank You, Lord, for Your Holy Spirit that guides us in all things. Help us to make wise decisions for us and our children.

'For the LORD gives wisdom; from His mouth come knowledge and understanding.'
—PROVERBS 2:6

Praying About Everything

As a first-time mom, the stress was high when my daughter was little. I'd never had a baby before, I'd not been around babies in a while, and I'd never had the responsibility of caring for someone else. Being a mom was totally new, and I was pretty scared I might do something wrong. I had read numerous books and blogs and we even did an online prenatal class, but I still didn't feel very prepared for when they handed me the baby and she was suddenly ours. One thing about living in the desert is it's hot. When our baby was born in December, it was pushing 25 degrees Celsius (80 Fahrenheit) during the daytime. So, air conditioning is something we live with around here on a daily basis. But during the winter and spring, temperatures fluctuate a lot between the daytime and nighttime temperatures, so it can be hard to figure out. I know,

See the Good/God in Everything

you're thinking, 'Seriously, Gina, air conditioning?' But it's really an area I struggled with. In the beginning, my prayers were literally, 'God, please help me to choose the right setting so she doesn't get too hot or too cold'. Actually, it's still a prayer I pray every night. But, thank God, I've gotten much better at it. One of our best purchases ever was a thermometer for her room. Now I know the ideal temperature she likes to sleep in, and I know based on the outside temperature how to get that. I still check in on her through the video monitor every night, but generally I've gotten better at gauging air conditioning settings. What's the point? Pray about everything. It may seem like the stupidest, ungodliest thing, but if it matters to you, it matters to God.

Thank You, Lord, that You know every hair on our head and every prayer we pray. Help us daily to lift up in prayer the things that matter to us. Let us not be anxious for anything but be ones who pray about everything.

> *'Be anxious for nothing, but in everything by prayer and supplication, with thanksgiving, let your requests be made known to God; and the peace of God, which surpasses all understanding, will guard your hearts and minds through Christ Jesus.'*
> —PHILIPPIANS 4:6–7

Empathy, Not Resentment

My dear 18-month-old toddler has officially reached the clingy and whiny stage. This is a pretty new thing for us, as before she would sit for ages and amuse herself with her play and self-discovery. She's always been attached to my husband and I, but now there is whininess involved, and the clinginess is at another level. There are some days where she wants Mommy and she wants her *now*, for no other reason other than that is her greatest need. It's been very trying on me as a mother. Sometimes I just want to do something that requires use of my hands, which is hard to do with a heavy 18-month-old on my hip. There are only so many things you can do one-handed. And the crying; don't even get me started on the crying! In trying to deal with this, I found an article which really helped me. It said kids aren't trying to manipulate you at this age, but are trying to communicate their needs, and that a parent's perception of the motivation behind their child's behaviour is the single most powerful determinant of the parent's response. That we should have empathy toward our child, not resentment. One of the key things that helped me is the advice to carve out more intentional special time; that can be playing, reading, running, anything really, but make sure you're disconnected from technology. And the other was to use bathtime and bedtime as a way to connect and to really cuddle her up. After just two days of following this advice, there's been a dramatic drop in the amount of clinginess and whininess she's been exhibiting.

Thank You, Lord, for the advice from others who have gone before us through the parenting journey. Help us to have empathy towards our children. Help us, Lord, to make wise choices in our parenting, so that we end up raising godly children.

'Show me Your ways, O Lord; teach me Your paths.'
—PSALM 25:4

See the Good/God in Everything

I Dropped My Baby!

When I was young, single, and childless, I used to pride myself in being young and athletic. If I forgot something up the stairs I wouldn't just walk, I would dash up, being proud of being young and fit. *Pride before the fall.* When my daughter was about four months old, right before the pandemic, I had plans to be an independent and adventurous mother. So, one day I planned to take my young baby in her stroller to the grocery store about a ten-minute walk away. I had everything packed and organized when I realized that the shop was about to close. I had to hurry! With my daughter in my arms, I raced quickly down the stairs. My flip-flop slipped on the tile and I fell backwards onto my back, sliding down on my backside a few steps down. My arms flailed and my little daughter slipped out of my hands, landing a few steps below me. I remember the sheer animalistic cry that came out of my mouth as she fell from my hands. No words could express my pain and terror. I grabbed her wailing self and called my husband while bawling my eyes out. It didn't help that my husband had instilled a rule when she was born that we should always hold onto the railing while carrying her up and down the steps. Did I learn my lesson? Without a doubt. Don't rush; hold the railing; it's better to go slow and be safe; and listen to your husband. Thank God she turned out to be okay when we had her checked by her doctor...who also told me to be more careful.

Thank You, Lord, that You give Your angels charge over us to keep us in all our ways. Help us not to be cocky, but to have more wisdom in our parenting. Help us, Lord, when we fail, to learn the lesson quickly, to forgive ourselves, and to do better next time.

> *'For He shall give His angels charge over*
> *you, to keep you in all your ways.'*
> —PSALM 91:11

Letting Her Go

So, my little girl is going to playschool in a month. She will be 20 months old, and she is definitely ready. I've been very privileged to be able to be a stay-at-home mom, so this is a huge new step for us. I'm feeling so many emotions about sending my little girl to playschool. I'm also dealing with anxiety, which is so unlike me. I've reacted by praying about everything making me anxious. For the fear-based thoughts, I throw those right out, and focus my thinking on how much fun she'll have, and how she'll enjoy her time there. Part of letting her go, even if it's just to playschool, is also realizing that our time with her is so limited. Our jobs as parents are time-restricted and we need to take advantage of every day. Our job is to raise them in His ways, period. To teach them the truth about God, to love them and show them how God loves them and others, to guide them to make godly choices and to show them how to be a light in the world. Our lives here are so short, and eternity is the end goal. So yes, she's starting playschool, but the emphasis is not really on letting her go, but on preparing her to go.

Thank You, Lord, for Your Holy Spirit that guides us in all things. Help us every day and in every moment we have with our children to train them up in Your ways.

'Dedicate your children to God and point them in the way that they should go, and the values they've learned from you will be with them for life.'
—PROVERBS 22:6 (TPT)

See the Good/God in Everything

You Don't Need a Lot of Stuff

Here's the thing—when I was pregnant and getting ready for my little girl's arrival, I didn't know what to get. So, I did what most people do, and searched the internet and blogs for the must-needed items for a new baby. I cannot tell you how much stuff I got that I didn't end up using, or ended up using so minimally that it wouldn't have made a difference at all if I hadn't had it. Everyone has the best intentions with must-needed items, but really, before babies turn one, you can still get away with very little. There's even this crazy train of thought that you should buy multiple items of the same thing, like bottles or pacifiers, in case baby doesn't take to one particular type or brand. (This is unnecessary, by the way.) Another one is to have multiple items of the same things in different levels or different rooms of the house, aka diaper caddies. It seems good in theory, but if you have a small house, it's totally unnecessary. With the logic of a naïve newbie, I ended up spending a crazy amount of money on stuff that I just ended up giving away. I know this isn't common advice, but you can buy baby stuff only as you need it. This is especially so much more possible now with how amazing online shopping is. So, don't stress so much, and don't put a huge dent in your wallet. Read the blogs, but be honest and realistic with yourself about what you need and don't need. Not every good idea is necessary for you and your situation.

Thank You, Lord, that You give us wisdom in all things. Lord, give us wisdom and practical sense when it comes to preparing for baby's arrival. Help us to know what to spend our money on, what to invest in, and what to forgo. Help us to be wise and sensible parents.

'Wisdom is the principal thing; therefore get wisdom.
And in all your getting, get understanding.'
—PROVERBS 4:7

You Don't Need a Diaper Bag

I loathe diaper bags. The person who invented that was a genius scammer. They're bulky, usually pretty ugly (even the best brands), waterproof, and just not stylish! A diaper doesn't need its own special bag! But, when I was pregnant, I was convinced I wouldn't be motherly enough if I didn't have a designated diaper bag. What a lie! But, I fell for it at the time, and even bought two. They were an absolute waste of money. They were rarely used, and I was pretty embarrassed to be travelling with a bag the size of carryon luggage every time I went out with my child. Here's the thing—if you don't feel you need a diaper bag, or if you're like me and are not sure it's a legitimate purchase, don't get on the damn bandwagon! What I ended up doing when I just couldn't stand using the huge diaper bag anymore was to use a large reusable tote bag I bought from a grocery store; it was less than ten dollars, but I loved it because it was light, large, and washable, and I didn't look like I was constantly on my way to the airport! I've even gotten to the point where I just stick the most necessary items, a diaper and spare pacifier, in my own purse at times for quick outings. Just because 'they' (all the mommy bloggers and YouTubers) say you need one, doesn't mean you need one.

Thank You, Lord, that You give us wisdom in all things. Help me, Lord, to have more wisdom. Help me to not follow the crowd but to go with my own gut, and help me to make wise choices with my spending.

> *'He stores up sound wisdom for the upright; He
> is a shield to those who walk uprightly.'*
>
> —PROVERBS 2:7

Sick Baby Heartache

My baby girl is sick, and it's making this mama's heart a bit sad. She had a bit of a vomiting episode yesterday, vomiting at school yesterday, then a bit of diarrhea at home. She was the stinkiest, saddest sight when I picked her up from school. It's most likely a bit of a stomach bug, we're thinking possibly from an undercooked hotdog the night before. My baby girl's appetite was non-existent, limited to a few crackers and a tiny bit of rice, some water and some electrolyte drink. She didn't want to nap at all yesterday, so we laid in bed and watched *The Sound of Music*. Since she missed her nap, she was overtired and cranky and wanted to constantly be in Mommy's arms, so I put her in her baby carrier where she promptly fell asleep. This is such a rare occasion; I can't even remember the last time she fell asleep like that. It was the loveliest and saddest thing, and I just wanted to hold her close. It's so hard to see your child sick, and it makes your heart go out to them. We prayed for healing and restoration, and that she would feel better after a good night's sleep. Sometimes it still surprises me, the amount of love and affection I have for my daughter. On days when she isn't well, you just want to do everything in your power to make them better. Life is tenuous and though we love our children so much, there's only so much protecting and caring we can do for them. It highlights to me the absolute importance of being prayerful and trusting God with our lives and theirs.

Thank You, Lord, that there is no circumstance that surprises You. You remain on the throne, no matter what we go through. Help me when my child is sick to be prayerful and patient, and to do all I can to help them. Help me also to trust in You, and to remember that You know and love my child even more than I do. That You will never leave them or forsake them.

'And the Lord, He is the One who goes before you. He will be with you, He will not leave you nor forsake you; do not fear nor be dismayed.'
—DEUTERONOMY 31:8

Toddlers Are So Smart and Pick Up on Little Things

I never knew how much kids pick up on things. It makes you wonder just how much they're aware of and see. My daughter has a bit of a routine when she goes to bed, where we must give her a kiss on the lips, as well as her stuffed animals; and if Mommy is putting her to bed, Daddy must also kiss Mommy on the lips before he says goodnight and leaves. She's been doing this for at least a few months now. The other day, my husband and I were going through some issues and were upset with each other (see 'Too Much Forgiveness for One Day'). So, when Daddy went to say goodnight, he kissed our daughter, then he kissed one teddy bear, and then the other. She then pointed to Mommy's lips, which is her norm. I wasn't happy, though, and there was no way I was going to kiss my husband, not with how pissed off I was with him. So, as he came towards my face, I averted my head slightly and he ended up kissing my forehead instead. As soon as Daddy left, she came in close to my face

See the Good/God in Everything

with puckered lips and kissed me on my lips and gave me the sweetest smile. It was funny that she noticed Mommy and Daddy didn't kiss on the lips and so she kissed me on the lips instead. It's also amazing that she just wants to share the love with her favourite people (and stuffed animals), all the time.

Thank You, Lord, for little children. I can see why You wanted the little children to come to You. Help me to be an easy forgiver and to be as loving and humble as a child. Help me to be more aware of the example I show my children, and to always be a godly and loving parent and spouse.

'Then Jesus called a little child to Him, set him in the midst of them, and said, "assuredly, I say to you, unless you are converted and become as little children, you will by no means enter the kingdom of heaven."'
—MATTHEW 18:2–3

Missing My Baby Girl

The first two weeks of my daughter's playschool was hectic, slightly traumatic, and nerve-wracking. She'd never been left with anyone other than Daddy before, and those times were few and far between. So, playschool was a very new thing. As she came in contact with all the other kids and their germs, she got sick a few times the first few weeks. Even after two weeks there was still a bit of crying and screaming as I dropped her off. But, things are slowly getting better. The cries and screams have lessened, and when I pick her up to leave, she smiles and waves goodbye to the teachers and assistants. Those first few weeks I was so concerned and anxious that I didn't really have a chance to miss her. But now I'm dealing with missing my baby girl. I try to move on because it is easy to get stuck in the sad-missing-her feelings. I'm actively taking each thought captive, and trying not to think about what she's doing, how she's feeling, and if she's okay. I just think about how she's having a grand old time, bless her, say a quick prayer, and move on. And I remind myself to make sure that I cover her with lots of kisses and cuddles, and tell her how much I love her when I see her again.

Thank You, Lord, that children are a blessing from You. Help me when I am sad and miss my child. Help me to not get stuck in that feeling, but to be prayerful, trust You, and trust the choice to send her to school. Help me to be a positive, nurturing, and strong mother, who is a godly example to my kids.

> *'Who can find a virtuous wife? For her*
> *worth is far above rubies.'*
> —PROVERBS 31:10

She Didn't Cry!

It took three weeks, but today my little girl didn't cry when I dropped her off at school!!! I have tears of happy mama joy!!! My little girl is growing up so quickly. We walked slowly to school, looked at the birdies, and saw the people going off to work. When we got to the door, I leaned down to kiss her and said 'have a nice day', then put her hand in the assistant's hand and off she went. No arguments, no screams, no trying to follow after me. I was so proud of her, but a little sad too. These little victories and these small steps of independence are amazing, and I'm so proud she was finally able to get there. I'm a little sad, though, because my baby girl is becoming a big, independent girl. I know it's a cliché that kids grow up quickly, but they really do. So, let's take advantage of every day to cherish our babies, teach them, equip them with life skills, pray over them, and pour our love over them. Their childhoods last but a season, and I want my girl's to be a blessed one, full of love, fun, friends, and family.

Thank You, Lord, that children are an inheritance from You. Thank You that they are a blessing to us, and never a burden. Help us to take advantage of every day to grow them in Your ways, and to love them and make their childhoods a happy one. Help us to have wisdom in our parenting and to love, protect, and cherish our children the way You do to us.

'But Jesus said, "Let the little children come to Me, and do not forbid them; for of such is the kingdom of heaven."'
—MATTHEW 19:14

Sleep Regressions

Before I became a parent, I had never in my life heard of a sleep regression. A sleep regression is when a previously good sleeper suddenly changes, and they suddenly find it difficult to sleep. They become fussier at bedtimes, and will most likely refuse to sleep or nap. Sleep regressions are good, because it shows that your child is developing. When they're learning new skills such as turning, crawling, walking, or talking, or having a growth spurt, their sleep will be affected. Here's the thing— when our baby was four months old we sleep-trained her. I had had enough of an irregular sleep pattern, short naps, and the fact that baby could only fall asleep while in my arms. So, we sleep-trained her with the 'cry it out' method. For parents who read this, don't lose your pants if you're not a cry-it-out person. It's not as harsh at it reads, and we didn't leave her to cry for hours on end, more like a few minutes the first day then increasing slowly over time. But seriously, it works; you just have to brace yourself for the crying. So, back to sleep regressions. Our daughter recently had not been sleeping well, and I had gotten into the bad habit of comforting her by holding her in my arms and waiting until she fell asleep to put her back in bed. Silly Mommy, I had forgotten all about sleep regressions and sleep crutches! I actually contributed to a sleep crutch, which is a negative sleep association. I was letting her get used to falling asleep in my arms, again a big no-no. So, after coming back to my senses, I had to go back to basics and fall back on the sleep training learnt earlier. Such a rookie mistake!

Thank You, Lord, that You guide me in the best ways to parent and look after my child. Help me when I fall short or make mistakes to have grace for myself, and to do better next time. Help me, Lord, to have more wisdom and discernment, and help me to find reliable and trustworthy parenting advice and mentors.

> *'For the moment all discipline seems painful rather than pleasant, but later it yields the peaceful fruit of righteousness to those who have been trained by it.'*
> —HEBREWS 12:11 (ESV)

See the Good/God in Everything

The Terrible Twos

My dear 21-month-old daughter is experiencing the Terrible Twos. I know she's not two yet, but trust me, she's got them already. She's got tantrums, defiant behaviour, mood swings, and an obscene amount of frustration. She knows what she wants, and when she doesn't get it, there's most likely going to be wailing, screaming, crying, and flailing body parts. I know it's really not her fault, that she has limited communication skills and a limited emotional ability to deal with her frustration, but sometimes it's just very hard for me to handle. I think part of my slow response is that I assumed it would be when she was two and not earlier, but all the online sources tell me it can definitely be before the child is two years old. Another reason I think I'm having trouble dealing with the changes is that she was the loveliest, most agreeable, happiest baby—she barely cried and was easily manageable. But alas, here we are, writing this after I put her down for a nap. It was the roughest morning. I was so frustrated from all the screaming and crying that I literally just cried. I had had enough, and I didn't know what to do. So, I started reading every blog on how to deal with the Terrible Twos, just for some guidance and more insight on how to deal with it. I know it's not her fault and she doesn't do it on purpose, but sometimes I just wish I had so much more resilience and patience.

Lord, Jesus, please help me to have resilience and more patience. Help me to have the tools and skills necessary for this next season in my daughter's life. Help me to have more wisdom, to be a quick learner, and to help guide my daughter in Your ways during this season.

> *'Have I not commanded you? Be strong and of good courage; do not be afraid, nor be dismayed, for the Lord your God is with you wherever you go.'*
> —JOSHUA 1:9

Your Own Time Doesn't Exist

I have this dear friend who has three children aged between 5 and 12 years old. She used to always tell me about how she would go to bed at two in the morning because she was always so busy. We were without kids at the time, and we had all the time in the world. So, I absolutely couldn't fathom why she was always so busy. But now I have an almost 2-year-old, and I get it, because now I have no time for myself as well. When my baby is at school or napping, I get to my laptop as quickly as possible to get some work done. You've gotta do what you've gotta do. I try to get as much done as possible when my girl is home and awake as well, but at this age she definitely needs attention, engagement, and stimulation. In the few hours I have between putting my daughter to sleep and going to sleep myself, I still seem to have a million things to do: try to get in a shower and wash my hair, make and pack the baby's lunch bag for school, fold another basket full of laundry, go back to my daughter and re-settle her because she won't sleep, have sex with my husband or just have a conversation without interruption, watch something mindless and relaxing on my phone, read the Bible, then go to sleep. Okay, maybe I do have some time to myself, but it's extremely limited and it's not as relaxing as it used to be.

Thank You, Lord, that my husband and my daughter are a gift from You. Help me to organise and prioritise my time during the day, to give time for them, and have some time for me too. Help me when things are too busy to let go of my standards and not worry about getting everything done. Help me to let go of stress and perfection.

'She opens her mouth with wisdom, and on her tongue is the law of kindness. She watches over the ways of her household, and does not eat the bread of idleness.'
—PROVERBS 31:26–27

See the Good/God in Everything

I Should Have Stuck to My Gut

So, it was one and a half months before my daughter started school. We had visited the school, met the principal, looked at the classrooms, got the schedule (8:00 am to 1:00 pm), and filled out the registration form. Things were looking good, and we looked forward to when she could start. Our daughter was on one nap a day at the time, at 11:30 am. She would sleep for a good two to two and a half hours, every day. It had taken her ages to get onto that schedule, and even longer for her to settle into it well. So, in the month and a half before school started, I contemplated changing her nap schedule to fit in with school. Her new nap time would change from 11:30 am to 1:30 pm. It was definitely doable, but would require some effort on my part to slowly change her naps by intervals until we got to 1:30 pm. Here's the thing—our girl is a good napper, but she needs a strong routine, and to follow her schedule to a T. So, I discussed this with my husband. He thought it was too much work, and that she would naturally tire out at school and be so exhausted afterwards that she would pass out for a nap when she got home. Yeah, not so much. So here we are, about three weeks since school started, and our dear girl is still not sleeping well for naptime or bedtime. It's not as bad as the first few weeks of school, but there's still some definite room for improvement. I love my dear husband, but I should have stuck with my gut. I allowed myself to get talked into what sounded like a fairly reasonable opinion, which turned out to be wrong. But I'm with my daughter more than anyone else, and I know her and her body clock better than even my dear husband. So, I should have stuck with my gut and changed her nap before school started.

Thank You, Holy Spirit, that You guide us in all things. Help me to stick with my gut, and to follow through with what I think is the best way forward, and not just the easy way forward. Help our daughter to adapt to this new sleep schedule easily and quickly, and to return to the good sleeper we know she is.

'I will both lie down in peace, and sleep; for You alone, O Lord, make me dwell in safety.'

—PSALM 4:8

VPLs

I had forgotten what it's like to make an effort in the way I look. During pregnancy and post-partum, I was focused mostly on comfort more than anything else. Everything I bought was with comfort in mind. If I looked semi-decent, that was merely a plus. In pregnancy, with my huge growing belly, my increasing hips and my swollen feet, beauty was a side note. And post-partum, with my mom belly, ever-fluctuating weight, and unacceptance of said extra weight, it was hard to look in the mirror and be content. I never understood mom jeans until I had a baby. Now I get why moms need their own special sort of jeans. Unflattering as they may be, I accept the necessity of it. One day I was getting dressed to bring my daughter to school when I noticed the unflattering VPL (visible panty line) on my backside. This was probably not a new occurrence, as I'd been wearing the same clothes for the past few weeks, but this was the first time I'd noticed it, and when I finally did, it bothered me. I'd gotten so used to being functional that I almost forgot about looking nice. Luckily, I had some other, more flattering underwear, so I put those on instead. But it was the most uncomfortable thing! I forgot that when you wear invisible underwear, it's highly uncomfortable. But it's not really about visible panty lines or invisible panty lines. The fact is that I had gotten too comfortable in my comfortable clothes and ways, and forgot to make a bit of an effort; if not for me, then at least for my husband, to look attractive and put together. (I know how I feel when I see him in his tracksuit bottoms all weekend, where showers have been elusive.) But really, it should be for me too. I should dress so I feel pretty

See the Good/God in Everything

and confident and not frumpy and overweight. As I care about inner beauty and being a godly, God-fearing women, I should also care that I look appropriate, lovely, and attractive.

Thank You, Lord, that You care about beauty. Help us to be godly women of inner beauty, but also women who are not afraid to look after ourselves and our appearance.

'You are altogether beautiful, my darling, beautiful in every way.'
—SONG OF SOLOMON 4:7 (NLV)

Working Moms Are My Heroes

Moms who work outside of the home are my heroes. That's not to say that stay-at-home moms aren't amazing, because they are. And hello, I'm a stay-at-home mom too, so you know I love you. But I have a newfound respect and appreciation for those moms who leave home, leave their baby in the care of others, and go to work. I have the greatest respect for my mom. My entire childhood, she worked as a nurse in a children's hospital. Depending on her shift she would sometimes leave before daylight, and I always remember that she would come into our bedrooms while it was still dark and give us a kiss goodbye before she left for work. She would then walk to the bus stop, rain or shine, to get the bus, then the train, to work in the city. I've started working now and I'm finding the transition hard. I have very limited time for my baby, even less for my husband, and the least amount of time for myself. I am feeling all the feelings of sending my baby off to playschool. It's also taking a toll on my husband and I, as normally I would do most of the housework, since my husband works full-time and I would be at home. But since I'm working now too, the parenting roles need to be more evenly distributed, because I just don't have enough time, patience, or mental energy to do it all by myself. So, working mamas, stay-at-home mamas, single parents, I salute you. You are my heroes. The job you do inside and outside the house, the sacrifices you make on the daily, and the love you pour out are commendable and praiseworthy. I am so proud of parents and mamas who make it work, who do what needs to be done to run a house and provide a living. I am praying for you to have strength, energy, more patience, lots of grace, and a community of loving people to surround you. Know that all you do does not go unseen, and the sacrifices you make do not go unnoticed. And you are an amazing example to your kids. We love you.

Thank You, Lord, that You are the ultimate Father. That You loved us all with such a great love, You sent Your son Jesus to die for us, so we can be restored to You. You are the greatest example of love in action. Help us to parent and love like You do, and to raise our kids in Your ways. Thank You that You always provide for all of our needs, and we never have any lack.

'For the children ought not to lay up for the parents, but the parents for the children.'
—2 CORINTHIANS 12:14C

She Had Fun

When I went to pick up my girl from school, I could hear wailing from outside the glass doors. I was thinking, 'Is that my baby?' and then the 'Mama, Mama!' cries could be heard, and I definitely knew it was her. She was a puddle of tears and had apparently seen me walking down the path and started crying. But, her teacher assured me that she had had

See the Good/God in Everything

fun at school and she only started crying when she saw me. That was a relief. I was so thrilled to hear that my baby girl had finally had fun at school that I almost burst into tears myself in front of the teacher and multiple assistants. It had taken about three weeks, but this was great news! It was such a joy to hear that she's actually enjoying school. There were so many times over the first few weeks of school when I seriously doubted if it was a good idea for her to go. And I know my husband definitely questioned if school was a good idea, especially after she kept getting sick. So, it makes this mama's heart happy to know she hasn't just adapted but has started to thrive and be happy there.

Thank You, Lord, that with You we can do all things. Thank You that our child has adapted and is finally enjoying school. Help her to have fun and learn lots of things. Surround her with good people and let her be a blessing to those around her.

'I can do all things through Christ who strengthens me.'
—PHILIPPIANS 4:13

Don't Project

When I was growing up, what I remember most is that seeing the world was an important aspect to our family. My parents got married young, and I think they felt they never had the freedom to travel around and see the world. I think perhaps they also felt they'd had a family too soon. This affected me in a few ways. Firstly, I grew up thinking travelling and seeing the world was the epitome of happiness. Secondly, because of this, I was also taught not to get married before I was 30 years old. Because my parents got married young, in their mind maybe too young, they often thought that if they had waited till they were older, like 30, they would have been able to have an adventurous life pre-kids and pre-responsibility. I understand why they would say that, and I can see their heart in the matter, but the emphasis was too strong. They were projecting their issues with getting married young, and their regret at not being able to do more before they had a family, onto me. So now, I am super aware of the issues I have in my own life that I need to deal with. And I need to deal with them and do the heart work (which is hard work). I need to sort out my own issues, so that the things that negatively affected me as a young person don't affect the way I parent my children, nor influence how or what I speak to them about.

Thank You, Lord, for our parents. Help us to learn from their wisdom and shortcomings. Help us to reflect on our childhood, and to see where negative things may be affecting our parenting. Help us to do the heart work, so we can be the person of God You called us to be. Help us to be more like Jesus, each and every day, and help us to parent Your way, all the time.

'Have mercy upon me, O God, according to Your lovingkindness; according to the multitude of Your tender mercies, blot out my transgressions. Wash me thoroughly from my iniquity, and cleanse me from my sin.'
—PSALM 51:1–2

Parent Shoptalk

Here's my take on becoming a parent. There are some days when all we talk about is what I call 'parent shoptalk'. It's the interesting and non-interesting things about our child: bowel movements, naps, new foods, new discoveries, new words. Sometimes these things enthral us,

See the Good/God in Everything

and we enjoy being caught up in the world of new parents. But there are also days when it's a drag. You ask yourself, 'Where has me gone to?' or, 'Is this child all we talk about now?' The answers, incidentally, are that You has taken a back seat while your child takes up your life; and yes, that *is* all you'll talk about, for the first year at least, before the novelty and newness will begin fading. Part of becoming new parents is finding the balance between being loving, doting, engaged parents, and being loving spouses keeping the fire and interest alive. (Hello, I'm speaking to myself here!) This does not come easily, which means you really need to prioritize quality time for you and your spouse. Once a child arrives on the scene, the marital relationship with your spouse can easily become a shoulder-to-shoulder-only relationship, where your focus is only on the kids and the marriage goes not just to the backburner, but down the drain. We must remember that children are an inheritance and we are rearing them in His ways, for a season. The season is not that long, and when they leave, your spouse is still there. So, I know it's hard, especially for parents of little kids, but we have to take time to prioritize our marriages too.

Thank You, Lord, for my spouse. Help me to prioritize my marriage and make time to connect with my husband. Help us to be wise parents in raising our children and protecting our marriage. Help us to be wise with our time each and every day.

> *'And Adam said: "This is now bone of my bones and flesh of my flesh; she shall be called Woman, because she was taken out of Man." Therefore a man shall leave his father and mother and be joined to his wife, and they shall become one flesh.'*
> —GENESIS 2:23–24

Grateful at All Times

There were many times when living abroad that finding certain things—things we're used to in the West, things we may even take for granted in the West—are hard to find. I remember the first day my daughter went to daycare. When I went to pick her up later in the day, the teachers and principal couldn't find her bag. It wasn't labelled on the outside (though it was on the inside), and they had placed it in the wrong classroom. After many minutes of searching, they finally found it, and I was told to put a label or tag on the outside of the bag. When I got home I tried to find something, anything, I could use to put her name on the outside of the bag. I didn't have much—duct tape, a permanent marker, and an old used airline luggage tag that was falling apart. So, I attached the luggage tag to her backpack, covered it with duct tape, and wrote her name with the permanent marker. It didn't look pretty, but it worked, and that was the most important thing. Many months later, when visiting my parents in Canada, one of our friends gifted our daughter with personalized labels and stickers. It even came with a personalized luggage tag for her backpack. It was very nice but I didn't think much of it at the time, since she wasn't at school then. After a few months we finally relocated to Australia and got all our documents in order to send her to daycare. When I was going through and organizing her stuff for the first day, I remembered the new luggage tags with her name on it that we had been gifted with, and took off her old hodgepodged one from her backpack. It was very poignant for me. I cried. Taking off that ugly old handmade luggage tag, and putting on the new pretty, personalised one, made me remember how good God is. I didn't have much at the time, but I had an old airline luggage tag, duct tape, and a permanent marker, which turned out to be enough. But now we had something pretty and new that I hadn't even thought of myself. You probably think I'm silly or overly emotional, writing about such trivial things. But to me, it was a God moment. It reminded me that He is there in the lack, and in the abundance, and I am so grateful.

See the Good/God in Everything

Thank You, Lord, that through all the things we go through in life, big and small, You are with us. Our needs aren't inconsequential to You, and You love us so much.

> *'Therefore do not worry, saying, "What shall we eat?"*
> *or "What shall we drink?" or "What shall we wear?" For*
> *after all these things the Gentiles seek. For your heavenly*
> *Father knows that you need all these things. But seek*
> *first the kingdom of God and His righteousness, and*
> *all these things shall be added to you. Therefore do not*
> *worry about tomorrow, for tomorrow will worry about*
> *its own things. Sufficient for the day is its own trouble.'*
> —MATTHEW 6:31–34

Parenting Disunity

Parenting disunity is very hard to deal with, and it makes the marriage stressful. Parenting styles are usually to blame, as one parent may be more disciplined and the other one may have a more laid-back approach. My husband and I have had issues in parenting recently. We left the Middle East and my husband's job in December, had two months in Canada on vacation, then one month in Australia settling in and getting all our documents sorted. During this three-month sabbatical, we and our two-year-old daughter were dealing with lots of travel, time zone changes, living with grandparents, her sleeping in a bed and not a crib, relaxed schedules, and me being newly pregnant again. During this time, we regressed into some very bad sleeping habits with our daughter, most notably co-sleeping, and basically all but forgot her sleep training. We used to do her nighttime routine then leave her in bed, drowsy but awake, and she would fall asleep on her own. But, with all the many changes, we regressed into some bad sleeping habits. When my daughter would wake up at night and I was too tired to go check on her, my husband would go to see her, but would end up falling asleep in her bed, or end up bringing her into our bed. I would tell him over and over again to leave when she fell asleep, or to just comfort her enough for her to stop crying, or give her some milk if that's what she wanted, then leave. He would say, 'Yes, yes', but in the end he would end up falling asleep there or bringing her into our bed. What can I say? We had problems. Finally, when my husband's new job was starting, I knew we needed to get rid of the co-sleeping and go back to the sleep training. What a headache! Firstly, our two-year-old would tell me she wanted Daddy to sleep in her bed. Then she would get up out of bed and bang on the door. But thankfully, she couldn't open the door yet, so we had a win there. But honestly, it wasn't our daughter who needed to change more; it was my dear husband's thinking. It took a few intense conversations, but in the end, he agreed sleep training was good, and that what he had been doing was instilling in her bad sleeping habits, which he agreed to stop.

Thank You, Lord, that You want us to be peacemakers, and to keep unity in our marriages and families. Help me in my marriage when my husband and I are in two different minds about something. Help me to be patient, humble, and gentle, and help us both make wise, united decisions for our children.

'Be completely humble and gentle; be patient, bearing with one another in love. Make every effort to keep the unity of the Spirit through the bond of peace.'
—EPHESIANS 4:2-3 (NIV)

See the Good/God in Everything

The Changes with Kids

Life without kids was very different. We were married for six years before our daughter arrived. I now understand why people say that 'life without kids is a honeymoon period', because it's pretty true. Kids are a blessing! Never get me wrong on that. But the changes are real. Before kids we used to go out to late dinners in nice restaurants. Now we feel more at home in a mall food court or family-friendly restaurant, places our daughter can make a mess, walk around, and have a tantrum without much notice. My husband and I used to have long, deep, meaningful conversations; now, if we can get a few minutes in edgewise, without our little dear interrupting us, it's a miracle! Also, we used to travel a lot. Since our daughter arrived we've had to consider what requirements are needed to travel with her. In my books, travelling with a lightweight, breastfeed-only baby is probably the easiest time to travel with a child. Once they're off the breast or eating more solid food, it gets trickier, since airplanes and airports don't have the best food options, and in a lot of countries you can't enter with fruit from another country, so you can't just travel with everything you need. But the biggest change with kids is you officially become a member of the parents' club—the club where life's most precious beings have been entrusted to us from God.

Thank You, Lord, for gifting us with these precious children. Help us to guide them and raise them in Your ways. Help us to have wisdom in our parenting and in how we live our lives.

'All your children shall be taught by the Lord, and
great shall be the peace of your children.'
—ISAIAH 54:13

WIFE

You Are Not Your Husband's Holy Spirit

Repeat after me: You are *not* your husband's Holy Spirit. I used to think the Lord was speaking to me things my husband should improve on or change, or providing revelation on some particular prayer topic we were having. And it's true that often the Lord will speak to one of us something, but usually it will be confirmed by an agreement or similar revelation by the other. I've come to realize that even if I have revelation on something my husband doesn't, I can't help him into getting revelation himself. I have to leave it, ponder it in my heart, pray about it, and let my husband get there on his own. And he usually does. But by letting him get there on his own with God, it gets him there in His timing and not mine. Sometimes I think we wives want our husbands to get revelation right at the same time we do, and I imagine most husbands regularly feel this way about their wives too. But we need to remember that all of us have our own journey to make with God. Sometimes we just need to pray and leave it, and let it come in His time.

Lord, help me to be the perfect helper for my husband, and not to think my timing is Your timing. Help me to trust in Your timing for all areas of my life.

> *'And we know that all things work together for good to those who love God, to those who are the called according to His purpose.'*
> —ROMANS 8:28

Every Man Has His Quirks

I love that old reality TV show *Duck Dynasty*. They were rednecks from Louisiana who had become millionaires from duck calls one of them patented and made. It was a funny, clean Christian show. Phil Robertson, the patriarch of the family, used to say, 'Every woman has her quirks'. I like to think that every man has his quirks too. That's something they don't tell you in the pre-marital classes or books, but your husband will have his quirks as well. Some quirks are cute, some are interesting, some are funny, some are downright weird, and some are downright disgusting. I find it interesting that the more questionable quirks don't usually appear until after the wedding. Either way, quirks or not, I'm still called to be the virtuous helper wife that God called me to be.

Lord, help me to focus on the good and not nitpick on the small inconsequential things. Help me to be the best helper for my husband and the best wife I can be.

'An excellent wife is the crown of her husband, but she who causes shame is like rottenness in his bones.'
—PROVERBS 12:4

Hard Conversations

I both hate and love hard conversations. I hate them because, let's be honest, they're hard. Usually they involve baring your soul, most often they include discussing expectations, and they're almost always heavily steeped in discussing deep heart issues. (Well, they usually are for me, anyways.) You have to make yourself a little bit vulnerable in these conversations, and I always find that hard. But, I also love these

See the Good/God in Everything

conversations, because it gives everyone a chance to say their piece and be heard. Usually, it leads to greater connection, but don't hold that against me if it doesn't.

Lord, help me to be a great listener, to be slow to speak and quick to listen. Help me to listen, to have wisdom and discernment. Help me also to respond the way Jesus would, and to always show love.

> *'So then, my beloved brethren, let every man be swift to hear, slow to speak, slow to wrath; for the wrath of man does not produce the righteousness of God.'*
> —JAMES 1: 19–20

Worth the Wait

I was 32 when I met my husband, and for some Christian single ladies, 32 years old feels ancient. I know it did for me. I felt like I was the only sucker without a husband or even any potential for one. It was a dreadful, sad, and very difficult time in my life. I had a lot of well-meaning relatives ask if they should set me up with some friend of a friend who was single. That was kind of them, but I just wasn't interested. I had followed what I'd been taught about praying for a promise (write the vision and make it plain—Habakkuk 2:2), and had listed things about my future husband that were important to me. This wasn't just the tall-dark-and-handsome kind of things, but also character traits and how I envisioned our marriage to be like. Ok, yes, I did want him to be taller than me, around 6'1", I will admit that, but other than that I didn't have any thoughts on how he looked. Okay, okay, I will admit as well that I did want him to be handsome. Who doesn't want a handsome husband?! When I finally met him in a service one day in March, I knew straight away there was something different/special/noteworthy about him. But he was divorced—oh my! And he had five adult children—oh my, oh my... It wasn't the perfect package on the outside, but my dear husband has a heart of gold, and is a man after God's heart. And though the wait was hard and long, he was worth it. He is my iron sharpening iron, my best friend, and my greatest encourager. He sees the best in me, even when I don't see it myself. Trust His process, and don't settle for anything but His best for you.

Lord, thank You that You have Your best for us. Help us to wait patiently in hope, and to grow and become the women of God You've called us to be, as we wait for Your promise.

> *'But the LORD said to Samuel, "Do not look at his appearance or at his physical stature, because I have refused him. For the LORD does not see as man sees; for man looks at the outward appearance, but the LORD looks at the heart."'*
> —1 SAMUEL 16:7

Be an Excellent Wife—The Crown on Your Husband's Head

Proverbs 12:4 says, 'An excellent wife is the crown of her husband, but she who causes shame is like rottenness in his bones'. This is one of my new favourites, and one I meditate on to remind myself of the woman of God I am, or should be. Not too long ago, I had a very bad day. I was hormonal, I was trying to be mindful of what I was eating, and I was reducing my sugar. I didn't take out my bad mood on my husband per se. I just kind of avoided him, put my head down, did what I needed to do, didn't talk much, wasn't affectionate, and wasn't happy. I kind of held on and rode the wave of life. Okay, this wasn't an ideal day, but to be honest, I handled it a lot better than previously. In the past I would have blamed my husband for everything and maybe even unwillingly caused a fight. So, I'm improving. Praise God. We have bad days, and that's fine, but even on our bad days we should be making slight improvements in our self-control, handling and managing our emotions, and being more aware of what's going on internally. Because we have a higher calling...and it is a high one! We are made to be the show-stopping masterpiece our husband wears on his head! What does this excellent wife look like? She's gentle and kind, strong and capable, anointed and powerful. She's wise, leads with wisdom and humility, is teachable, and submits to authority. She's hospitable, loving and prayerful, honours her husband and tends to his needs, makes her family feel loved and accepted, and brings joy wherever she goes. She's not a gossiper nor time waster. She's good and does good things. Yes, we go through bad days. But our ultimate goal should be to be getting closer and closer to the excellent wife God has called us to be. To be the beautiful masterpiece, the person our husband loves and adores, who brings him joy, not evil, all the days of his life.

Thank You, Lord, that You desire us to be women of inner beauty and character. Help us each and every day to strive to be the woman of excellence that You call us to be.

'An excellent wife is the crown of her husband, but she who causes shame is like rottenness in his bones.'
—PROVERBS 12:4

Wife Fails

I have bad days. I'm only human. Some days I am patient and kind, I've got my house in order, and I'm totally on top of everything. I'm an efficient multitasker and feel on top of the world! Then I have bad days. Sometimes they aren't even full days, just a part of a day that isn't up to my high standard. I'm exhausted, my house is a mess, I'm lacking energy and patience, and I may resort to turning the TV on to distract my child for a bit while I try to collect myself. It happens. I do a quick self-assessment and see where my problems lie. Maybe I didn't sleep well the night before, maybe I didn't eat well, maybe I'm hungry, maybe I got upset over something irrelevant, maybe I need to forgive, maybe my thinking has been bad. If I can get help, I do, but if I can't then I pray for strength to get through the day, outsourcing what I can. I'll forget about tackling the to-do list and take it easy with my house. I might get takeaway for dinner. Maybe I won't finish folding the laundry, and maybe I won't bathe my daughter that night. If I've been thinking wrong, or I've let my human nature get the better of me, I repent to the Lord. If I've been rude, unpleasant, or unkind to my husband, I repent and ask for forgiveness quickly. Sometimes against all odds, days just don't turn out well, but we are still children of God, always loved, and always a work in progress.

Thank You, Lord, that You always love us. Thank You for all our days; when they are good and when they are bad. Help us to have humility, and to trust in You every day. Help us to be like Jesus more and more.

'But those who wait on the Lord shall renew their strength; they shall mount up with wings like eagles, they shall run and not be weary, they shall walk and not faint.'
—ISAIAH 40:31

See the Good/God in Everything

Sin Lurks at Every Corner—Be Wise!

Have you ever wondered why there are so many scriptures about adultery and sexual immorality? Read Proverbs again, and you'll see it's not a topic to be trifled with. Sexual immorality, adultery, and the adulteress lurk around every corner, and we must be extremely careful in all our dealings with all people. We must also watch our thinking about ourselves and our spouse. Once we start thinking negative, demeaning thoughts about our spouse or our marriage, we allow an open door. Don't be deceived—sin lurks at every turn, so be wise in all your ways. I recently heard about a pastor who admitted to having an adulterous affair for months. My heart broke! Guess where he met the women he had an affair with? In a park. Yes, in a park! I know meeting someone in a park can be so innocent, but sin will seize you if you aren't careful in all your dealings, with everyone, everywhere. You could be a housewife and stay home 90 percent of your time, and still fall into sin. I know, I've been there. (I didn't have an affair, but I got too close to someone online while I was once taking an online course.) When you get excited to see someone, or to speak to someone, of the opposite sex who is not your spouse, let me tell you, you have a problem, or are at least close to having a problem. There's excited, and there's *excited*. You know the difference; you don't need me to explain it to you. Everyone knows when they are in sin. I heard of a Christian politician who follows the Billy Graham rule to avoid any situation that would have even the appearance of compromise or suspicion. The Billy Graham rule includes not traveling, meeting, or eating alone with a woman other than your wife. There's wisdom in that. We must be wise like serpents.

Thank You, Lord, that if we lack wisdom we should ask You for more wisdom. Lord, give us more wisdom! Help us to be wise, shrewd and cunning like serpents, but also to be gentle as doves. Lord, help us to be wise and to guard our marriages.

'If you do well, will you not be accepted? And if you do not do well, sin lies at the door. And its desire is for you, but you should rule over it.'

—GENESIS 4:7

Be an Encourager

I don't know about your husband, but my husband is a strong weight-of-the-world type of person. He doesn't often share things weighing on his heart, nor does he like to unnecessarily burden me with matters. One thing I've realized with my husband being so strong is that he doesn't often ask for or even seem to want encouragement. But I've noticed that though he doesn't seem to want encouragement, it is one thing that really makes a difference to him. He values my encouragement and gratitude, though he may not always vocalise it. And it makes a difference to him. When I encourage my husband, when I'm his cheerleader, I show him that I'm for him, that I'm his supporter, in his corner, will do everything I can to help him be the best version of himself. Being an encourager, being positive, and not holding any grudges or unforgiveness towards my husband helps me to regulate and determine the spiritual atmosphere in our home. It's an essential assignment. When I encourage him and say I believe he can do it (whatever the 'it' may be), I'm having faith and calling those things that aren't as though they are. I'm also prophetically declaring the Word of God over my husband and aligning him with the Word. It's an important and integral part of our marriage, and of me being his helper. We as wives wield so much authority and power in our homes and marriages, and we play a huge part in determining what kind of atmosphere our households and marriages have.

Thank You, Lord, that You give us the ability to impact and influence our marriages and households. Help us to be the type of helper to our husbands that You called us to be. Help us to be encouragers to our husbands, and to see the good in all things.

'Therefore encourage one another and build each other up, just as in fact you are doing.'
—1 THESSALONIANS 5:11 (NIV)

Manage Your Expectations

Something I haven't seen in the premarital books, nor have I heard about it in premarital counselling, is anything about managing expectations. Now, I'm really looking at you, ladies. Let's be honest. We have expectations, and sometimes quite a lot of them. But what I want to say to you is that if we can manage our expectations, it will make our lives, and especially our marriages, much better! Maybe it's just me, but if I've told my husband something once, I kind of just expect him to remember it. Also, is it wrong that I simply want my husband to read my mind and know exactly what I want, and when I want it? *Doesn't he know me by now?!* This is so unrealistic. Firstly, when we discuss managing expectations, the most important rule is to vocalise them. I can't tell you the number of times my husband and I had major problems because I didn't vocalise my expectations. (I focus on us wives, but my husband has been known a time or two to not vocalise his as well, so it works both ways.) The second, supremely important rule with managing expectations is to lower them. Sometimes we wives just have such high expectations. We need to have more realistic ones, combined with vocalising them to help ensure our married lives run as smoothly as possible.

Thank You, Lord, that You give us Your wisdom. Help me to be a good communicator and help me to be loving, kind, and humble at all times.

'Better to be of a humble spirit with the lowly, than to divide the spoil with the proud. He who heeds the word wisely will find good, and whoever trusts in the Lord, happy is he. The wise in heart will be called prudent, and sweetness of the lips increases learning. Understanding is a wellspring of life to him who has it. But the correction of fools is folly. The heart of the wise teaches his mouth, and adds learning to his lips. Pleasant words are like a honeycomb, sweetness to the soul and health to the bones.'
—PROVERBS 16:19–24

I Wish He Understood Hormones

According to my fertility tracker app, I'm in my fertile period, and should be ovulating any day now. I wish my husband was more aware of and knowledgeable about hormones. You would think after seven years of marriage, he'd be a bit more cognizant about mine. Yesterday and today I have gone through ridiculous mood swings. My patience is non-existent, I'm easily and highly irritable, and I'm uncommonly upset and angry. I wish my husband knew that when I go through these hormones and mood swings, I'm literally trying to hold on. It's not my conscious decision to be irritable or to have no patience or sense of humour. You know what I mean? I used to think I *was* my hormones, that it was my personality to be a generally moody person. This is incorrect. It's nice to be older and wiser and to have things in perspective. I now know that these mood swings are temporary and that they aren't my

See the Good/God in Everything

personality. So, I pray to God that these mood swings will pass easily, that my husband will have patience and understanding towards me, and that I come out unscathed. Once I'm feeling back to my old normal self, I will have to have another discussion with my husband about mood swings and hormonal changes.

Thank You, Lord, that my body is fearfully and wonderfully made in Your image. Thank You that my body is the way it is, so that I can grow and carry children. Help me, Lord, when mood swings and hormonal days occur. Help me to have patience and peace and for there to be unity, love, and peace in my marriage and family during those difficult days.

'Finally, brothers and sisters, rejoice! Strive for full restoration, encourage one another, be of one mind, live in peace. And the God of love and peace will be with you.'
—2 CORINTHIANS 13:11 (NIV)

Let Him Do What's in His Heart (Even If It Doesn't Make Sense)

Sometimes my husband has weird ideas. I don't always understand them, and I usually find them strange, but I've learnt that sometimes I just need to let him do what's in his heart. When our daughter started crawling, he went into hyper-childproofing mode. I understand that he wanted her to be safe, and that he wanted to do what he could to ensure our house was childproof, but he went a bit over the top. Almost every inch of her room is now covered in childproofing padding and foam. I thought he was going a bit over the top, and I originally tried to stop him, but he just really felt compelled to do it, so I let him. It wasn't worth getting into an argument over. I'll admit, though, that she's never had any accidents in her room; and when she's fallen, she's been injury-free due to the padded floor and padded corners. Sometimes when my husband has an idea, he just needs to have the freedom from me to follow through with it. It may or may not work, and I may or may not agree, but I allow him the freedom to do what he feels compelled to do (within reason). Sometimes it's just him, but sometimes it's the Holy Spirit. But by giving him the freedom, if it works out and turns out to be a good thing, he has complete ownership of that.

Thank You, Lord, that You speak to us in many ways. Guide us in all things. Help me to give my husband the freedom he needs to make his own choices. Help me not to be controlling or manipulative of my husband.

> *'For as many as are led by the Spirit of*
> *God, these are sons of God.'*
> —ROMANS 8:14

Get Your Head in the Game

Ladies, get your head in the game. My husband says he's always ready for sex, that he just needs a bit of a push and he's good to go. But that isn't how I work. I need good engaging conversation, affection, and declared undying love. And if something's on my mind, or I'm distracted with life and running a household—which, hello, is every day—I'm usually not even thinking about sex. One of my husband's frequent phrases to me is 'get your head in the game', that all the things keeping me from sex is usually between my ears. He's right, as he quite normally is. I think too much, I worry too much, and I've got a thousand tasks on my mind at once. So, when he tells me to get my head in the game, I actively engage. I force my mind to think about the task at hand. If it's lovemaking then I think about that, and I don't allow myself to be distracted by what we'll have for dinner tomorrow, when my Amazon package is coming, or whether I should add bananas to my online grocery order. I know we females are amazing at multitasking; but when it comes to romance time, be single-minded to the task, and get your head in the game.

Thank You, Lord, that we are fearfully and wonderfully made. Help us to keep our marriage in the highest priority and to be fully engaged in our dealings with our husbands. Help us not to be distracted by life, but to give our husband our full attention when necessary.

'Marriage is honorable among all, and the bed undefiled;
but fornicators and adulterers God will judge.'
—HEBREWS 13:4

How Often Do You Pray?

I was speaking recently to one of my relatives who with her husband were going through some really tough times. We were talking about how our husbands handle different situations and she asked me, 'How often do you pray for him?' My answer was 'as often as possible'. I pray daily about his work, his relationships with friends and family, his spiritual life, and just about anything else I can think of to pray for. I also ask the Holy Spirit to lead me how to pray, and see if there's anything He's highlighting for me to pray about. I also pray about the future—if I know there's change coming, like a new job, or a move to a different place, I pray in advance about that too. I pray for his growth in the Lord, and that he isn't being stagnant but growing wiser and closer to God all the time. There's only so much we can do in the physical, but in the spiritual we can affect everything with our prayers.

Thank You, Lord, that You hear all our prayers. Help us not to grow weary in praying, but to be prayerful in all aspects of our lives. Help us to lift up our spouses, families, communities, and country to You in prayer. Help us to live righteously.

> *'Rejoice always, pray without ceasing, in everything give thanks; for this is the will of God in Christ Jesus for you. Do not quench the Spirit. Do not despise prophecies. Test all things; hold fast what is good. Abstain from every form of evil.'*
> —1 THESSALONIANS 5:16–22

See the Good/God in Everything

MARRIAGE

Marriage is Not a Romance Novel

I used to love romance movies and Jane Austen books. For many years I had *Pride and Prejudice* on constant replay, first via VHS, then DVD, then on my phone directly through iTunes. And then I got married, and I realized all those movies and books don't actually show marriage. They show the drama and excitement of courting and falling in love; but actual marriage, they just don't touch on it. What can I say? Firstly, that Jane Austen will not prepare you for marriage! Marriage can be fun, exciting, and romantic, yes. But it can also be boring, mundane, and ordinary. Courting and falling in love is the super exciting bit, but it's the being married that's hard work. It's the everyday moments of a marriage you need to work on. Work to keep things interesting, work at growing closer and more intimate, and work at growing more in love with each other. It's easy to fall into a routine-driven, shoulder-to-shoulder, doing-oriented type relationship (especially when you have kids). But to keep things going for the long term in marriage, you need to continue to build your heart-to-heart relationship. What you don't see in the Jane Austen books and romance movies is the daily work of marriage. That marriage is like a garden and you must tend to it, take out weeds, and water it with time and love.

Lord, we thank You for marriages. We thank You that You are in our marriages. Lord, help us to work on our marriages, to never take our marriage for granted, and to also see the best (not the worst) in each other.

'Blessed is everyone who fears the Lord, who walks in His ways. When you eat the labor of your hands, you shall be happy, and it shall be well with you. Your wife shall be like a fruitful vine in the very heart of your house, your children like olive plants all around your table. Behold, thus shall the man be blessed who fears the Lord.'

—PSALM 128:1–4

Communication Can Be Hard, But Is So Necessary

I grew up in a family where we discussed how we felt upfront, sometimes with loud angry voices. That was the norm. If we didn't discuss things outright, our body language and facial expressions would make you know how we felt. I know it's not an ideal way of communicating, but that's just what I grew up with. My husband, on the other hand, just doesn't do things like that. He'll pretend as if everything's normal, even though he might be seething on the inside. He'll put a fake smile on his face, try to be polite, and even speak calmly. But you can pick up on someone's vibe and emotions, and I'll know that though he's acting as if everything's okay, he's actually pissed off at me. I really dislike this type of behaviour, because I'd rather just say what's on our minds when things happen and not let it stew, or pretend to play happy family when we aren't a happy family. Oh, but my husband will let things stew away for hours, days, weeks, even months. And then one day he'll basically explode and say, 'You did that one thing that one time, months ago...' and I'm like, 'Dude, so much time has passed, and you were acting all normal, how was I to know you were pissed off?!' So, after many serious confrontations and discussions (and years) we finally have the communication lines clear and open. I've learnt to just force the conversation with my husband. Force him to address his feelings, anger, and expectations, and hash it out with me. It may not be nice to do at the time, but honestly, it clears things up so much faster, and you don't have resentment and bitterness building up towards each other.

Lord, help me in my weaknesses. Help me to have wisdom in my marriage, to be a good communicator, and to be self-reflective so I can do my part to better our marriage. Help me to forgive quickly and thoroughly, and to not let resentment or bitterness build up towards my husband. Help me to always keep the peace in my marriage.

'Be angry, and do not sin: do not let the sun go down on your wrath, nor give place to the devil.'
—EPHESIANS 4:26–27

BEST

When we got married, the wonderful pastor who was to preside over our wedding ceremony did a short pre-marital course with us. It was known as BEST: Blessing, Edification, Sharing, Touch. Blessing is ensuring we use kind words and actions, show appreciation and thankfulness to our spouse and God, and pray for each other. Edification is building up, not tearing down. A husband edifies his wife by praising her, and the wife edifies her husband by her loving response to him. Included in edification is refraining from criticising the other. Sharing includes time, activities, interests, concerns, objectives, and goals. Touch includes sexual intimacy as well as non-sexual affection. It's a very simple teaching but an important one. We must always strive to be our BEST in our marriages, and treat it as a blessing.

Thank You, Lord, that You give us the wisdom, ability, and desire to be a better person for our spouse. Help us to be more and more like Jesus each and every day. Help us every day to be a blessing to our spouse and to build them up. Thank You for the joy, love, peace, and unity that will flow from our marriage, because we put You and Your ways first.

'Therefore let us pursue the things which make for peace
and the things by which one may edify another.'
—ROMANS 14:19

'BEST' model taken from Love Life for Every Marriage Couple *by Ed Wheat and Gloria Okes Perkins.*

Be Flexible with an ADHD Diagnosed Spouse

My husband has ADHD. He was diagnosed by a psychiatrist when he was in his forties. He relates his experience with ADHD like this. For many years when he was at work there was an open window that would bother him tremendously because of the traffic noise. The day after he was finally medicated for ADHD, he went to work, and after some time realized the window had been open the whole time and it didn't bother him at all. Living with a spouse with ADHD is a bit of a learning curve, especially if your spouse is not regularly medicated, and especially if it's something new and different to you. My dear husband, when he's not medicated, is very relaxed and lackadaisical. I find it difficult but not impossible to have a serious or meaningful conversation with him. He views his unmedicated self as creative, fun, and funny. When my

See the Good/God in Everything

husband is medicated he's engaged, communicative, and compelling. He can be a bit intense sometimes, like when one has an energy drink. When my husband first told me he had ADHD, I didn't really think anything of it. In the excitement of courting, who has time to think about things like that? I never thought what life with a husband with ADHD would be like, but it's taken an enormous amount of patience, willingness to listen and learn, and a desire to understand my husband. It isn't always easy, but we must be flexible in our marriages. We must move with compromise and grace, and be adaptable in our ways.

Thank You, Lord, that You teach us and guide us in all things. Help us to be adaptable and flexible in our marriages. Help us to administer grace often, and to be accommodating. As well, help us to be flexible to You and Your ways, and to be sensitive to the leading of the Holy Spirit.

> *'For God has not given us a spirit of fear, but of power and of love and of a sound mind.'*
> —2 TIMOTHY 1:7

My Wise Husband Is Really Good at Ignoring Me

My husband wanted me to call this entry 'My Amazing Husband'. Well, he is pretty wise. He's actually so wise, he knows when to ignore me. Some of you may think that's harsh, but it actually isn't. Ever get so hormonal you can't see straight? Maybe you're exhausted or stressed and the things coming out of your mouth aren't very pleasant or nice? Or maybe you're just a little pissed at something, and you're banging the cupboards a bit too hard? Hello, ladies, I'm speaking to you! Hello, this is me too! The other day I had strapped my 25-pound baby to my back and decided to vacuum the house. It was a good idea in theory and it worked pretty well. The only problem was I didn't account for the backlash of absolute exhaustion and pain in my body afterwards. So, my husband came home from work, and after dinner the exhaustion hit me like a ton of bricks. It was like the exhaustion just came out of nowhere. I put the baby to sleep, and the general rule is when one person puts the baby to sleep, the other cleans the kitchen. Well, I came back down after putting the baby to bed and there was my husband sitting on the couch watching YouTube, with our kitchen a disaster area. This led to the both of us cleaning up, but I was pissed, slamming cupboard doors and huffing under my breath. It's lucky I didn't break any dishes! Finally, it was clean and I stormed up to bed and almost passed out. I finally realized with my achy body and unclean kitchen fiasco that I'd been very rude. I apologized to my husband for letting my exhaustion affect my behaviour and attitude. He pointedly told me he was wise and just ignored me. Sometimes in the process of being more like Jesus, we have slip-ups. This was one of mine. But my dear, wise husband knows the art of ignoring me. Sometimes a bit of ignoring works to keep the peace until the other one comes to their senses.

Thank You, Lord, for Your wisdom. Please give us more wisdom and strategies to keep the peace in our marriages, families, and relationships. Help us to be like Jesus more and more, and to have less slip-ups in our walk with You.

'Depart from evil and do good; seek peace and pursue it.'
—PSALM 34:14

See the Good/God in Everything

Catch Your Husband Doing Something Good

Recently with my energetic and opinionated toddler, I've been noticing that I've been focusing on her negative behaviour too much. I noticed I was catching her doing bad things, like throwing food off her highchair. I was reading a parenting blog that mentioned catching your child doing something 'good'. Instead of commenting when she throws her food off her table, I now comment on how well she's eating (before she throws the food off the table). This is also called 'descriptive praise'. It's a proactive and positive way to reinforce good behaviour. Well, I told my husband about the descriptive praise, and he reminded me that he'd already told me about the concept a few months previous. Okay, I forgot that bit. But, then he reminded me that the same thing goes for husbands. It's super easy to catch him at a moment when his behaviour isn't ideal, like when he's weeing with the door open. Or he leaves the toilet seat up. Or all his dirty clothes are all over the floor. But after telling him off this morning for another lapse in judgement, he jokingly said to me as he kissed my cheek goodbye, 'Catch your husband doing something good'. He's right.

Thank You, Lord, for my husband. Thank You that he is such a blessing. Help me to catch him doing something good, and not always focus on the negative. Help me to be an encourager and not a discourager or nagger.

*'A merry heart does good, like medicine,
but a broken spirit dries the bones.'*
—PROVERBS 17:22

More Than a Husband

Husbands are what we make of them. In the first few years of marriage, my husband was just my husband. We did everything together, we had a few common interests, and we enjoyed each other's company. But by going through harder times—family problems, infertility, working through insecurities, developing godly character—we moved from being just husband and wife to best friends. We're now confidants, each other's champions and supporters. Being best friends didn't just happen overnight. It took time and a decision. You have to want to be each other's best friend, and you have to do the work that comes with being a best friend. Best friends are those who know our hearts. They know what will make us laugh and cry. They know our hidden fears. They'll defend us to others. They'll protect us and keep us safe. They encourage. They know when to make us laugh and when to be quiet and listen. They value our relationship and work to protect it at all costs. They see the best in us. Best friends are the best friends. And our husbands can be more than husbands; they can be our best friends if we want them to.

Thank You, Lord, for our husbands. Thank You that they are godly men after Your own heart. Help us to respect our husbands and be their greatest encouragers and champions.

*'As iron sharpens iron, so a man sharpens
the countenance of his friend.'*
—PROVERBS 27:17

See the Good/God in Everything

Sometimes My Husband Is a Jerk

Sometimes my husband is a jerk. That's a harsh statement, but it's true. There are days when he's woken up on the wrong side of the bed and life in a non-Western, non-Australian country is just too much for him. People don't speak English very well, we're all wearing masks, there are loudspeakers going off everywhere, and the drivers are pretty crazy. All of that can make my husband a very unpleasant person to be with. He was once upset with life and the wild driving and he took it out on me with his unkind words and tone. While I was in the bathroom forgiving him and very angry, I thought to myself, even though I love my husband and he's my other half, my worth doesn't come from him. Whether he's amazing, a jerk, or somewhere in between, my worth comes from God. God defines who I am. Days like these remind me so much that God really is the defining factor in my life. People, no matter how great, are human and fallible. So, though my husband today was a jerk, I still have to forgive him and love him, and have grace for him. One day at a time.

Thank You, Lord, that You are my confidence. Help me to have grace even when I am angry and upset. Help me to forgive quickly and easily, to have wisdom, and to keep the peace in my marriage.

'My child, never drift off course from these two goals for your life: to walk in wisdom and to discover your purpose. Don't ever forget how they empower you. For they strengthen you inside and out and inspire you to do what's right; you will be energized and refreshed by the healing they bring. They give you living hope to guide you, and not one of life's tests will cause you to stumble. You will sleep like a baby, safe and sound—your rest will be sweet and secure. You will not be subject to terror, for it will not terrify you. Nor will the disrespectful be able to push you aside, because God is your confidence in times of crisis, keeping your heart at rest in every situation.'
—PROVERBS 3:21–26 (TPT)

Ground Rules in Marriage

These ground rules are a collaboration of what my husband and I deem as foundational in marriage.

Address things quickly
Apologize quickly
Always forgive
Love of God that equals changed behaviour

If you know you've done something wrong, apologize quickly. Don't wait for your spouse to drag it out of you. Even if you're not sure you were in the wrong, but there is no peace, apologize first and figure it out later. Always forgive. This doesn't mean be a doormat, nor does it refer to abuse. It refers mainly to forgiving your spouse and restoring them to the high place. It means don't bring up past incidences unnecessarily, and don't hold onto grudges. It means forgive thoroughly. When you love God, you should want to be more like Jesus, period. We are imperfect humans. You should be willing to recognise behaviour, traits, and habits that aren't godly, and be willing to try with God's help to address and maybe change. Sometimes in marriages it's just easier to ignore things. This usually leads to a build-up of resentment and cataloguing of issues. As much as possible, address things quickly and in a timely manner, and don't let issues build. Be willing and open to change for the betterment of your marriage, and to keep the peace.

Thank You, Lord, for bringing our spouses into our lives. Help us to have wisdom and discernment in our lives and marriages. Help us to have joyful and peaceful marriages, so that our marriage would glorify You. Help us to always have unity in our marriage.

See the Good/God in Everything

'Set me as a seal upon your heart, as a seal upon your arm;
for love is as strong as death, jealousy as cruel as the grave;
its flames are flames of fire, a most vehement flame.'
—SONG OF SOLOMON 8:6

Keep the Peace

Peace is something you don't notice until it's gone. As born-again believers, filled with the Holy Spirit, peace surrounds and envelops us. We can easily take it for granted. And we probably don't even notice the peace that surrounds us and that we have within us, until it's gone. Gone by arguments, unforgiveness, sin, and attack. When my husband and I have an argument, or if there's something I need to forgive but haven't, I can instantaneously feel the absence of peace. It's funny, but when things are good I don't realize that I'm actually engulfed with peace. I've learnt that the best way to keep the peace is to not be too uptight, to laugh things off, and to not get easily offended. To humble myself and self-reflect. To humble myself enough to be the first to apologise. We need to learn how to shrug off insults and keep the peace.

Thank You, Lord, for Your peace. Help us not to take peace for granted, and help us to be peace makers in all aspects of our lives.

'If you shrug off an insult and refuse to take
offence, you demonstrate discretion indeed.'
—PROVERBS 12:16 (TPT)

The First Year Was Our Worst

Let me just say that our first year of marriage was the worst. It was not the honeymoon period others have. Why was it so bad, you wonder? I think it comes down to a few things. Firstly, when we got married I was 32 and had been living abroad for almost ten years. I was an extremely independent and opinionated person, maybe even difficult and set in my ways. Another was that my husband was in his fifties. He'd been through a divorce after twenty years of marriage. He knew what kind of psychological and behavioural issues had contributed to his previous failed marriage, and he didn't want to go through that again. There were a lot of confrontations and butting of heads. Another was that before we got married there was a lot of drama, which resulted in us being estranged from my family. It was a super tough time for me. I was hurt and I knew I'd also hurt a lot of people. It was a heavy weight on my shoulders and it would take a long time for me to forgive, heal, and reach out to my family. There were many tears involved, lots of journaling and heart-to-heart conversations with God. We had to work through a lot of issues, both my husband and I. But in the end, we survived and are the better for it. We know that our marriage has been through difficult waters, but with God it came right in the end. What's my point about all this? Be willing and open, because none of us are perfect. Marriage is not about perfection or idealism but about peace, love, harmony, and unity. We need to address the issues, insecurities, and fears in our life so that we don't bring into our marriages baggage from our past.

Thank You, Holy Spirit, that You are working in us to have the Fruits of the Spirit and to look like Jesus every day. Help us to self-reflect, address, and acknowledge our shortcomings, fears, and issues, and to deal with them in the appropriate way so that they will not hinder our marriages.

See the Good/God in Everything

*'Not that I have already attained, or am already perfected;
but I press on, that I may lay hold of that for which Christ
Jesus has also laid hold of me. Brethren, I do not count
myself to have apprehended; but one thing I do, forgetting
those things which are behind and reaching forward to
those things which are ahead, I press toward the goal for
the prize of the upward call of God in Christ Jesus.'*

—PHILIPPIANS 3:12–14

Sometimes You Need to Be the Strong One

The seasons often change in our marriage and in our lives. When we were battling with infertility and trying for a baby, I went through a dark valley. My husband had to be the strong, sane one. The positive one. The encouraging one. I was going through probably the hardest time in my life. Battling myself to remember and trust that God is good. Focusing on the fact that I would make it out of the valley stronger, more faithful, and more in awe of His goodness. It took a long while for me to make it out of that valley. I went through periods where it got better, then got worse. I battled with a lot of insecurity. Things have shifted now in our marriage and I'm having to be the strong, sane one. My husband's dealing with work issues, stress, and the desire to leave and return to Australia. It's a balancing act—being supportive of my husband, making sure I'm listening to his complaints without letting it get into a whinging fest, being prayerful, and being open to hearing from God on all this.

Thank You, Lord, for my dear husband. Thank You that You are with us whether we are in the valley, or on the mountaintop. Help me to be a supportive and prayerful wife.

> *'This is my command—be strong and courageous!*
> *Do not be afraid or discouraged. For the LORD*
> *your God is with you wherever you go.'*
> —JOSHUA 1:9 (NLT)

When Things Changed for Me

When I first met my husband, all I saw was a middle-aged divorced man, slightly handsome, slightly weird, Australian, with a lot of baggage. But, I remember there was something different about him, though I couldn't put my finger on it. We ran in similar social circles though neither of us were dating anyone. We had a mutual friend who lived in the apartment next door to me. She worked with me, but she was closer in age and background to my husband-to-be. She once got quite ill suddenly and I accompanied her to the hospital for an appointment. Right before she went into the examination room, she informed me that John (my future husband) was going to be stopping by the hospital to drive us to the airline office so she could get a flight back home to Australia. I didn't have a second to think about it before she was taken into the examination room and John arrived. He came with a bag on his shoulder which I thought was odd for some reason, so I asked him about it. He said he brought the bag because he was carrying various things. He said, 'Because [our mutual friend] is sick, I brought Teddy to comfort her', and proceeded to take out a teddy bear. Then he said, 'And because ladies tend to like chocolate, I brought her that too', and pulled out a box of chocolates, and then said, 'And I brought scriptures to pray over her for healing'. It was at that moment that something changed for me, and I saw him in a different light. I didn't see a weird middle-aged divorced man, but I saw him as a godly man, kind, considerate, and with good intentions. It's funny how one choice interaction can change the way you view someone.

Thank You, Lord, for godly husbands and divine appointments. Help us to see the way You see, and to love the way You love. Help us to love our husbands more and more each day. Help us to be the best wife for our husbands and to live our lives and marriages in a way that is pleasing to You.

> *'But the Lord said to Samuel, "Do not look at his appearance or at his physical stature, because I have refused him. For the Lord does not see as man sees; for man looks at the outward appearance, but the Lord looks at the heart."'*
> —1 SAMUEL 16:7

I Need Communication and Conversation

My husband came home from work a few days ago, and we tried to have a conversation over our daughter babbling and vying for Daddy's attention. Our daughter hadn't had much dinner an hour earlier, so I asked my husband if he could give her some of his chicken as he ate his dinner, as baby girl loves to share Daddy's food. She won't always eat what I give her, but if Daddy's eating it, she wants it and will gobble it down! I think it's obvious who should be doing all the feeding... Anyways, my dear husband was 'trying' to multitask, attempting to feed our daughter while trying to talk to me at the same time. It didn't work. I got peeved off since I was being ignored, but I forgave him. It affected me because I know that I thrive on communication and conversation, and I wasn't getting it. I wouldn't call it a marriage fail, but it definitely didn't work. It is important that we as wives know exactly what we need, especially from our husbands. And we need to be able to vocalize our needs to our spouses, not keep it all in and let it grow into resentment.

Thank You, Lord, that You clothe us in strength and dignity. Thank You, Lord, that life is good and we can laugh without fear of the future. Help us to know ourselves and what we need as women, and to communicate our needs with our husbands. Help us to have united and happy marriages, where You are at the centre.

*'She is clothed with strength and dignity, and
she laughs without fear of the future.'*
—PROVERBS 31:25 (NLT)

Post-coitus is Not the Time to Tell Him to Use Mouthwash (Explicit)

It's funny how women can be in the middle of lovemaking and also be very distanced from it. In another entry I wrote about how we need to get our head in the game when it comes to lovemaking. Another important issue is timing and not saying things at inopportune moments. In my defence, I'm getting better at not blurting everything I think of straight away (usually at the wrong moment), but the urge is still there. The other day we were in the middle of lovemaking. As a general rule, my husband must use mouthwash beforehand. It's just a thing. I'm sensitive to smells and tastes and, let's be honest, a man's mouth could always use a good brushing and a swig of mouthwash. So, in the middle of lovemaking we were kissing and I was really noticing how his mouth didn't taste nice at all. It was like he'd just had a bit of smelly parmesan cheese, but I knew he used mouthwash. I contemplated if this was a good time or a

See the Good/God in Everything

bad time to mention this to him. I concluded that he'd be pretty pissed if I mentioned it at that time, as we were in the middle of lovemaking, so I kept it to myself and got on with it. Yes, it was a bit unpleasant, but I survived. Then, post-coitus, I was also considering if it was a good time to mention the mouthwash thing…I again decided it was probably better to keep it for another time. Timing is so important, and not ruining lovemaking or its afterglow with unpleasant comments is a good thing. So, let's work hard at keeping the peace in our marriages and continue to be aware that the timing of our comments and statements is so important to keeping the peace.

Thank You, Lord, that You give us Your peace, and that You want us to be peacemakers. Help us to remember that sometimes it is best to keep our mouths shut. Help us to know when the time is right to say something.

> *'Even a fool who keeps silent is considered wise;*
> *when he closes his lips, he is deemed intelligent.'*
> —PROVERBS 17:28 (ESV)

Heart to Heart

A shoulder-to-shoulder relationship consists of being united to achieve a shared goal. Think of soldiers in the army marching, for example. It's not the most intimate type of relationship, but more goal-oriented and focused. A heart-to-heart one, on the other hand, is a close, intimate, honest relationship. You know the inner depths of the other person's heart. You know their fears and their dreams. The goal in our marriage is to stay heart to heart; but let's be honest, when we had our daughter, heart-to-heart moments took a long holiday. There was very limited time for loving, intimate chats. It was more blurry-eyed 'hellos', 'goodbyes', or 'do a wash because everything has vomit on it'. Admittedly that time doesn't last very long, but you get into the habit of becoming super baby-focused. The baby becomes the centre of everything, and the centre of all your conversations. It came to the point months after our baby was born where I felt like I was living with a roommate, not a husband. So, we're now actively working to get back to a place where we're not just shoulder-to-shoulder in doing the work of being parents, but we also strive to keep our marriage heart-to-heart.

Thank You, Lord, that You desire intimate relationship with us. Help us not to forsake our relationship with You, or be distracted by the everyday. Help us to keep our marriages strong, close, and pure. Help us not just to do the work of being parents, but to strive for true intimacy with You and our spouse.

'The Lord is my shepherd; I shall not want. He makes me to lie down in green pastures; he leads me beside the still waters. He restores my soul; he leads me in the paths of righteousness for His name's sake.'
—PSALM 23:1–3

You Might Need to Plan Lovemaking in Advance

We had a baby, life got busy, work got stressful, we gained a lot of weight, and we just got lazy with lovemaking. It would seem that every few weeks, something would happen; I'd get my period, my husband would get sick, or we'd have a string of nights where the baby wouldn't settle and sleep. We'd just put off sex for another day in the future. We got really good at making excuses for not having intimate time. There was a scene in a movie I once watched where a husband and wife scheduled sex on Wednesdays. We watched it many years ago when we were having sex regularly, and we just couldn't comprehend that scene; we thought it was laughable. Oh, how the tables have turned! My husband now remembered that scene and thought it was a good idea. So, we now have a dedicated day of the week for lovemaking. It sounds pretty comical, but these days if we don't plan for intimate time, it just won't happen. Until our kids get older and we get back into the swing of things again, we just need to pick a day and make it happen. Sometimes you just need to do what you need to do to keep the love alive and physical needs met.

Thank You, Lord, that marriage was Your idea. You put husbands and wives together. Help us to do what is necessary to address the issues that keep us from being physically united in our marriages. Help us to have the time, energy, and desire to keep the love alive in our marriages and to have intimacy with each other.

> *'But because of the temptation to sexual immorality, each man should have his own wife and each woman her own husband. The husband should give to his wife her conjugal rights, and likewise the wife to her husband. For the wife does not have authority over her own body, but the husband does. Likewise the husband does not have authority over his own body, but the wife does. Do not deprive one another, except perhaps by agreement for a limited time, that you may devote yourselves to prayer; but then come together again, so that Satan may not tempt you because of your lack of self-control.'*
> —1 CORINTHIANS 7:2–5 (ESV)

Be Humble When Discussing Marital Issues

So, my dear husband and I were talking about our terrible day last night (see 'Too Much Forgiveness for One Day'). It was a touchy subject, as we were both upset with each other, and there were a few issues we needed to discuss. As we were talking things through, I had to constantly remind myself not to get provoked, not to get aggressive, and to humble myself. To speak kindly, openly, and honestly, and to not get worked up or defensive. I find that speaking about marital issues is one of the hardest things in marriage. You have to humble yourself, get rid of your ego, and be open to self-reflection. Maybe you're not as perfect as you think you are; maybe you need to apologize as well; and maybe you actually need to try better next time. It's never easy to have these conversations, but I find once you've cleared the air and you've all had your say, spoken your mind, and spoken about what bothered you, both the relationship and the marriage get better. It gives you the chance to get rid of issues and baggage, and deal with them head-on. But if you're not humble and self-reflective when having these conversations, it just won't go anywhere.

Thank You, Lord, for Your example of humility. Help me to be humble and self-reflective so I can be the best person for my spouse and marriage. Help me to deal with issues and to be more like You, Jesus, each and every day.

*'Pride goes before destruction, and a
haughty spirit before a fall.'*
—PROVERBS 16:18

See the Good/God in Everything

Emotionalism Isn't Good Enough; You Need to Actually Change

No one's perfect; let's get that clear from the get-go. When you get married, you're still not perfect. Even if you're a 'good' Christian, that still doesn't make you perfect. When we first got married, I used to think I was a pretty good, slightly perfect person. Boy, was I wrong! When we used to get into an argument, especially when I was in the wrong, I would be a bucket of tears, bawling and begging to be forgiven. I would say, 'Of course I'll change', but then kind of leave it at that. You see, I used to think I was pretty perfect and surely my husband was over-reacting. But he wasn't. You see, for my husband, emotionalism wasn't good enough; he wanted to see a commitment to change from me. Over time I realized actual change wasn't necessary for him per se, but simply the desire and intent to change through self-reflection, and a desire to better our marriage by becoming a better person. Apologies are good, but change is better.

Thank You, Lord, that You desire us to be more like Jesus and to represent Him well. Help us to desire and allow the Holy Spirit to renew and change our attitudes and character to be more like Jesus. Help us to develop the Fruit of the Spirit in our lives. And help us especially to be the kind of people who will work on our marriages, and do what is necessary for it to be fruitful, lasting, and a blessing.

> *'Since you have heard about Jesus and have learned the truth that comes from him, throw off your old sinful nature and your former way of life, which is corrupted by lust and deception. Instead, let the Spirit renew your thoughts and attitudes. Put on your new nature, created to be like God—truly righteous and holy.'*
> —EPHESIANS 4:21–24 (NLT)

When He Finds It Difficult

When things are difficult for me, I'm usually dealing with fertility issues, issues of insecurity, waiting on God for promises, or problems with friends or family. But my husband's main issues tend to be difficulties at work—dealing with many different people with different backgrounds, of various nationalities, and the high stress of it all. Working here in the Middle East is different as the culture, way of working, and way of communicating is different from Western countries. So, when my husband is going through difficulties I support him through prayer, gentle reminders of God's goodness, and listening. Sometimes the listening involves him venting. Venting, though, has to be kept in check, because it can get to be too much and end up turning into constant complaining. This was the case with my husband and I had to veto him venting. I actually had to very seriously ask him to stop saying bad things about his colleagues because it was too much. I had to gently remind him that life and death is in our control, and his unsaved colleagues need our prayers instead. I often need to gently remind my husband that the hardship he's going through is a chance for him to learn something, an opportunity to develop fruit of the spirit such as patience, and a chance for him to bless others and learn to be content in every situation. And then after I've said my piece, and been prayerful about his situation, I have to let him be, and let him work it out on his own.

Thank You, Lord, that You are with us even in our hardships. Help us to be prayerful and supportive wives when our spouses are going through difficult times. Help us to have wisdom, kindness, and compassion when speaking to them about their troubles.

'These things I have spoken to you, that in Me you may
have peace. In the world you will have tribulation;
but be of good cheer, I have overcome the world.'
—JOHN 16:33

See the Good/God in Everything

He Has to Learn the Lesson Himself

Here's the thing about my dear husband; sometimes I think he's a bit slow on the uptake. I'm not saying he isn't a smart guy, because he is, but what I'm saying is that sometimes I wish he'd learn the God lessons quickly and move on. I see what I believe is the lesson he needs to learn, but he doesn't listen to me when I tell him. Take for example one of his co-workers. He has a love-hate relationship with this guy, an alpha male versus alpha male, mano y mano type of thing. There are days where things are great and they're best buds, working in tandem together; and then for a month after that, my husband has nothing positive to say at all. He's the source of most of my husband's stress, and they butt heads like bulls often, over just about everything. But I see his relationship with this co-worker as an opportunity for my husband to pray for this co-worker, as in 'pray for those who spitefully use you' (Matthew 5:44), and as well for his salvation. I also see it as an opportunity to learn contentment. Let's be honest—life isn't perfect, and there will always be people in our lives who we don't get along with, we don't want to be around, and we really don't like. But we have to love them as God tells us to, and be light around them. I've mentioned all this to my husband who thinks it's all a very good idea, and sometimes he kind of gets it; then other days he has no idea what I'm talking about and has only complaints. So, I'm learning that he has to learn the lesson himself. I'm not his Holy Spirit, and I can't do the heart work or the mind revelation work for him; he has to figure it out and learn it himself. But we all have lessons we're learning, and I know he sees areas where I myself need improvement. In those moments, I know that he stands by, prayerfully and patiently, trusting God to do the work in me, as I know God will do the work in him to make him more like Jesus.

Thank You, Lord, that You are constantly doing a work in us to change us into more like Jesus. Help us to be pliable, mouldable, and quick learners.

'You have heard that it was said, "You shall love your neighbor and hate your enemy." But I say to you, love your enemies, bless those who curse you, do good to those who hate you, and pray for those who spitefully use you and persecute you, that you may be sons of your Father in heaven.'

—MATTHEW 5:43–45

See the Hero in Your Husband

As mentioned before, I have this obsession with *Pride and Prejudice*, the book and the various movies. I've seen them all but I love the 2005 Keira Knightley version the most. At the climax toward the end of the film, Mr. Darcy (the love interest) comes walking through a field in the early morning. It's the hero shot and it's awe-inspiring. With dramatic cinematography, framing, lighting, and music to instil admiration, it's like the perfect man shot. He was a bit of a jerk in the beginning of the movie, but then rectifies his mistakes and becomes a redeemed man. Doing all this for his love, who still hates him (apparently), he becomes the epitome of a good man. I watched this movie again recently and when I saw the hero shot, I thought about how we need to see our husbands like that. We need to see the greatness, goodness, kindness, effort, and consistency in them, and treasure them like the heroes they are. Too often when we've been married for some time, it's easy to see the failures and shortcomings of our spouses. But we need to frame them in a good light, see their heart, and think good redeeming thoughts about them, not just focus on their imperfections.

Thank You, Lord, for our husbands. Help us to see them as the heroes they are. Help us to see the best and think the best of them. Help us to build them up into the men of God You are calling them to be, and

See the Good/God in Everything

help us to be the kind of godly, loving helper wives You call us to be. Help us not to nag or get caught up in the unimportant things so that we can be all that You call us to be in Christ.

'And now, dear brothers and sisters, one final thing. Fix your thoughts on what is true, and honorable, and right, and pure, and lovely, and admirable. Think about things that are excellent and worthy of praise.'
—PHILIPPIANS 4:8 (NLT)

Staying in Love

I'm a bit of a romantic. Some of my all-time favourite movies are romantic comedies, or period pieces that also have dramatic intrigue and happily ever afters. I grew up watching *Notting Hill* on VHS almost daily when I was a teenager. But now that I'm a 40-year-old mother of almost two kids, and having been married for almost a decade, what I can say is that movies are not real life. Movies are fantasy!!! The movies show the easy bit of love and marriage. They show the courting period. The period when you fall in love and everything is hunky dory and wonderful and life is fun and exciting. To be honest, before having kids, life really was like that. We travelled around the world when we wanted to, went out for late-night dinners to nice restaurants, and had long intense conversations. We did fun things and life was pretty easy and manageable. We had time, energy, and freedom. Life was easier then. Then we had a baby, who grew up to a toddler, who is still growing up. Children are a blessing, don't get me wrong, but marriage with kids is hard work. I find the hardest part of marriage with kids is staying in love and having time for yourselves. Keeping the romance alive when you have schedules, bedtime routines, and active and noisy toddlers is all but impossible. So, make time for the romance. Wait, let's lower our expectations a bit. Make time to talk and have an adult conversation. I'm definitely speaking to myself here! But, let's just try to make time to connect with our spouses, even for just a few short minutes. Happy mommies and daddies make happy family and happy kids.

Thank You, Lord, that You have made us fruitful and multiplied us. Help my husband and I to have the wisdom to keep our love alive and our marriage strong even with our growing, busy family.

> *'A new commandment I give to you, that you love one another; as I have loved you, that you also love one another. By this all will know that you are My disciples, if you have love for one another.'*
> —JOHN 13:34–35

See the Good/God in Everything

FORGIVENESS

Forgiveness and Prophetic Release

Sometimes even when I say I forgive my husband, even if I do actually forgive him, there can be a part of me that still holds onto something. Sometimes it's a bad attitude, or an emotion like anger, or a bit of ego. These aren't godly characteristics. When my husband repents and I forgive him, he's restored to the high place as if he hadn't sinned in the first place. And all aspects of my heart and mind should be in line with that. Part of what helps is our forgiveness routine which goes like this: The one who did something wrong must repent to the other person, something along the lines of, 'I'm sorry that I (insert what needs to be forgiven). I'll try not to do it again (which they actually have to try to do). Will you forgive me, please?' The other person says, ' I forgive you', then must release. We do a prophetic act of releasing. As if I was holding a bunch of leaves I throw them into the air. I prophetically release the anger, bad attitude, or ego. If we've released correctly we usually laugh, because it's pretty stupid and funny. But if we aren't laughing yet, we do it until we do laugh.

Lord, help me to be an easy forgiver. Help me not to hold onto disrespect, ego, or a bad attitude. Help me to forgive my spouse wholeheartedly.

'For if you forgive other people when they sin against you, your heavenly Father will also forgive you. But if you do not forgive others their sins, your Father will not forgive your sins.'
—MATTHEW 6:14–15 (NIV)

Check Your Heart Often

I realized recently that I had deep-rooted unforgiveness towards a member of my family, due to an incident a few years ago. At the time I was new to the family, and to be honest I was quite self-conscious about my new position. We were visiting this family member in a different city. We had been taken out to an event. While at this event, this family member brought someone to my husband and I, introducing my husband and totally ignoring me. My husband, aware of this blunder and outright disrespect, said, 'And this is my wife Gina'. At first, I didn't think anything of it, other than that this family member was being very rude and inconsiderate. In this family member's eyes, I obviously wasn't important enough to warrant introduction. But over time I realized it had affected me very much. Whenever I would think about that family member, I would have very mean thoughts. In my head I was always vindicating myself for being ignored. I realized I was actually very angry that I didn't stand up for myself at the time. I realized I needed to do a full heart check. I needed to forgive this family member for blatantly ignoring me. I also had to repent to the Lord for allowing my self-worth and value be affected by this family member. We must constantly remind ourselves that our value comes from God. God loves us so much that He sent His son to die for our sins. People may love us, and people may hate us, even within our own families (Luke 12:53). It's just a fact that even within my family, there will be some people I get along with and some I don't. But it's important that we check our heart and our thought life regularly. The direction of my thoughts actually highlighted to me the unforgiveness I was harbouring. Sometimes we can get prideful and think we're immune to harbouring unforgiveness, because we're so familiar with the teaching of forgiveness. But we must check ourselves regularly to ensure our hearts are clean.

Thank You, Lord, that You remind us to forgive seventy times seven times. Help us to always forgive, and to forgive quickly.

See the Good/God in Everything

'Get rid of all bitterness, rage and anger, brawling and slander, along with every form of malice. Be kind and compassionate to one another, forgiving each other, just as in Christ God forgave you.'
—EPHESIANS 4:31–32 (NIV)

Forgive and Forgive and Forgive Some More

I've come to realize that a lot of the forgiving I've had to do was towards family members. When we open our hearts towards people, we allow ourselves to be vulnerable. When we're vulnerable, we're more susceptible to feeling hurt. It's a fact. Family especially, because they're the nearest and dearest to us, are quite frequently the ones we need to forgive the most. I feel like forgiveness is an area the Lord has been really making me press into. Recently, the smallest things have rubbed me the wrong way, and I've needed to forgive, even if it seemed so stupid and inconsequential. I had an incident recently where I was upset that a family member didn't reply back to my text message. It seemed like such a stupid little thing, but I was still a bit upset. Because I thought I was being stupid for getting hurt and upset over such a silly inconsequential thing, I put it on the back burner and tried not to think about it. Many days later I realized I was actually upset, and that I had unforgiveness. I always assumed forgiveness would be for big things and big gestures, but that's wrong. Sometimes even things that seem small need to be addressed and forgiveness needs to be given.

Thank You, Lord, that if we confess our sins, You are faithful and just to forgive us our sins and to cleanse us from all unrighteousness. Thank You, Lord, that You care about the things we care about, even the small things.

*'Are not two sparrows sold for a copper coin? And not one
of them falls to the ground apart from your Father's will.
But the very hairs of your head are all numbered. Do not
fear therefore; you are of more value than many sparrows.'*
—MATTHEW 10:29–31

Forgive a Hairdresser?

I'm being taught a lot on forgiveness recently. I'm being taught that forgiveness may come in many different shapes and forms. During the pandemic, for example, I had limited access to beauty treatments, particularly getting my hair cut. But after ten months my hair can grow pretty long, especially as I have long hair to begin with. So, I Googled a few places, read some reviews, then booked in an appointment. Note that I live in a country in the Middle East where English isn't the native language. It's generally spoken by most but not always. I had high hopes, though, as when I called the salon, the person who answered spoke very good English. So I went to the salon and, to make a long story short, it was bad customer service from the beginning. I should have turned around and walked straight out. Hoping for the best, though, I stuck with it. But when I met my hairdresser who spoke very limited English, I should've known better. It wasn't the world's worst haircut; I've had that too, so I know it wasn't that. But it wasn't a nice haircut. I got home and proceeded to complain, a lot, to my husband. It wasn't until I was lying in bed trying to sleep that night and mulling the day over that I realized I was pretty upset at the salon and the hairdresser, and that I needed to forgive them. So, I proceeded to forgive the salon and the hairdresser. As always, I also repented to the Lord. I think we unknowingly disguise unforgiveness with complaints. We need to stop complaining, recognize we've been hurt, and forgive, not just mask our hurt with complaints.

See the Good/God in Everything

Thank You, Lord, that You are constantly making us into Your image. Help us to quickly recognize when we have been hurt, and to forgive. Help us to always keep our heart clean.

'Blessed are the pure in heart, for they shall see God.'
—MATTHEW 5:8

Sometimes I Get Tired of Forgiving

On my daughter's first birthday (during the pandemic) we had planned two Zoom birthday parties—the first with our extended family, and the second with our fellowship in another city. (We had recently moved, and our friends from church were in another city.) These were planned in advance with everyone. That day I also had a medical procedure in the morning. The procedure was fairly quick and painless, but left me groggy and bloated. After a good nap and some pain meds, we put on our special birthday outfits, made sure the balloons and birthday decorations were in place, and got in position in front of my laptop for our Zoom meetings. The first party with my family and relatives turned out very well. Slightly less people than anticipated, but still enjoyable. The second party I had high expectations for. All of our friends had RSVPed and planned to join the Zoom meeting; many of them had been friends for years. Well, the call came and went and we ended up having one friend join us. I cannot tell you my level of disappointment. Over the next few hours I received countless apologies and excuses. Each time I received another message I just replied 'no worries' and then in my heart forgave them. Yes, I know my expectations were too high. But I was so sure this would go down without a hitch, and I wasn't expecting a lack of attendance. As well, these were people I never thought in my life I would need to forgive for any reason. They're just so loving and godly!

And human. And there are always firsts, I guess. But part of me was just tired of forgiving. I knew I had to, but I just wanted a bit of a break. I had other things on my plate and I didn't need this as well. But I did what I needed to do. I forgave and forgave and forgave them again until I was no longer offended and easily provoked.

Thank You, Lord, that there is no limit to how much we should forgive. Even when we feel we have forgiven numerous times, help us to keep forgiving. Help us to keep our hearts clean towards You, and to not hold offences against others. Help us to be gracious and thankful in all aspects of our lives.

> *'Since God chose you to be the holy people he loves, you must clothe yourselves with tenderhearted mercy, kindness, humility, gentleness, and patience. Make allowance for each other's faults, and forgive anyone who offends you. Remember, the Lord forgave you, so you must forgive others. Above all, clothe yourselves with love, which binds us all together in perfect harmony. And let the peace that comes from Christ rule in your hearts. For as members of one body you are called to live in peace. And always be thankful.'*
> —COLOSSIANS 3:12–15 (NLT)

Forgiven but Not Fixed…Yet

I take seriously what it says in Ephesians 4:26–27: 'Don't let the sun go down while you are still angry, for anger gives a foothold to the devil'. But, let's be real about forgiveness in marriage. There are times when mishaps and disagreements are only discussed and spoken about in the privacy of our bedroom, after the day is done, and normally when our

See the Good/God in Everything

baby is asleep. Sometimes we're able to sort things out straight away, but there are other times when we need to give each other breathing space or thinking space. Even if things aren't thoroughly sorted, I try to ensure we've at least acknowledged the need to forgive each other and apologized, even if we don't totally make up that evening before bed. It's better than nothing. I would always prefer to take as much time as needed to hash our thoughts out, but life gets in the way, especially with kids. We do what we can. As long as apologies and forgiveness has been given, I'm willing to put in a pause and sort the rest out the next day. It's not ideal, but it's real life.

Thank You, Lord, for our spouses. Help us to be united and of the same mind. Help us to humble ourselves and to keep the peace in our marriages. Change us to be more like Jesus every day.

'Now I plead with you, brethren, by the name of our Lord Jesus Christ, that you all speak the same thing, and that there be no divisions among you, but that you be perfectly joined together in the same mind and in the same judgment.'
—1 CORINTHIANS 1:10

Forgive Until It Stops Hurting

Let's be real. There are different types of hurt. There's hurt when your spouse doesn't consider you in a decision, and there's a different level of hurt when your spouse is having emotional and unwarranted communication with a person of the opposite sex, and has hidden it from you. There is hurt, and there is more hurt. I've noticed that when it comes to forgiveness, there are different reactions depending on the level of hurt. If a slight hurt, when I forgive, the release from the pain and hurt can be instantaneous and very freeing. But for a more intense hurt, even after I've forgiven, sometimes I don't feel any different. This is when I apply the 'Forgive Until It Stops Hurting' rule. I forgive every day. I forgive when something triggers me. I forgive when I think about the situation. I forgive and forgive and forgive some more. I forgive until I'm no longer hurt. I forgive until I don't get triggered. I forgive until I'm no longer dwelling on the hurt. Sometimes forgiving alone won't trigger the release. This is when I start blessing. I bless their work, their relationships, their finances, their health, and their future. You forgive and bless and forgive and bless, then forgive and bless some more until you have freedom and peace.

Thank You, Lord, that You give us the answers and directions for life. Thank You that You desire us to live life to the fullest and not be held down by bitterness and unforgiveness. Help us to forgive, especially when we are hurt deeply by others.

'Fear not, for I am with you; be not dismayed, for I am your God. I will strengthen you, yes, I will help you, I will uphold you with My righteous right hand.'
—ISAIAH 41:10

Forgiving a One-Year-Old

My husband laughed at me when I told him that I had to forgive my one-year-old. But it's true. I love my daughter, but especially now that she's an opinionated and vocal toddler, there have been instances where I've been upset with her and needed to forgive her. Like the time when she slapped my face—it hurt! Or the time when I was washing the dishes and she came up, grabbed my leg, then forcefully bit me! Yes, I know she

See the Good/God in Everything

doesn't (probably) do these things purposefully and with bad intentions. But it still got me vexed and offended! I'd really like her to go and bite her father, because he'd think it's endearing and laugh. I know his reaction is the one I should probably have. Nonetheless, even with knowing all this, I've still had to forgive my one-year-old at times. It's all about keeping your heart clean.

Thank You, Lord, that everything in my life, whether big or small, matters to You. Thank You for guiding me, Holy Spirit. Help me to keep my heart pure and clean, and to not let unforgiveness, anger, or bitterness take root.

'Blessed are the pure in heart, for they shall see God.'
—MATTHEW 5:8

Pre-emptive Forgiveness

I'm learning something new. I'm calling it pre-emptive forgiveness. It's forgiving before I get upset, before my emotions catch up with me, and pre-emptively before arguments can start. So, for example, one time it was the weekend and I was making French toast for the family. I was finished making theirs so I told them to sit down and start eating. This isn't actually what I wanted. I actually wanted them to wait for me to finish making the whole lot, then for us to eat together at the table. But they listened to my instructions and ended up finishing eating before I'd even had a chance to sit down. I could feel my emotions starting to bubble up inside me. So, I forgave my husband for eating without me, and I forgave myself for not communicating my expectations clearly. I started to feel anger rising within me, so I forgave again. I repeated in my head a few times that I forgive my husband. Surprisingly, the anger never made it to the foreground, and I was lucid enough to clearly tell my husband that I actually wanted us to eat together. Pre-emptively forgiving my husband actually diverted an argument and saved us all some strife. It also helped in mitigating my emotions. Even before I felt the anger rising, I knew my expectations weren't being met, and that I could either pre-emptively forgive my husband and stop the emotional train, or allow the emotions to play out, which would've been messy to say the least.

Thank You, Lord, for Your Holy Spirit that teaches us and guides us in all things. Help us to be pre-emptive forgivers and ones who keep the peace. Help us to keep our hearts clean and to forgive quickly and easily.

'Be joyful. Grow to maturity. Encourage each other. Live in harmony and peace. Then the God of love and peace will be with you.'
—2 CORINTHIANS 13:11 (NLT)

Forgiving My Child, Again

As I was about to give my daughter a bit of mac and cheese for lunch one Saturday, my dear husband made a comment that I wasn't feeding her 'proper food'. So, to counteract that, I went on a cooking frenzy the next few days to ensure there was enough 'proper food' in our fridge. I made pasta bolognese, chicken tikka masala with veggies, hardboiled eggs, and butternut squash soup. I then attempted to feed some of the proper food to my daughter for lunch. She had a few bites then dumped the rest of it on the floor in an extravagant fashion. Yes, a lot of that was my fault. I shouldn't have given her the whole lot at once, and I should have been

See the Good/God in Everything

paying more attention. But alas, the food was all over the floor. I'd spent goodness knows how long preparing it, as well as all the pre-cooking, buying, defrosting, etc. And do you know how hard it is to make food with a child on your hip? Mama got pretty darn pissed off. I know, she's only 18 months old, and I know she didn't intentionally mean to push all my buttons, but the result was still a pretty upset Mommy. Even though I know my child didn't do it intentionally, the need to forgive her was still undeniable. My husband tells me often that I shouldn't let it get to me, and to not take it too seriously, which I'm trying often to do, but until I get there I'm forgiving frequently.

Thank You, Lord, that Your Fruits of the Spirit are growing in my life. Help me to easily overlook offences, even from my daughter. Help me to have the correct balance between discipline and fun and to have more wisdom and grace in my parenting.

'Bear with each other and forgive one another if any of you has a grievance against someone. Forgive as the Lord forgave you.'
—COLOSSIANS 3:13 (NIV)

I Forgive Australia

My husband and daughter are Australian; I was born Canadian, but am currently an Australian Permanent Resident. When the pandemic hit, almost every country closed their borders and went into a hard lockdown. One thing most countries did was continue to let in their citizens and their families without exception. Some countries even went the extra mile to repatriate their citizens from certain countries, even organizing flights for them. But, Australia...well, they let their citizens back in, but they had a limited capacity on how many of them could enter the country per week, and then after a bit of time they decided to halve that number. In the Australian state my husband is from, this number went down to 200 people per week. This upset me very much. As a seasoned traveller living abroad, just the freedom and knowledge that you'll be let back into your country when you want to go back is comforting. It's like that scene from that old '90s Val Kilmer movie *The Saint*, where the American lady living in Russia is chased by some bad people, she runs to the American embassy and screams, 'I'm American, open the gate!!!' She falls into one soldier's arms, while the others close the gate behind her and multiple soldiers with guns stare menacingly at the bad guys. This cap on international arrivals to Australia was very disconcerting because it directly affected us. It made me very upset with Australia. I was starting to think some unpleasant and loathsome thoughts about Australia, which for me is a sign that my heart isn't right. I know it may sound weird to some to have unpleasant thoughts about an entire country, but it's possible, trust me. So, I realized it stemmed from the capacity rule, which undesirably kept us stuck overseas for over two years. So, I had to forgive Australia. I also had to remind myself that we're just passing through on this earth, and the politicians who make these decisions are fallible humans too.

Thank You, Lord, that our citizenship is heaven, and we are only passing through the earth for a time. Thank You that You are our provider and help. Help us not to focus on the things that could go wrong, or be anxious or worrisome for the future. Help us to trust in You with everything. Help us to be prayerful, and flexible, knowing that in every situation You are with us, and provide for us.

> *'But our citizenship is in heaven. And we eagerly*
> *await a Savior from there, the Lord Jesus Christ.'*
> —PHILIPPIANS 3:20

Forgiving the Stupidest Things

Some people think that forgiveness is only forgiving the big, important, meaningful things in our lives—arguments, disagreements, differing opinions, moments we've been greatly wronged or treated badly. But I say that forgiveness is also for the small things, things we may even think are stupid or ridiculous. Forgiveness is also needed with unmet expectations. I'm speaking to you, ladies. Let's be honest. We usually have an expectation about everything. Case in point, the other day we got Mexican takeaway. If you know me and my husband, we'll take anything Mexican or Tex-Mex; it's one of our favourite cuisines. Well, we both got the taco sampler of four hard tacos. They were delicious. My dear husband had finished his lot, but I had one taco left. I'm sure you see where this is going. I put it in the fridge before we rushed to bathe and put our baby to bed. I even remember thinking in my head as I put it in the fridge that I'd finish the taco tomorrow for lunch and it would be delicious. So, the next day I went to the fridge to get my taco for lunch, and it was gone! My husband who had woken in the middle of the night had it as a midnight snack, thinking it was free for the taking. Yes, I should've definitely communicated its 'taken' status a bit better to him. But I was still annoyed and upset—he had eaten my taco! Some people would let it go and not worry about it, but I had an expectation of eating that taco for lunch! He was embarrassed he ate it, but didn't say sorry, which kind of pissed me off even more. About five minutes later I realized I was pissed at my husband, so I forgave him until I didn't feel upset anymore. Sometimes we need to forgive even the things we think are irrelevant, stupid, and ridiculous, to keep our hearts clean.

Thank You, Lord, that You teach us to have no limit on forgiveness. Help us to forgive when things are big and important, and when things seem small and inconsequential. Help us to be frequent and thorough forgivers.

> *'Catch for us the foxes, the little foxes that ruin the vineyards, our vineyards that are in bloom.'*
> —SONG OF SOLOMON 2:1

Forgive Them Even If They're Dead

Parents have a way of impacting us in a manner that affects us like no other. Oftentimes their words, actions, or attitudes, if negative and stinging, can have a life-long lasting impact. One time, for example, when living abroad, I was feeling ill. So, I decided to call my mother at work. It was a random decision; I rarely called my mother at that time in my life, and rarely at work. But, for some reason I just needed to speak with her. But she, being the busy nurse she is, didn't have time to talk to me and quickly said she'd call me back. It was so long ago that I honestly don't even remember if she called me back or not, but the feeling of being brushed aside by my mom when I needed her hurt. I have family members who have been traumatized by their parents. Manipulation, violence, accusations, contempt, abuse; these are only some of the things my relatives have gone through. The hurt and anger cut so deep that even when their parents passed away, the emotions remained. And hurt doesn't just disappear because the person who inflicted it is gone. Even if they've died, we still need to forgive them. God doesn't want us to cling to past hurts, but to move forward with our lives. So, let's forgive everyone, even our parents, even if they're not present with us, and let's let God heal our hearts.

Thank You, Lord, that You call us to forget the past and look forward. Help us to forgive even the most traumatic things we have been through. Help us to forgive our parents. Help us to recognize that

See the Good/God in Everything

even when our parents fail, though the hurt is great, You still call us to forgive them.

'No, dear brothers and sisters, I have not achieved it,
but I focus on this one thing: Forgetting the past and
looking forward to what lies ahead, I press on to reach
the end of the race and receive the heavenly prize for
which God, through Christ Jesus, is calling us.'
—PHILIPPIANS 3:13-14 (NLT)

Forgiveness Doesn't Always Lead to Restoration

Forgiveness and restoration are two totally different things. Forgiveness is the act of forgiving someone. Maybe someone upset you or wronged you; maybe you had unmet expectations that weren't fulfilled. As it says in Mark 11:25, if you have anything against anyone, forgive him, that your Father in heaven may also forgive you your trespasses. When we forgive, it's not a huge act that anyone sees. Really, only God sees when we forgive the other person. But, we do it to keep our heart clean towards others, and so God will forgive us of our sins. Restoration is when things are renewed and restored. It's when our relationship with the other person is fixed. A lot of times people think forgiveness automatically leads to restoration. It doesn't. Forgiveness is one-sided. The other person or party doesn't need to apologize or change their behaviour, yet we still forgive them. Restoration requires the other person to be involved. You can't restore a relationship on your own. It needs two people to rebuild a relationship. Usually restoration is the end goal, but it can take a lot of time and effort, and both sides need to want to rebuild for this to happen.

Thank You, Lord, that when we forgive others, You forgive us of our sins. Help us to recognize quickly when we need to forgive, and help us to be generous forgivers. Help us to have restored relationships. Help us to have patience, understanding, and the awareness that sometimes restoring a relationship can take a while.

> *'Pursue peace with all people, and holiness, without which no one will see the Lord: looking carefully lest anyone fall short of the grace of God; lest any root of bitterness springing up cause trouble, and by this many become defiled.'*
> —HEBREWS 12:14–15

Forgiving My Daughter, Again

There seems to be a theme here, as I've needed to forgive my dear daughter again and again. It's not her fault, I know. But that doesn't stop the fact that I've needed to forgive her. She started daycare last week and has been in contact with all those kiddie germs, which has resulted in a runny nose. On top of that, she's been finding it hard to transition to the new routine; sleep has been lacking, naps have been lacking, and there have been a lot of post-daycare tears and meltdowns, which the internet tells me is a normal thing. This resulted in a terrible night last night, in which the whole family was up and she couldn't go back to sleep unless we co-slept with her. It started with her crying literally every time I closed my eyes to sleep. I was half-tempted to turn off my baby monitor and ignore her all night; I didn't, but that just made me upset and annoyed. I could feel the anger rising every time I had to get up from my bed to try to console her. I'd be knocked out of sleep with her crying and have to forgive her again and again, before getting up to attempt to settle her down. I know it's not her fault—she's a child, everything is overwhelming, and in her eyes, I'm the answer to all her problems—but still, I needed to forgive. I was upset, sleep-deprived, and tired, but I still forgave her.

Thank You, Lord, that You are helping me to know the fruit of the spirit which is patience. Help me to be gracious and understanding with my child. Help me not to take things too seriously or to take her meltdowns to heart. Help me to forgive even the little things, and to lead by example. Help me to be loving and nurturing, even when things are hard.

'Rejoicing in hope, patient in tribulation, continuing steadfastly in prayer.'
—ROMANS 12:12

Too Much Forgiveness for One Day

I know God will say you can never forgive enough, but on days like today, I'm sure there's a limit. My husband has pissed the bejesus out of me today. First, he was a prick. He was unmedicated and was just super sensitive. Today, none of the questions he asked me seemed to be answered properly or correctly in his eyes. WTF?! He wanted clear yes or no answers, and if I didn't answer like that, I wasn't communicating properly to his liking. God help me. We've been married for almost nine years, yet today he's got a problem with how I respond to him? No, that's definitely not my problem. So, I had to forgive him for that. Then, while I spent almost an hour trying to put our daughter to bed, I find out he ate his dinner but left the kitchen a mess. Have you seen my kitchen? We have a 20-month-old who can destroy the kitchen in less than two minutes, and he didn't help to clean it?! Lord, have mercy! I can ignore the rest of the house, but the kitchen is where we spend the majority of our time. So, I had to forgive him for that as well. There were other times I needed to forgive him, but let's just leave it at that. Today he pushed my patience, pushed my self-control, and pushed me to keep my mouth shut; because if I hadn't, I would've totally lost it on him, and it wouldn't have ended well. Seriously, I know God says you can never forgive enough, but today I was just about at the end of my limit of forgiveness.

Lord, help me. Today was one of those days. I felt like I had to forgive and forgive, and have patience and more patience. I feel like I am at the end of my forgiveness and patience quota. I am still angry and upset with my husband. Help me to forgive more, and to forgive thoroughly. Help me to have grace, mercy, and patience with my husband. Help me not to sin, even though I am very angry. Help us as we work through our issues, help there to be peace, love, and unity in our marriage, and help that things will get better from now on. Thank You, Lord.

> *'Therefore, as the elect of God, holy and beloved, put on tender mercies, kindness, humility, meekness, longsuffering; bearing with one another, and forgiving another, if anyone has a complaint against another; even as Christ forgave you, so you also must do. But above all these things put on love, which is the bond of perfection. And let the peace of God rule in your hearts, to which also you were called in one body; and be thankful.'*
> —COLOSSIANS 3:12–15

See the Good/God in Everything

Forgiving My Sick Husband

My husband has pretty ridiculous allergies. Living in the Middle East hasn't helped him much, with all the dust and sand that goes around. We went out to the park the other day, and it turned out to be a bad idea. The next few hours after the park, I kept noticing he was sneezing a lot, but didn't think twice about it. It wasn't until a few more hours had gone by and he said he wasn't feeling well did I put it together. I asked him if he'd taken some allergy medication, to which he said no. We dosed him up as we normally do when he's got some allergy irritation, but it was too little too late. The runny, itchy nose, sneezing, and general unwellness had started, and that would take a good medicated day or two to fix. The thing is, I'm working now. I need to have time alone to sit at my computer and write, and Saturday is one of those days I count on to work. My husband has agreed to take our daughter out for a few hours on Saturdays so I can get work done. And his allergies kicked in on Friday evening, so my Saturday of working went out the window. I know it's not his fault, but there's no babysitter to fall back on, so here we are. There's literally nothing I can do but accept that it's no one's fault and move on. But I won't lie—when I realized I wouldn't be able to work, I was pretty agitated. But I forgave him and moved on, as we must.

Thank You, Lord, that You will perfect the things that concern me. Help me to have more grace. Help me to use my time wisely and to make the most of the time that I have. Help me not to take my feelings out on my husband, and to have grace for him during this time.

> *'The LORD will perfect that which concerns me; Your mercy, O LORD, endures forever; Do not forsake the works of Your hands.'*
> —PSALM 138:8

Forgiving Our Cleaner

We have a cleaner. He's a fellow Christian, and was recommended to us by some friends. Now, we've worked with other Christians before, and our previous cleaner in our old house was amazing. She was very discreet and professional; you could trust her with almost anything, and we did. This guy, um, not so much. A few months ago when we made our latest payment to him, I realised that with the number of hours he was working for us, he was making a very good salary. But knowing that we were leaving in a few months' time, I felt a little bad for him. So, my husband and I discussed it and decided that we should give him the benefit of a doubt and tell him we'd be leaving in a few months' time. In particular, we asked him not to mention this to anyone, as we had a few mutual acquaintances at both work and church, and my husband hadn't yet notified his work of his intent to shortly give his notice. Well, just the other day, one of the mutual acquaintances came to my husband and congratulated him on leaving. My husband was surprised and asked who'd mentioned this to him, to which he replied our cleaner and Christian brother. It turned out he's a blabbermouth, and not even a discreet one at that. I'm a bit peeved. I mean, wouldn't you be? The one thing we specifically asked him not to do, he did. So, I'm not sure what to do, if anything. If this was a company, I would've given him a disciplinary notice. Anyways, here we are. I'll leave the what to do for now, but I'll do the part I know to do, which is to forgive him. I'm really not pleased about it, and I'll definitely have to make sure we don't give him any more confidential information. But still, I will forgive him.

Thank You, Lord, that You have no limit on forgiveness. Help me to forgive thoroughly, but also help me to be wise. Help me to have wisdom in dealing with people we work with and to have better boundaries.

See the Good/God in Everything

'Then Peter came to Him and said, "Lord, how often shall my brother sin against me, and I forgive him? Up to seven times?" Jesus said to him, "I do not say to you, up to seven times, but up to seventy times seven."'

—MATTHEW 18:21–22

I Forgive Him for Not Letting Me Drive

We live in a country in the Middle East where women have only recently gotten the go-ahead to drive. The norm for women prior to this was to have a driver or their husband/male family member drive them. Since I'm a woman, I was subject to this too. I didn't have a live-in driver, but I had a dedicated driver who I would always use to drive me places. When the law was changed, I asked my husband if I could drive and he adamantly said no. The roads are admittedly crazy in this country, and he didn't want me to be driving in those conditions. Fair enough. We'd gotten into a car accident a few years previously, and if not for the fact that we'd been driving a large pickup truck, it likely would've been very bad. Anyways, that was a few years ago, and since then the roads have gotten better and the amount of people driving has decreased. So, when we decided to send our daughter to daycare, it seemed like a good opportunity for me to drive. It would be in the fall, and the weather would be cooling down, which meant my husband would start walking to work. Our car would then be sitting in the driveway; and instead of getting a driver to take me, it just made sense for me to drive our car and take our daughter to school. So, I asked him and this time he said yes! But then a series of unfortunate events led to the misplacement of my Canadian driver's license, and an easy way to get a license was no longer possible. I guess what I'm forgiving him for is the fact that I could've easily gotten my license if I've done it years ago, while my license was still valid and not misplaced. Or, if I'm being real, the actual forgiveness is probably to forgive him for saying I couldn't drive all those years ago. It seems that that's actually the root of my discontent. So, I forgive him for not letting me drive when I asked him a few years ago.

Thank You, Lord, that You forgive me of my sins as I forgive others of their sins to me. Help me to forgive quickly and easily. Help me to know the root of my discontent, so that I forgive the root of the problem.

'Love prospers when a fault is forgiven, but dwelling on it separates close friends.'
—PROVERBS 17:9 (NLT)

Forgiving a Pastor for No In-Person Services

When the pandemic started and most of the world went into lockdown, it took some getting used to, but I attended church online. It wasn't the same, and the worship and fellowship was different, but I know Holy Spirit never leaves us, so it was manageable. Then a year went by, then another. Malls were open but practicing social distancing and with limited capacity. People were thinking about things getting back to normal. Vaccines had started to show up in many countries, and in the country we're in, there was a hard and fast vaccine drive. By this time, I was growing tired of online church. I wanted to be in fellowship with people in person. Our church in the previous city we lived in had limited-seating in-person services, and a rota for those who wanted to attend in person. My parents' church in Canada also had a ticket-style program for those who wanted to be in fellowship in-person. I wish the church we attended had this type of system. It didn't, though, only online

See the Good/God in Everything

services. My heart ached. I could go shopping in the mall and go out to a restaurant, my daughter could go to playschool, and my husband could go to work, but we couldn't attend church in-person! The outrage!!! I was super pissed at the pastor of the church we were still attending only online. I know there are probably many reasons why he couldn't hold in-person meetings, but it still bothered me very much. We eventually started to attend another church service that had simultaneous online and in-person meetings. But I still had to forgive that pastor. It's a tough season for all of us, and he was probably doing the best he could. But, you also cannot stay where you are when church is draining you, and you're not getting anything out of it. So, we blessed him and moved on.

Thank You, Lord, for pastors. I know they have so much work to do to tend to the flock You have given them. Help me to make wise choices and decisions. Help me to find a church group where I can get fed, have fellowship, and freedom of the Holy Spirit.

'And let us consider one another in order to stir up love and good works, not forsaking the assembling of ourselves together, as is the manner of some, but exhorting one another, and so much the more as you see the Day approaching.'
—HEBREWS 10:24–25

Forgiving My Husband for Not Pulling His Weight

There's been a bit of a disproportionate distribution of household work and parenting in my home, since I'm a stay-at-home mom/wife, and my husband works long hours. Before we had our daughter, I was quite used to doing everything at home—cooking, cleaning, laundry, etc. When our daughter came along and I was a new mom, it was hard to do everything I used to do plus look after my daughter, but I managed somehow, though it was difficult. But when I started working again and it required me to spend time on my computer, managing both the home and the growing baby full-time was no longer possible. My husband, because it'd been over a year of me doing everything, wasn't accustomed to pulling his share of the parenting. He used to call me to help him change a poopy diaper, or to help him take our daughter out of the bath, because he found both difficult while 'I was good at it'. Ha! This is what happens when you don't train and teach your husband from the beginning to help with the baby! So, after an intense confrontation, he agreed to pull his weight, and he's no longer allowed to call me to help with the baby at every turn.

Thank You, Lord, for our families. Lord, help us to communicate our needs with our spouses more regularly and openly. Help us to not let resentment and bitterness build up because we do not ask for help when we need it. And help us to trust our spouses when they help us, and to be grateful and gracious, and not to nitpick them.

'Bear one another's burdens, and so fulfill the law of Christ.'
—GALATIANS 6:2

See the Good/God in Everything

FAMILY

Listen to Your Mother—She Has More Wisdom Than You Know

I don't know when it started, probably sometime in my teens, when I would petulantly disregard almost everything my mother said. I often had an exasperated tone of 'oh Mom!' It was horribly egotistical of me, as well as dishonouring. This continued until I got pregnant with my daughter. You see, my mom is wise, and her wisdom really came to the forefront when I was pregnant, because she was a paediatric nurse for 40 years, in the best children's hospital in Canada. And when I got pregnant with my daughter, she was the quickest and most informed person I knew (other than my doctor). She was also an incredible support, which I didn't expect. When our daughter was a few months old, anytime she was going through some health issue, my husband would say, 'Ask your mom'. Though hindsight is 20/20, don't be like me. Listen to your mother and value, respect, and honour her thoughts and opinions, even if you don't agree with it. She has a lot more wisdom than you realise.

Lord, thank You for our mothers. Thank You for their love, patience, and sacrifice. Help us to honour our mothers the way You want us to.

'Honor your father and your mother, that your days may be long upon the land which the Lord your God is giving you.'
—EXODUS 20:12

Teach Forgiveness

Forgiveness isn't mainstream. You don't really see a lot of movies where someone who's been wronged, or treated badly, forgives. Usually the common reaction is to cut off all ties and move on, or seek violent revenge. Forgiveness and reconciliation are topics infrequently talked about outside the church. I think those not churched may have only heard the 'forgive and forget' saying, which doesn't truly capture the breadth of forgiveness. I want to make sure, especially now that I'm a parent, that I'm a good example of a quick forgiver. That I don't hold onto grudges; that though I forgive someone else, I'm not a doormat; and that I'm wise about my relationships. That when I forgive, I forgive thoroughly, and restore the person to their rightful position. That I don't 'forgive' them but then treat them badly and think awfully about them, because that isn't really forgiveness. When God forgave us of our sins, He did it so thoroughly that He doesn't hold a grudge against us, or remind us of our sins. I'll be the first to say that forgiveness isn't easy, but nothing about the narrow path is, and that's why few walk on it.

Lord, thank You that You forgive us so completely. Help us to forgive others who have wronged us, and to raise our children in Your ways.

'For if you forgive men their trespasses, your heavenly Father will also forgive you. But if you do not forgive men their trespasses, neither will your Father forgive your trespasses.'
—MATTHEW 6:14–15

A Gentle Answer Turns Away Wrath

There's a reason the Book of Proverbs is called the book of wisdom. Take Proverbs 15:1 (NIV)—'A gentle answer turns away wrath but a harsh word stirs up anger.' Have you ever been in a situation where everyone's against you and you feel like you have no friends in the world? I was there once. The emotions are overwhelming. I was feeling anger, guilt,

See the Good/God in Everything

anxiety, confusion, sadness, and contempt. I remember there was a moment that felt like the calm before a storm. It felt like a half-second, though I don't actually remember how long it was. But it was a definitive moment where I had a choice, a God-given moment. It was the moment I could use a gentle or soft answer, to be kind and let the Holy Spirit speak to me and through me; or choose the harsh word and let the emotions dictate my choice. I don't know if you can tell which one I chose, but it didn't end well. It led to years of estrangement, and having to forgive daily. Living with that bad choice of choosing the harsh word, because I was upset and indignant, led to a lot of regret and pain. I learned it the hard way. But you, be wise—when you get that second, that moment, where you have a choice between a gentle answer and bringing peace, or speaking a harsh word and stirring up anger, I beg you, choose the gentle answer. It will save you years of pain.

Lord, we thank You that Your Holy Spirit is with us always. Help us to choose Your way, and not the ways of the flesh. Help us to be gentle and kind, and not to stir up anger. Change us to be more like You, all the days of our lives.

'A soft answer turns away wrath, but
a harsh word stirs up anger.'
—PROVERBS 15:1

What's Your Heritage?

I grew up Catholic, but when I became a born-again believer, I kind of just thought everything from my past church and religious experience was irrelevant. After a few years and the Lord doing a work in me, I realized that even though there were some irredeemable aspects of my past church background, there were also some very highly admirable aspects. One of them was that my family believed in prayer. My mother and grandmother were adamant and steadfast that we should pray constantly. One of my most memorable memories of my grandmother was her sitting on her small single bed in her small bedroom, with a small bedside lamp on. She would pray into the late hours of the night, way past when everyone had gone to sleep. She believed in the power of prayer, and she was unashamed of anyone knowing that. What a heritage! And one I didn't even realize I had until quite recently. You may or may not have a heritage like I speak of; if not, make one. Get with the Lord and build an inheritance in the Spirit you can give to those you love.

Thank You, Lord, that You are our portion. Help us to be wise to leave a spiritual inheritance and heritage to our children's children. Help us to be such unashamed lovers of God that our relationship with You would impact our whole family for generations.

> *'O Lord, you are the portion of my inheritance and my cup; you maintain my lot. The lines have fallen to me in pleasant places; yes, I have a good inheritance.'*
> —PSALM 16:5–6

I Want to Be Like Her!

When I was living in the UK, I had a good friend from church who was from Malaysia. She was in university and often doing exams. I remember during one exam period, she told me that every morning her mother in Malaysia would call her and pray with her over the phone. I couldn't believe it! I didn't know any mother and adult child duo that close, nor had I ever thought a mother would do something like that. It blew my

See the Good/God in Everything

mind. It makes sense to me now that even if my child leaves home and goes abroad, I would call her often. That during trying times in her life I would support her, be there for her, and pray for her on the phone, not just pray for her from a distance. There are many inspiring women in the Bible, but my friend's mom was one of the first times I came across a really inspiring godly mother in real life. When I heard about her, I just knew I wanted to be like that. I want to be a godly mother and be impactful in my child's life even when they get older and leave home.

Thank You, Lord, for godly women we can learn from and emulate. Thank You for the good example they are. Help us to learn from them and to raise up our children in Your ways so when they are old they will not depart from it.

'Let no one despise your youth, but be an example to the believers in word, in conduct, in love, in spirit, in faith, in purity.'
—1 TIMOTHY 4:12

What's Your Legacy?

When my mother-in-law passed away, her eldest son (my brother-in-law) gave the eulogy. Her most impactful and longest-lasting legacy was that she was the first Christian in her family, and that she prayed for her husband and children to be saved. Her prayers were answered and there are many in our extended family who are faithful Christians. I know for a fact my husband credits his mother's prayers as an integral part in his life and salvation. We often forget that when we leave this earth, we take nothing with us, and what we leave behind will either be remembered or forgotten. And let's be honest, a lot of it will be forgotten. So many things in life are fleeting and superficial; we must focus on the eternal. One thing I remember, value, and cherish about my grandmother was that she always prayed. She would sit on the side of her bed and pray late into the night. It could be midnight and we might have been out at a family gathering all evening, but she would always say, 'I'll just pray first' before going to sleep. This instils in me joy of inheritance that I come from a family of God lovers and prayerful women. Let's ensure we pass on things of lasting value, and intentionally build into the lives of our children and their children for their posterity.

Thank You, Lord, for our families. Thank You that You tell us in Your Word to train and teach our children about You and Your ways. Help us to be diligent and purposeful to leave a godly, eternal legacy.

'We will not hide them from their children, telling to the generation to come the praises of the Lord, and His strength and His wonderful works that He has done.'
—PSALM 78:4

Don't Pass On Cultural Insecurities

Don't pass on your cultural insecurities to your kids. The things we say and talk about affect our children in numerous ways. I have a nose. It's not a bad nose, it's just a nose. It's the type of nose that, if I were to go back to where my parents are from, the Philippines, I would probably find many people with a similar nose. Noses are a popular topic of conversation in my family, and I'm guilty too of making it a topic. And my nose, of all my facial features, makes me noticeably Filipino, or at least those who know would say so. But because of the focus on noses, it made me very insecure and hyper-conscious of my nose and appearance.

See the Good/God in Everything

This is especially true because my parents emigrated to Canada in the '70s, and as a first-generation Canadian it was always more prized to look less Filipino. When my husband and I got married, he couldn't understand my obsession with my nose. He thought it was beautiful as it is. He didn't make any comments about it or its size. Then our daughter was born. She has a nose very similar to mine. Some family members commented about her nose and advised us to pinch it regularly as a baby, in the hopes that the shape would improve as she got older. When my husband heard that, he was appalled and unequivocally told me not to do that. Our daughter is beautiful and we unanimously decided we didn't want to pass on the nose insecurity I had onto her. So, we leave her nose as it is and are thankful for the beautiful daughter we have. No nose conversations here.

Thank You, Lord, that we are fearfully and wonderfully made. Thank You that we are made in Your image and are beautiful. Help us to break free from the bondage of cultural insecurities and the lies spoken over us that we are not beautiful as we are.

*'Do not let your adornment be merely outward—
arranging the hair, wearing gold, or putting on fine
apparel—rather let it be the hidden person of the heart,
with the incorruptible beauty of a gentle and quiet
spirit, which is very precious in the sight of God.'*
—1 PETER 3:3–4

Living Abroad Is Never Easy

I originally left home when I was 25 years old. It was for a year-long stint to Japan where I would teach English. I would go from there to England, where I would get a Master's degree and stay almost ten years, to finally ending up in Saudi Arabia where we're pushing close to the ten-year mark again. When you're young, travelling is easy. The rush of living abroad, the freedom and independence, exploring new cultures and people, and making a good salary make it easy and fun. But I'll tell you, living abroad is never easy, especially when the years get on. Yes, FaceTime, instant messaging, and WhatsApp can make staying connected easier; but even so, when it comes to relationships, nothing beats being face-to-face with family. The hardest thing about living abroad is the decline in familial relationships. The one question my husband gets very frequently when he speaks with one of his kids is 'when are you coming home?' Let's be honest, FaceTime is great, and WhatsApp is great, but it's really difficult to have a heart-to-heart conversation. Missing out on important events and moments, and building and maintaining relationships, all get put on the back burner when one is living abroad. One must work doubly hard to maintain relationships when abroad. So, we try really hard with what we've got. My daughter and I religiously FaceTime my parents every week. If we're lucky and schedules permit, we aim for two video chats a week. My husband with his work schedule tries to call one of his kids every few weeks. We have family chats as far as the eye can see. We do what we can with what we have. We pray for our family and for the time when we can be reunited with them.

Thank You, Lord, for our families. Thank You, Lord, that You watch over them when we are absent from them. Help us to cultivate our familial relationships even from a distance.

'May the Lord watch between you and me
when we are absent one from another.'
—GENESIS 31:49

See the Good/God in Everything

It Gets Harder

It was a rough day for Mommy. It was church day and we were trying to watch the service online. It wasn't going so well. Our pastor is doing a series on the Book of Revelation and is on chapter 10. It's not the easiest listen week after week, I'll admit. My dear husband was finding the message hard to listen to and was complaining and nodding off. It was our daughter's lunch time, so I got her lunch ready and dragged her highchair to the living room so she could see the service online. She had a few bites of food, then started to play with it, then dumped the rest on the floor. I had had enough. It was like pushing a rock uphill. My husband wasn't interested in watching the service, and our daughter didn't want to eat. I felt like I was forcing everyone to do something they didn't want to do. After that incident, my husband and I had a discussion. He agreed that in the future, he won't complain but will sit and watch the whole service. He also said that regarding kids, it will get harder. That I should just relax and not take things too seriously. So, I sat and pondered that for a while, the idea that things will just keep getting harder with my kids. Are my reactions, views, and mindsets well-placed for me to deal with the 'harder'? It's an easy, resounding 'no'. If these little things rattle me so easily, how will I deal when things get more challenging? So, I turn to the only one who can help me change my mindsets, give me more grace and patience, and help me to be more relaxed, capable, and collected. Being a parent is a very different type of challenge. There are so many little things I need Daddy God to help me with, each and every day.

Thank You, Lord, for Your inheritance. Help me to be the kind of godly, loving parent You have called me to be. Help me in all aspects of my parenting, and help me lean not on my own understanding. Help me to be prayerful and sensitive to the Holy Spirit's leading throughout my day.

'I will instruct you and teach you in the way you should go; I will guide you with My eye.'

—PSALM 32:8

FOMO (Fear of Missing Out)

Before the days of the pandemic, we used to travel a lot. *A lot.* We used to fly back to see family and friends, and especially for big family events, weddings, funerals, new babies, and graduations. Then the pandemic hit and going to places like Australia was extremely complicated and difficult, even as citizens. During the time of lockdown and closed borders, my husband's mother died (not from COVID), one son got married, and two new grandbabies were added to the family. The FOMO couldn't have been worse. Of course, video calls were made, and that's better than nothing; but let's be honest, it's not the same as being there in person. I've had to learn to manage my expectations and not let the FOMO get out of hand. God is always with us and though we may be disappointed, He has a purpose and plan for us where we are. So, we trust in Him, and we trust His timing. We won't always be living abroad and away from family. And when I really feel the FOMO, I pray. I pray that weddings will go as planned, I pray for the new marriages, I pray for the new grandbabies and the new parents, and I pray for the time when we'll be there in person.

Thank You, Lord, that You teach us how to be content in our circumstances. Help us when we do not feel contentment to pray, bring our worries to You, and be grateful for what we have.

See the Good/God in Everything

'Not that I was ever in need, for I have learned how to be content with whatever I have. I know how to live on almost nothing or with everything. I have learned the secret of living in every situation, whether it is with a full stomach or empty, with plenty or little. For I can do everything through Christ, who gives me strength.'

—PHILIPPIANS 4:11–13 (NLT)

Don't Cut Off Ties—It Is Very Hard to Fix

When we first got engaged and were planning to get married, there were a lot of familial disputes and disagreements. In the end, I was hurt, offended, and pretty upset with everyone in my family. So, I thought the best way forward would be to cut off all ties with my family. I got rid of all my social media accounts and I unfollowed and unfriended just about every member of my immediate and extended family. I wanted nothing to do with them at the time. The hurt was too deep, the sadness boundless, and it was just easier for me that they be out of sight and out of mind. Fast forward eight years. We're still living abroad and have only returned to Canada twice since getting married, so have only had very limited contact with my family. If it wasn't for us having a baby, I think the relationship with all of my family would still be pretty constrained. What's the takeaway from all this? That it may seem like the easiest thing to do is to cut off all ties, but in the long run it's actually not. Building up relationship, confidence, trust, and respect is tough; and if it's lost, it'll take a long time to rebuild. So, don't do what I did and cut off familial ties hastily and without deliberation or pause. Take a moment, breathe, and humble yourself. Do whatever you need to do to keep the peace in your family, because once relationships are cut, you may or may not be able to get it back.

Thank You, Lord, that You give us the fruit of the spirit and wisdom. Help us in our families to keep the peace. Help us to be peacemakers and people who bring love and unity into our families.

'Bless those who persecute you; bless and do not curse. Rejoice with those who rejoice, and weep with those who weep. Be of the same mind toward one another. Do not set your mind on high things, but associate with the humble. Do not be wise in your own opinion. Repay no one evil for evil. Have regard for good things in the sight of all men. If it is possible, as much as depends on you, live peaceably with all men.'

—ROMANS 12:14–18

Praying for Them to Know God

I have a lot of family, and a lot of my family aren't Christian. Some were brought up in the church, some not; some are from a Catholic background, others not. My heart aches for them, as some just outright reject God. I was thinking about one of my relatives recently. She loves nature and showing others the beauty of nature. She takes others out to see lovely sunsets, or to go on hikes to see the land. She's one of my favourite relatives, but sometimes I don't understand how she can see the beauty of things in nature and not see the Creator Himself in it all. When I read Romans 1:20 (below), my heart aches more for them, because it says that they are without excuse. That God is clearly seen, even in nature. Probably even more so in nature. The beauty of nature is breathtaking; how could you not see a higher power in it? All other things aside, my greatest desire is that I would be a light. That who I am as a person, how I live my life, how I am as a person, wife, mother, etc., would give glory to God. That my family would see the goodness of God

See the Good/God in Everything

in me, and it would turn them to Him. Above all I want to love my family unconditionally, and without judgement. Part of what led me to Jesus was being welcomed by Christians who didn't know me, but welcomed me with open arms and without judgement. We need to channel more non-judgmentalism and inclusiveness.

Thank You, Lord, that You did not come into the world to condemn the world, but that the world, through You, may be saved. Help me to be a light, to love unconditionally, to be inclusive and non-judging. Help me to show Your love to my family, and especially to my unsaved family. And Lord, we pray that You would remove their heart of stone and put in a heart of flesh.

> *'For since the creation of the world His invisible attributes are clearly seen, being understood by the things that are made, even His eternal power and Godhead, so that they are without excuse, because, although they knew God, they did not glorify Him as God, nor were thankful, but became futile in their thoughts, and their foolish hearts were darkened.'*
>
> —ROMANS 1:20–21

BEING A
WOMAN

Today or One Day

You know the saying 'there's no time like the present'? Well, it's true. What are your goals and dreams? What have you put on the back burner because life is busy, but that you hold dear to your heart? Do you want to start a business, open an Etsy shop, be a writer? This is something I have to remind myself every day. If I keep waiting until the perfect time, it's just not going to happen. I have a husband and now I have a child, so let me tell you, there's no time unless you make the time. And it's true that every day is a gift. We have the opportunity every day to start, to do something, to do the thing that sparks the fire in our spirit. It's also true that if we mess up, things don't go according to plan, or we lose the day due to a cranky sick baby, that's okay too. There's always tomorrow. But don't let life and the busyness of life cripple your dreams. I think the dreams that God gives us goes hand-in-hand with Matthew 19:26, quoted below. I think He gives us the seemingly impossible dreams so that we must rely not on man, but on Him to accomplish them.

Lord, we thank You that You give us dreams and amazing things to accomplish. We know we can only do it with You. Help us to rely on You every day, and not try to do things in our own strength.

'But Jesus looked at them and said to them, "With men this is impossible, but with God all things are possible."'
—MATTHEW 19:26

Learning Not to Get Easily Offended

In 1 Corinthians 13:5 it says '(love) is not provoked'. Other versions use the words 'angered', 'irritable', 'resentful', 'quick-tempered', or 'quick to take offense'. So that means that if I'm easily offended, I'm unloving. This is an area in my life I'm actively trying to improve. Recently I hadn't heard from a few friends for a couple of weeks. Whenever I messaged them, I would get the shortest response, if any. Okay, granted, the way they responded wasn't amazing, but it wasn't the end of the world. Either way, I was incensed. I was pretty much convinced they were ghosting me, and that our friendship was over. I had even written about it, in this devotional, in an entry titled 'When Friends Hurt You' which I have since deleted. I had to go through the motions of forgiving them, and I had to deal with my hurt over not being acknowledged. I had to remind myself constantly that it's not really all about me. They're busy people with stressful jobs. Sometimes they just aren't able to reply back in the timeframe I'd like. I also have to be conscious of the fact that because of the pandemic, my social circle basically revolved around my household. So, I've needed social interaction. I've put disproportionate pressure on my friends unknowingly. I'm learning not to get provoked or offended. I think part of my learning is letting things slide. Being a bit like water over a duck's back. Yes, my friend could have done better, but I also could have not jumped to conclusions so quickly, not thought the worst about them, and not gotten offended so easily.

Lord, thank You for Jesus' perfect example. Help me to love like He loves and to think the best in others.

'I, therefore, the prisoner of the Lord, beseech you to walk worthy of the calling with which you were called, with all lowliness and gentleness, with longsuffering, bearing with one another in love, endeavouring to keep the unity of the Spirit in the bond of peace.'
—EPHESIANS 4:1–3

Be the Warrior You Were Called to Be

The Bible tells us that our struggle is not with flesh and blood. It's true. There's a whole other realm of reality we don't see with our physical eyes. But the Bible tells us all about it so we know how to war. I've always been an intercessor. From the time I was a young baby Christian I have always been the type of person to attend the weekly prayer meetings. I love to pray prayers that God sees, and have always felt and known that my prayers are powerful. I love the images of female warriors of God (Google it), wearing their full armour. We must rise up as the warrior women of God we've been called to be. We mustn't assume someone else will pray if we don't. We're all needed, and we're all powerful, and we're all well-equipped and strong.

Thank You, Lord, that greater is He who is in us than he who is in the world. Thank You for Your Holy Spirit guiding us, and thank You, Lord, that You give us the keys to the kingdom. Help us, Lord, to rise up as the warrior daughters of God You have called us to be. To be strong and courageous and to fulfil Your purposes in our life.

> *'Finally, my brethren, be strong in the Lord and in the power of His might. Put on the whole armor of God, that you may be able to stand against the wiles of the devil. For we do not wrestle against flesh and blood, but against principalities, against powers, against the rulers of the darkness of this age, against spiritual hosts of wickedness in the heavenly places. Therefore take up the whole armor of God, that you may be able to withstand in the evil day, and having done all, to stand.'*
> —EPHESIANS 6:10–13

Learn Something

Since I got married, I've come face-to-face with the fact that I'm not perfect. It really hit me in marriage. Before that I could almost convince myself that I was a pretty great, almost perfect person. But when I got married, life threw me curveballs. There were family problems, insecurities, and unfulfilled desires. There was the fact that I'd been single and independent for a long time, and I didn't really know how to be a wife, let alone a good one. My husband, with his background of being previously married and divorced, also wouldn't let anything slide. If there was a character flaw, a slight hint of victim mentality, or a bad thought in me, he'd address them immediately. So, what did that teach me? It taught me that there's always something to learn. There are lessons in life, everywhere. We can sit back and let life go by, get caught up in our issues, and not ever change ourselves, or we can strive for godliness. Life is about humbling ourselves and learning, growing to be better representatives of Jesus in everything we do and with everyone we come in contact with. There's always more wisdom to gain, always more love to share, always more goodness to dispense. And though we may think we're almost a perfect person, like I did, the truth is that our character can always, always, always be more like Jesus. But only if we let Him.

Thank You, Lord, for Your Holy Spirit living in me. Help me to allow the Holy Spirit to change me to be more like Jesus in every area of my life. Let my life glorify You.

'He must increase, but I must decrease.'

—JOHN 3:30

See the Good/God in Everything

Getting Off the (Social Media) Grid

I never understood those people who go 'off the grid'. Those interesting folks who buy a piece of land and live in the woods somewhere, far away from people. You see them on YouTube. Maybe it's just me, but I like malls, big superstores, and sushi! Give me a really good Japanese restaurant any day and I'm a happy camper. But one thing I do agree with those 'off-grid' people about is not having other people know your business all the time. You see, I'm not on social media. I am off the social media grid. I don't know about you, but on social media, I always felt like I was trying to portray the perfect me. When I was taking pictures, they had to be perfect so I could post them to my accounts. I was trying to look perfect and beautiful and living the perfect life—and that's when I knew I had to get off. Plus, I was also always checking who was liking my updates and who was viewing my stuff. It got pretty wild. Not just that, but the amount of stalking that can occur is just insane. So, I deactivated all my accounts and deleted all my apps. I'll admit, it's hard for my friends to find me online. But for me to keep my heart clean, not waste time, and not compare myself to other people, it's a huge win.

Thank You, Lord, that You guide us by Your Holy Spirit. Help me to do what is necessary to keep my heart pure, and to live a life of godliness and righteousness. I want to be more like You each and every day. Help me in my weaknesses and help me to walk on the narrow path that few are on.

> *'Create in me a clean heart, O God, and*
> *renew a steadfast spirit within me.'*
> —PSALM 51:10

My Unborn Baby

When I was young and living at home, my mom used to say it was a woman's choice whether or not to have an abortion. I never really thought about what that meant, though. One day while on YouTube, I saw Abby Johnson on FlashPoint. I had heard of her, of course; she's the former Planned Parenthood director who had a transformational experience. There has also been a movie made about her life. Abby had helped a doctor perform an ultrasound guided abortion in her clinic, and the experience dramatically changed her life. When I saw Abby Johnson on FlashPoint they were discussing the millions of babies' lives that had been lost because of abortion. Something about hearing it this time really impacted me. It made me value human life, even if unborn. (Now, don't get offended; I'm not judging anyone or any circumstance.) But something changed in me, because when I was pregnant with our daughter, she was actually a twin. We bought the books on multiple babies, and I even started purchasing double the amount of clothes. But when we went for another routine ultrasound, there were no longer two heartbeats, but only one. One of our babies had died in my womb. It was a very difficult time for both my husband and I. This unborn child, who once had a beating heart in my womb, was our child. Her life was precious to us. We never got to see her smiling face, but she was our child and a part of us. She was created from my husband and I. Her life, though unborn, was significant and valuable.

Thank You, Lord, that even before we are formed, You knew us. Help us to be defenders for all children.

> *'Your eyes saw my substance, being yet unformed. And in Your book they all were written, the days fashioned for me, when as yet there were none of them.'*
> —PSALM 139:16

What's Your Superpower?

I've always loved quotes and inspiring phrases and encouragements. Sometimes they're biblical, but sometimes they're inspiring but not directly from the Bible. I have a board on Pinterest with these types of quotes and one of them says 'What's your superpower?' Each of us has a superpower, some purposeful God-given destiny that we're to accomplish in our lives. It might be to be a teacher and inspire and impact children's lives. Or it could be to be a part of a ministry and to play a part in bringing heaven down to earth. But, sometimes the superpower is something you've been through. In the entry on abortion, I spoke about Abby Johnson, a former Planned Parenthood director who had a transformational experience. She's now a proactive advocate and defender of life, and has a ministry to help women who work in abortion clinics but desire to leave that industry. What hard, life-changing experiences have you gone through? Maybe it's infertility, maybe it's relationship issues, maybe it's a divorce? God will use what you've gone through as a catalyst to affect change in others. God wants to use what you've gone through—your struggle, your pain, your suffering, and your breakthrough—to be an inspiration to others and to instil hope in others that they can and will get out of their hardship, when we have faith and hope in Jesus. A friend recently got in contact with me because they had questions about IVF. I felt like a superhero! I'd been through both the ups and downs of successful and unsuccessful IVF rounds, and I knew what it was like. I'd been through the hard walk of infertility and trying to get pregnant, and now my story and experience was helping someone else.

Thank You, Lord, for Your Holy Spirit that is with us always. Thank You, Lord, that because of You we are overcomers. Help us to know the purpose and plans You have for us. Help us to be a changemaker and to impact those around us, and bring heaven down to earth.

*'And they overcame him by the blood of the
Lamb and by the word of their testimony, and
they did not love their lives to the death.'*

—REVELATION 12:11

Get Community—But Be Careful

For many years on my infertility journey, as well as my stepmom journey,
I felt alone. I felt like a lot of people just didn't understand the journey.
Some people cared, but couldn't commit to long-term moral support.
Others didn't really care, because it just wasn't of interest to them. And
some people genuinely cared but weren't close enough to me to provide
the support necessary. So over time, for both infertility and being a
stepmom, I turned to Facebook groups. A quick search of Facebook
groups will bring up quite a handful of groups related to those two
categories. In my experience, these groups on the onset will seem like a
haven, a place with like-minded people going on a similar journey. But to
be honest, they can often be more like Negative Nancy meeting rooms.
Of course, I don't speak for every group, and this is only my opinion, but
I found that many people in these groups have nowhere else to go, so
they give detailed posts about their troubles and hog up these groups'
chats. Plus, unless you actually develop close relationships with people
on these groups, it can leave you wanting. I've found that when I joined
an online group like this, those with negative posts seem to dictate the
tone of the group, and it often caused you to see your own situation in
a much worse light than it is. These types of groups can seem like an
ideal place to get connection; and to a point, yes, maybe for you it will.
But I'd suggest instead to prayerfully share your journey with one or two
close friends (and your husband), or engage a counsellor or psychologist.

See the Good/God in Everything

I know not everyone is open to professional help, but they can be the best kind of paid friends to have.

Thank You, Lord, that there is a friend closer than a brother. Help us to be friendly to others to gain godly friends. Help us have wisdom, divine appointments, and favour to find community and support for our life's journeys.

'A man who has friends must himself be friendly, but there is a friend who sticks closer than a brother.'
—PROVERBS 18:24

No One Will Fully Understand

For some reason I used to think that my husband should or would understand everything about me. That he'd be the one person in my entire life who would know and understand the highs and lows of my life. But, a few years into marriage, I started to question if my assumption was correct. Even though my husband's my best friend, and he knows almost all the inner workings of my mind and heart, he still doesn't always grasp or fully understand the joys and hardships in my life. When we were trying for many years to have babies, it was one of the most difficult times of my life. It was a battle of keeping my faith and hope alive, and rejecting despair and disappointment. Yes, my husband desired children as I did, but he didn't have the same battle, nor experience it the same way I did. Then I read Proverbs 14:10 in The Passion Translation: 'Don't expect anyone else to fully understand both the bitterness and the joys of all you experience in your life'. It really took a load off of me. I didn't have to try so hard to make my husband understand. There will be parts of my life that literally no one will fully grasp, and that's okay. But as believers, we're so lucky and blessed that God knows our innermost parts, our thoughts, and our weaknesses like no other, and that He loves us, and is with us, through it all.

Thank You, Lord, that You are the one, and only one, who will ever fully understand me, and who will always be with me. Thank You so much, Lord.

> *'O Lord, you have searched me and known me. You know my sitting down and my rising up; you understand my thought afar off. You comprehend my path and my lying down, and are acquainted with all my ways. For there is not a word on my tongue, but behold, O Lord, you know it altogether. You have hedged me behind and before, and laid your hand upon me. Such knowledge is too wonderful for me; it is high, I cannot attain it. Where can I go from your Spirit? Or where can I flee from your presence? If I ascend into heaven, you are there; if I make my bed in hell, behold, you are there. If I take the wings of the morning, and dwell in the uttermost parts of the sea, even there your hand shall lead me, and your right hand shall hold me.'*
>
> —PSALM 139:1–10

Happiness Is an Inside Job

For some reason, we grow up with this idea that when we get married or when we have a baby, we'll be happy always, because our dreams have come true. Yes, those are wonderful life events, but too often we base our happiness on a specific event or outcome. Or, we base our happiness on our life circumstances, thinking once everything is aligned and

See the Good/God in Everything

perfect, happiness will come. Or, we think when our husband dotes on us, shows us affection, and fills our love bank with our love language, we'll be happy. This is all folly. Happiness is an inside job that starts with a choice. You have to choose to be happy daily. You have to choose to be happy regardless of your circumstances, and regardless of the people around you. There was a time when my husband was absolutely miserable. He was tired of work and he wanted out. Nothing would make him happy. He'd sit around absolutely miserable, and it was a pretty awful home environment for some time. I had a choice to make. I could let my husband's unhappiness affect me, or not. So, I made a choice; he could be as unhappy as he wanted to be, but his unhappiness wasn't going to rub onto me. I would continue to be happy and grateful no matter what.

Thank You, Lord, for Your redemption, provision, forgiveness, and love. We trust You in every area of our lives. Help us to always be grateful and to choose to be happy, knowing our true joy comes from You.

> *'A happy heart makes the face cheerful,*
> *but heartache crushes the spirit.'*
> —PROVERBS 15:13 (NIV)

Insecurities about Being Asian

As mentioned, I'm a first-generation Canadian. My parents individually immigrated to Canada when they were teenagers. They met in Canada, got married, and had me. I'm not sure exactly how it happened, but I've ended up with a lot of insecurities about being Asian. I think most of it originated from my parents being immigrants, and because there's such a focus on our physical appearance being Asian. In my family, it was always considered more prized to look less Asian. It's a surprise I even married a Caucasian man. When I discuss these things with him, he reiterates that he doesn't see me as Asian. He sees me as Gina, and as beautiful. He doesn't see my facial features as large or small, or as Asianesque or not. What a reminder of how God sees me. Sometimes with deep-seated issues with a long history, we can get caught up thinking it's normal to fixate on cultural physical features, when it's definitely not. We mustn't live in that space. God doesn't want us to live with insecurities, whatever the issue may be. We must take our insecurities to God, and let Him uproot our issues, expose and deal with our hearts, and bring us back to the truth—that we are beautiful, redeemed, and made whole, because of the sacrifice and blood of Jesus. That we are *His*, that we are conquerors, and that we are confident in Him.

Thank You, Lord, that You redeemed us by the blood. Thank You, Lord, that we can come to You with our fears, anxieties, and insecurities. That You do not want us to be held back by these things, but to live in Your freedom. Help us to address and unroot every fear that is holding us back in our lives.

'To the praise of the glory of His grace, wherein He has made us accepted in the Beloved. In Him we have redemption through His blood, the forgiveness of sins, according to the riches of His grace.'
—EPHESIANS 1:6–7

See the Good/God in Everything

Sometimes Life is Blah

There's a scripture (Psalm 118:24) and song that goes, 'This is the day the Lord has made, let us rejoice and be glad in it'. We sing it with our daughter. But still, sometimes life is a bit boring. We're glad and thankful to God, but I've been feeling like our lives are still a little bit boring. Things are good, and we're healthy, so glory to God for that. But we're still in the pandemic, so a lot of socializing options are out, most trips are out since I'm not fully vaccinated yet, and it's summer here in the desert, so it's pushing 40-plus degrees Celsius (105 Fahrenheit) on a good day, which means we don't do a lot of outdoor things. So, our options are limited and our social circle is limited. Welcome to 2020 and 2021. When we go through these boring times, I'm thankful. At this time in our lives, my husband is not so stressed with work, and I'm not stressed with trying to get pregnant or with childrearing. It's one of those times, maybe fleeting and passing, but nonetheless a season of rest and quiet. A season where things are slow. A time to refocus and settle. To focus on the core of being a wife and mother, focus on my walk with God, and be even more thankful for all He's done and all He continues to do.

Thank You, Lord, for our seasons of rest. Forgive me for thinking this time in our lives is boring. Help me to focus on the important things in life, my walk with You, and resting. Thank You for this time, and thank You that You are so good to us.

'Come to Me, all you who labor and are heavy laden, and I will give you rest. Take My yoke upon you and learn from Me, for I am gentle and lowly in heart, and you will find rest for your souls.'
—MATTHEW 11:28–29

Increase Your Faith

We'd been trying to get pregnant naturally for many years before looking at IVF. When the IVF was successful on the first try, it was a shock. But, to be honest, I was a bit numb to it all. I was happy and grateful to be pregnant, but I didn't really feel super excited about it. I didn't want to get my hopes up. So, I did the only thing I could think of, which was to pray. We had gotten the book *Supernatural Childbirth* by Jackie Mize many years back, on the off-chance/miracle we may get pregnant. In her book there are many great testimonies and prayers you can read and declare over yourself during pregnancy, and even when trying to conceive. So, we made a good habit of it, and declared the Word of God over our unborn child daily. We prayed about even the littlest details of pregnancy and childbirth, and increased my faith for a natural and quick childbirth. When you get the Word deep into your spirit and you've prayed about everything, and you've committed everything to Him, things are easier. The outcome was a miraculous and quick three-hour unmedicated labour and delivery. There was no fear and no anxiety. When you're so filled with faith, you just get it done.

Thank You, Lord, that You are faithful to Your word. Help us to increase our faith, and to believe in the impossible.

*'Now faith is the substance of things hoped
for, the evidence of things not seen.'*
—HEBREWS 11:1

See the Good/God in Everything

I Cried Over a Cat

I'm a bit ambivalent about cats. Sometimes I like them because some of them are really darn cute. But sometimes I don't. Where we live in the Middle East, cats are prevalent...like *really, really, prevalent*. Stray and feral cats are literally all over the place. There used to be a family of cats living under my husband's car, so it can be unpleasant. My husband is also allergic to cats, so we just try to avoid them as much as possible. We used to shoo away the cats hanging around our house. But when my daughter was bigger and showed an interest in cats, it got tough. One of the regular cats around the neighbourhood had kittens who would sit on our patio, and my daughter was enchanted. I was too! Who doesn't love kittens?! Well, I started to feel compassion for the poor little kittens. I wanted to feed them some food. Spoiler alert—feeding cats can be a bad idea. The problem was, the minute I put cat food out, the kittens were gone and we were left with their mother only. Still a super cute cat. The problem wasn't her, it was me. After about a week of feeding it, my husband mentioned that I had gotten quite attached to it, and asked me what I would do when we returned to Australia at the end of the year, barely six months away. Well, if you know Australia, you know that biosecurity laws are pretty intense, so it just wouldn't work out. I couldn't take the cat with us, and if I kept feeding it, I would just grow more attached to it. I had to cut ties with the cat. This is what happens when you live abroad, people. You love 'em, then you leave 'em. My heart ached for the poor little cat I wouldn't be able to feed and befriend anymore. I felt a bit silly that I was crying over a cat, but that was just my reality. It would be worse for me and the cat if the feeding continued for months and then one day we were just gone. I had to make the hard but responsible choice.

Thank You, Lord, that You give us pets to look after and love. Help us to make wise choices regarding them for their welfare and for ours.

'How much better to get wisdom than gold! And to get
understanding is to be chosen rather than silver.'
—PROVERBS 16:16

Getting Older

I don't like to admit it, but in a few days I will be turning forty years old.
It's a different type of view now. When I was young and in my twenties
and thirties it was like, work hard, build a career, travel to as many
places as possible, see the world, and live life to the fullest. Now, days
away from turning forty, my view on life has changed. Life now is: be
grateful for each and every day, appreciate and love those around me,
build relationships, accept that sometimes life might not turn out as I
think, and that's okay, God's still in the journey, and life is beautiful.
It's more important for me now that my life showcases the goodness of
God than having numerous stamps in my passport or a fancy job title.
I guess this is part of getting older and wiser.

**Thank You, Lord, that You walk with me in this journey of life. I am
not afraid to be alone, for You are always with me. Help me to grow
wiser as I grow older. Help me to remain humble and be teachable.
Help me not to grow stagnant and bitter as I grow older, thinking I
know everything. Please help me to be more gracious and loving and
to display more fruits of Your Spirit throughout my life.**

'The glory of young men is their strength, and
the splendor of old men is their gray head.'
—PROVERBS 20:29

See the Good/God in Everything

The Cat Came Back

The journey of the cat isn't over. The cat came back. So, I had stopped feeding and being friendly to the cat a few weeks ago and shooed her away whenever she came by. I thought that was it! Boy was I wrong. When she used to hang around the house, my husband suspected she was pregnant, but I wasn't so certain. Well, he was right, she was pregnant, again. After a few weeks of not seeing her, we returned home one day to see Mama Cat and three tiny kittens sleeping in our flower bed. It looks like the cat adventure isn't yet finished. I guess when it comes to life, things aren't always clear cut and easy. It looks like instead of having nothing to do with the cat (or, cat family now, I guess), I'll have to figure things out. There were really only two choices: let the pest control people come and take the cats away to goodness knows where and do goodness knows what to them, or let the kittens grow a little, look after and care for them, then give them away to a shelter. I honestly wanted an easy way out, just to cut all ties and not have anything to do with them again, but it seems like that isn't going to happen. It seems like every day I need God's wisdom for something, even for something as trivial as the stray cats living in my garden.

Thank You, Lord, that Your wisdom is not limited. Thank You that it is not limited to godly things only, but to all aspects of our lives. Help me to make wise choices, even to things that may seem insignificant to me.

> *'Are not two sparrows sold for a copper coin? And not one*
> *of them falls to the ground apart from your Father's will.'*
> —MATTHEW 10:29

Safe Shows

Let's be honest, shows today are not what they used to be. There's a whole lot of ungodly things out there that pass off as entertainment. I don't know about you, but when I watch certain shows, it doesn't end well. I end up with bad dreams, nightmares, or horrid ungodly thoughts. I end up regretting watching it, and need to repent, because let's be honest, I knew better. I'm thankful that where we live we don't have regular TV, or Netflix or any of those other streaming networks. We have YouTube and Apple TV and that's it. But it's already more than enough. Because of the amount of dodgy shows out there, I have what I call my safe shows. When I watch my safe shows or movies, I don't have to worry about any ill effects or spiritual attacks. My safe shows do not include things many people in the world today would not even bat an eye at, like pre-marital sex, cohabitation, any form of sexuality, homosexuality or witchcraft. My safe shows don't include anything with immoral or questionable values. For example, the 'Ocean's' movies used to be a safe show until I realized I kept watching movies about thieves! A definite no. We must pay attention to what we're watching—not everything is worth watching!

Thank You, Lord, that You give us Your wisdom and understanding. Help us to live a pure and godly life. Convict us where we can improve in purity and godliness, so we can represent You well.

'The lamp of the body is the eye. If therefore your eye is good, your whole body will be full of light. But if your eye is bad, your whole body will be full of darkness. If therefore the light that is in you is darkness, how great is that darkness!'
—MATTHEW 6:22–23

See the Good/God in Everything

God Gave Me a Cat...?

My friends are busy and isolating themselves because of their life dramas, and my husband is too stressed at work to talk to me, so God gave me a cat? I could be wrong; I don't actually know if he really sent me a cat or not, but he definitely knows I could use some company these days, as well as distraction. Honestly, I've never been a pet person. My parents have a dog, but it wasn't their choice to have him, and he came into our lives when I was already living abroad. It was just a known fact that as a frequent international traveller, a pet was an added liability. But God works in mysterious ways, and life these days has been very slow and mundane. It's never nice when your friends are too busy with their own lives to actually be a friend, but this is how life goes. So, I take it in stride and I deal with what I have. If a cat is the only friend I've got for this season, I'll take it. Sometimes things seem weird at first, but when you look back in hindsight, it makes sense why things happened that way. With all the talk of us leaving the Middle East, I wouldn't be surprised if God actually did plan for me to have just a cat as a friend. No one wants a friend who's only thinking and talking about leaving, and it could just be emotionally easier for both me and them (my friends). But who knows? I'm just thinking out loud. Either way, God knows my needs and He always provides for them, even the need to have a friend.

Thank You, Lord, that You know all my needs even before I ask You. Thank You that You bring comfort and peace in every season. Thank You that every season is purposeful and You are with me through it all.

'Therefore do not be like them. For your Father knows the things you have need of before you ask Him. In this manner, therefore, pray: Our Father in heaven, hallowed be Your name. Your kingdom come. Your will be done on earth as it is in heaven. Give us this day our daily bread. And forgive us our debts, as we forgive our debtors. And do not lead us into temptation, but deliver us from the evil one. For Yours is the kingdom and the power and the glory forever. Amen.'

—MATTHEW 6:8–13

Seriously, Drink Water

We live in the Middle East, and it's hot! The winter temperatures feel like early summer in North America, and the summer temperatures are around 45 Celsius (113 Fahrenheit) on a regular day. When I was new and naïve to the country, I joined an outdoor hiking group, which was a popular type of social event for Westerners at the time. On one such hike, my friend and I were lagging behind when she started to show signs of heat exhaustion. She was dizzy, excessively sweating, and had clammy skin. We rushed her to a car and got her cooled down with some water, but it was a close call which really highlighted the effects of the heat, and the importance of hydration. A few years later, my husband and I took part in a desert trip with our church fellowship. But because of my experience with my friend getting heat exhaustion, my husband and I drank five litres of water every day for the week prior to the desert trip. We weren't taking any chances. What resulted was us looking like absolute superheros. We had so much energy and vitality for the whole trip in the desert. Others were hot, bothered, and tired from the heat, but we weren't. We ended up being vital to the trip, as we had so much energy we basically packed up camp ourselves while everyone

See the Good/God in Everything

else recovered from the heat. It was remarkably noticeable what good hydration can do. So, for real, drink water. If you live in a hot place like me, drink even more water.

Thank You, Lord, that You give us wisdom, healing, and divine health. Help us to look after our physical bodies, just as we look after our spiritual bodies.

'Beloved, I pray that you may prosper in all things and be in health, just as your soul prospers.'
—3 JOHN 1:2

Godly Mentors

I've been lucky in my life as a born-again Christian to have had the most amazing mentors. Some were official mentors, and others were fellow leaders in church who I looked up to and admired. The first advice I received from my first mentor, when I was a wide-eyed baby Christian, was to watch her. Watch how she did life, watch how she worshipped, watch how she walked with the Lord. This was so key to me. Up until this point, I'd only been in the world or in the religiosity of the Catholic Church, so I didn't know what it was like to have a relationship with God, but she showed me how to do that. She corrected me when I needed correcting, like when I was hanging out with dodgy people in church (those who went to church but never really got plugged in and always criticized it), or when I purposefully went against her sound advice. Watching godly women do life is so key to me, so I surround myself with upstanding women. I watch and learn how they live, how they mother, how they parent, and there are always lessons I can learn. One thing noteworthy about these godly mentors and friends is the way they treat their husband. They are all extremely strong women of God, and some of them are very vivacious and chatty, but they still always hold their husband in the highest honour. They are kind to their husband and will always consider them and speak well of them. Another thing noteworthy is that they are worshippers. God is always worthy to be praised and they will sing and worship at all times.

Thank You, Lord, for godly women. Help us to surround ourselves with godly upstanding women we can learn from. Help us to be more like You, and to be the type of women, wives, and mothers You call us to be. Help us to be joyful in all things.

'Older women likewise are to be reverent in behavior, not slanderers or slaves to much wine. They are to teach what is good, and so train the young women to love their husbands and children, to be self-controlled, pure, working at home, kind, and submissive to their own husbands, that the word of God may not be reviled.'
—TITUS 2:3–5 (ESV)

Body Image Issues—Weight

After I had my daughter, I lost a good majority of my pregnancy weight in the first few months afterwards. It was a miracle, as I had put on a lot of weight, but it made me very happy. I could even fit into most of my pre-baby clothes. I do tend to wear baggy clothes, so it worked in my favour. But, nonetheless it was a good confidence boost. However, when we started doing IVF again, pretty aggressively, to get pregnant a second time, everything went downhill. Hormone drugs aren't fun. I had increased my eating and was even comfort-eating. Don't comfort-

See the Good/God in Everything

eat! But that's an entry for another time. When we took a break from IVF to deal with other fertility-related issues, and I finally looked at the scale, I realized I had put on a huge amount of weight. I was the heaviest I'd ever been while not being pregnant, by a long shot. I no longer fit into any of my pre-baby clothes, and was needing a whole new set of clothes. I can't tell you the absolute horror I felt. I was feeling disgusted and very ugly. I couldn't look in the mirror without getting depressed. It highlighted to me how much my self-confidence was linked to my body image, and in particular my weight. It forced me to address a few things: 1. Don't weigh yourself daily unnecessarily. 2. Don't do anything that will make you depressed (such as analysing yourself in the mirror or trying on clothes you know you don't fit into). 3. Address the overeating. This includes recognising that you do it, finding all the triggers, addressing them, and changing eating habits. 4. Make healthy choices. 5. Focus on inner beauty and how God sees you. Yes, we should be healthy and not overeat or comfort-eat; but more importantly, we need to separate our self-confidence from our body image. Our self-confidence doesn't come from being a certain weight. For me, this is still a work in progress, but I'm definitely addressing the points above and asking God for wisdom to be a healthy person with a healthy body image.

Thank You, Lord, that I am fearfully and wonderfully made in Your image. Help me where I comfort-eat and overeat. Help me to address those issues and other root issues related to my body image. Help me to not focus on my body image, but on attaining godliness and being the woman of God You called me to be.

'For physical training is of some value, but godliness (spiritual training) is of value in everything and in every way, since it holds promise for the present life and for the life to come.'
—1 TIMOTHY 4:8 (AMP)

You Can Change Your Thinking

I have a wild imagination. I can live in a story in my head. Since I didn't grow up in a Christian household, I didn't know anything about controlling your thoughts or thinking about good things. It just wasn't there. So, when I became a Christian, all those 'thoughts and thinking' scriptures really spoke to me. It was the answer to the question I didn't realize I should be asking. The process to renew my mind and control my thinking was a tough one. It's taken about 13 years so far, and I'm still working on it. In the beginning, I couldn't even just meditate on a scripture and think about it silently. My mind was overactive and unrenewed. So, what I did for many years was have scriptures all over my walls. I would put up plain brown wrapping paper, or just use regular A4 printing paper, and write the scripture I wanted to meditate on, in large writing, so whenever I saw it I would read it and think about it. Slowly over time, seeing those scriptures regularly, even multiple times a day, will affect your thinking. This is why your eye gate is so important. What you see, and what you watch, does affect your mind and your thinking, so be careful what you look at, see, and watch. The next big step for me in changing my thinking was controlling my thoughts and making sure I only thought about good things. This is a tricky one, because my mind is slightly melancholic (or so I think). This is also difficult because controlling your thoughts and only thinking about good things is mental exercise. If you aren't used to it, it'll take you a long time to get it into shape. But there's hope for us all!

Thank You, Lord, that You give us the words of life. Help us to renew our mind, and to actively think about what we are thinking. Help us to be wise about what we let into our minds via our eyes and ears. Help us to constantly renew our mind and to think about beautiful, good things.

*'And do not be conformed to this world, but be transformed
by the renewing of your mind, that you may prove what
is that good and acceptable and perfect will of God.'*
—ROMANS 12:2

Save Yourself for Your Husband (But Everything Is Under the Blood)

When I was young, purity wasn't really a topic we talked about. In high school we had to take the mandatory sexual health classes, but to be honest, a lot of kids my age were having sex. When I was 17, my aunt signed me up to a Charismatic Catholic youth camp, which I wasn't so keen on attending at the time, but I ended up loving it. During that camp they talked about abstaining from sex until marriage, and we signed a card saying we were saving ourselves for our spouses. But purity doesn't just mean abstaining from sex. This was an area of confusion for me, because I thought it only meant intercourse. But when I became a mature Christian, I realized purity doesn't just mean sex, but a whole lot of other areas. My goal for the future with my kids is to have an open dialogue about purity and how God wants us to treat our bodies. We have to remember that even though we may have sinned in this area in the past, when we repent of our sins, God forgives us of them; everything in our past is covered by the blood.

Lord, thank You that we are fearfully and wonderfully made. Thank You that Your Holy Spirit dwells in us, and our body is a temple for You. Help us to be pure in thought, actions and deeds.

'But if we walk in the light as He is in the light, we have fellowship with one another, and the blood of Jesus Christ His Son cleanses us from all sin.'

—1 JOHN 1:7

The Important Things

So, I recently got laser eye surgery. I didn't get the quick and easy LASIK, with the fast recovery time, as I could've. Maybe I should've. Instead I chose PRK, which my ophthalmologist said was safer, but has a much longer recovery time. And boy, do I mean a long recovery time. The first three days I basically spent in my bedroom with the lights out and sunglasses on, putting eye drops into my eyes almost every half-hour. And even now, eleven days post-surgery, my vision is still pretty hit-and-miss; at times excellent, and at other times blurry but manageable. The only way I can currently type is by using my husband's huge 27-inch computer monitor, with my computer screen on 200%. But, having said all that, my point is that during these past eleven days, the important and unimportant have become very evident and stark. When you can barely see, you can do very little, and only the most important things matter. With limited phone use, you realize a lot of things don't really matter at all. It gets down to the most basic issues. Do we have food? Is my family fed? Is my child happy and okay? Do we have clothes to wear? The important things in life are really pretty basic. All the other things we distract ourselves with—basically almost everything on our phones—aren't really that important. It just goes to show how unimportant and meaningless most of our phone apps are, yet we spend so much time on them.

See the Good/God in Everything

Thank You, Lord, that You care about us and all aspects of our life. Help us to get rid of the unimportant time-wasting things in our lives, and focus on the important things that bring life and peace into our homes.

'But solid food is for the mature, whose spiritual senses perceive heavenly matters. And they have been adequately trained by what they've experienced to emerge with understanding of the difference between what is truly excellent and what is evil and harmful.'
—HEBREWS 5:14 (TPT)

It Comes Down to Fear or Faith

I'm battling with a few anxieties these days. I'm battling with the desire to have more children, and the fear of providing for them in the future. I'm anxious about this because I'm a housewife and have been for the past eight years. My husband, who is much older than me, wants to retire soon, and then I'll be the sole provider. Thankfully, our house will be paid for by then, so that's one huge expense I don't need to consider, but everything else will be on my shoulders. Talk about stress. I say 'stress' but what it really is is fear. Fear for the future, fear of the unknown, fear that I can't do it, and especially fear that God won't provide for me and my family. So here I am, at a crossroads. I'm at the corner of fear and faith and I have a choice to make. I can choose to be fearful, anxious, and stressed, or I can choose to believe that He is faithful. Fear is the easier option, that's for sure, and it's the one I'm more familiar with. But faith is more rewarding and life-building. So, though it may be tough, I'm going to have to choose faith. We know the Bible says that He is faithful to His word. It says we are never forsaken nor will His children go begging for bread. So, if He looks after the birds of the air and clothes the lilies, how much more for His children? I'm crazy scared but will still choose faith, and believe that He is faithful.

Thank You, Lord, that You constantly remind us not to worry! And not to worry about tomorrow! Not to worry about our life, what we eat, and what we wear. That You will look after us and provide for us. Thank You for Your constant provision. Thank You that You know every aspect of our lives, and that nothing is hidden from You. Thank You that You love us and care for us, and You never leave us. Help us to trust in You, and live a faith-filled life.

'Therefore I say to you, do not worry about your life, what you will eat or what you will drink; nor about your body, what you will put on. Is not life more than food and the body more than clothing? Look at the birds of the air, for they neither sow nor reap nor gather into barns; yet your heavenly Father feeds them. Are you not of more value than they? Which of you by worrying can add one cubit to his stature? So why do you worry about clothing? Consider the lilies of the field, how they grow: they neither toil nor spin; and yet I say to you that even Solomon in all his glory was not arrayed like one of these. Now if God so clothes the grass of the field, which today is, and tomorrow is thrown into the oven, will He not much more clothe you, O you of little faith?'

—MATTHEW 6:25–30

See the Good/God in Everything

Praying for Celebrities

In my pre-Christian days I used to be a huge follower of celebrity news. I had my fair share of actors or actresses that I'd follow pretty religiously. I've been out of the loop for a while, but recently saw that one of these celebrities had broken up with her fiancé, and was now dating someone else. Who am I but a middle-aged housewife, but my heart hurt a little to hear that she was again dating someone else. I felt for her. This celebrity is a middle-aged superstar, who's amazing at what she does, but my heart goes out to her as she seems to go from relationship to relationship. I know she's a celebrity and I'll likely never meet her, but that doesn't mean I can't pray for her. It's been on my heart recently to pray for celebrities and people in the public eye. They need our prayers as well—actually, they may even need our prayers more, as they influence millions of people by their work and social media influence. So, my new job, instead of reading the gossip mags, is to pray for the celebrity who comes to mind. They need Jesus, salvation, love, wholeness, redemption, and forgiveness, and to be healed, saved, and delivered as well. So, let's not downplay celebrities, but keep them in our prayers.

Thank, You, Lord, that You didn't come into this world to condemn it, but that the world through You would be saved. Lord, we lift up to You these celebrities and people in the public eye. Lord, we pray that they would be blessed and prosper in every area of their life and work. Help them to see Your goodness in their lives, and help them to know that You love them.

'For God did not send His Son into the world to condemn the world, but that the world through Him might be saved.'
—JOHN 3:17

Goodbye and a New Purpose

So, we're finally leaving this country in the Middle East. We've been here almost ten years, and it's left a noticeable mark on my heart. Here in the middle of the desert is where I found love, grew as a woman, overcame insecurities, met the most amazing people, prayed up a storm, had a baby, and developed as a mother. With a few months left until we leave, we have lists upon lists of things to do before we go, and lists of things to do to prepare for where we're going. But in the meantime, I'm cherishing the everyday. Sometimes it takes knowing you will be leaving a place for you to really appreciate it. But the one thing I'll miss the most is the purposefulness of it all. Here, I felt moved to pray for people all the time. As my first mentor used to say, 'If you don't go, pray'. So, I may not have been in the workplace and I may not have made many local friends, but I know my prayers changed things in the spiritual. I'll never know how exactly until I get up to heaven and God shows me how it all worked together. So, I'm praying for the next thing. I'm praying about what God wants me to focus my prayers on and where to put my spiritual energy. Because I know how important and powerful prayer is, I want to make sure I'm focused on what He wants me to pray for.

Thank You, Lord, that You know all about our everyday. Help us to be more aware of You in our everyday routines and lives. Help us to be more sensitive to pray and follow Holy Spirit in the things we do, say and act, that we would affect those around us, for Your glory.

'Therefore I exhort first of all that supplications, prayers, intercessions, and giving of thanks be made for all men.'
—1 TIMOTHY 2:1

See the Good/God in Everything

Give Yourself Grace, Not a
Free Pass for Bad Habits

When we say to give yourself grace, we're often talking about giving yourself permission to forgive your mistakes, being aware that we aren't perfect, and understanding that it's okay not to have it all together all the time. When I have grace for myself, it goes one of two ways. Sometimes I just need to forgive myself for being human and making mistakes, but at other times I use it as an excuse to lose control and fall back into bad habits. Like comfort-eating, I'll say I 'deserve' it since I had such a bad day, which falls into my having 'grace for myself', so I'll order a few donuts. This isn't grace. Or, I'll fall into another one of my bad habits and waste too much time on the internet or watching too much YouTube. I know too many Christians who are in hard circumstances who use those hard circumstances as an excuse to 'have grace for themselves', but it just contributes to a cycle of encouraging bad habits. So, let's be honest with ourselves and call it what it is. Having grace for ourselves is sometimes forgiving our human mistakes or being aware that we aren't perfect. Having grace for yourself is not a free-pass card to fall into bad habits, or to lose self-control. Speaking to myself here.

Thank You, Lord, that You want us to have the fruit of self-control. Help me not to make excuses, under the heading of grace, to fall into bad habits. Help me to be honest with myself, and to deal with my circumstances in a way that is honouring to You.

> *'It is not good to eat much honey; so to seek one's own glory is not glory. Whoever has no rule over his own spirit is like a city broken down, without walls.'*
> —PROVERBS 25:27–28

Be Your Own Cheerleader

I have a sister-in-law who is amazing. So's so focused and driven, and knows exactly what she wants. She works hard and is extremely dedicated towards her goals. I never really understood her drive and purposeful nature before, but now I can see that she's just focused on attaining her goals. You see, I on the other hand have been a bit of a waffler. I've done a lot of different things half-heartedly. For a long time I wasn't focused on one particular thing or goal, nor did I feel really driven for anything. That is, until I started writing. Actually, it started when I first felt the desire to write a book about my brother. Everything fell into place then. Then one day, I decided to share a bit of writing with my husband. It was an entry for this devotional that I thought was pretty good. I was happy with it, and I wanted to share it with him. I thought he was going to be all happy, supportive, and encouraging, but he wasn't. He read it, paused, then said, 'Do you want to know what I think?' That should have been my clue, and I should've firmly replied no. Anyways, he had two critiques. Afterwards I said thank you, then left to take a shower to regain my centre. Here's the thing, people. I used to think our spouses needed to be our greatest cheerleaders in life. I'm now amending that thought. Yes, I think the role of a spouse should be to support and cheer the other spouse on in their life and work, but I think firstly we need to be our own cheerleaders. We need to fill ourselves with vision, focus, and purpose, so that even if our spouse fails to be a good cheerleader one day, as mine was that day, it almost doesn't matter. We can cheer ourselves on because we know what we're working for and what we're hoping to attain and achieve, and that drives us forward. We need to know the greatness of God inside of us, and our purpose. They should be the driving force in our lives.

Thank You, Lord, that You have a purpose and a plan for my life. Thoughts of good and not of evil to give me a future and a hope. Help me to be focused in my work and life. Help me to know that I can do

See the Good/God in Everything

all things through You. Help me to be my own self-motivator and cheerleader, knowing that with You I can do all things.

'The Lord will perfect that which concerns me; your mercy, O Lord, endures forever; do not forsake the works of Your hands.'
—PSALM 138:8

Be Thankful When You Are in a Good Church

The last few years have been tough spiritually, as we've found it so hard to get plugged into a good church. We moved cities (and away from our amazing church) just as we got pregnant. We were lucky at the time to find a good church with a pastor we really liked in the new city. However, as soon as baby came, I was a super-anxious first-time mom. I was so anxious about taking her out and even taking her to church, especially since it was quite a way away. And then less than three months after she was born, COVID hit. That church we were at basically disintegrated, and the pastor abandoned the fellowship. There were never any online meetings, no more emails with information about what was happening. It just died. Many months later and we were still on the hunt for a new church. The other churches we knew of were okay, but there wasn't one we particularly connected with, though we tried very hard on multiple occasions. Then, we finally connected with a church with some mutual friends, but it was a little different to what we were used to. I can't tell you how hard it is not to have a church you really enjoy. So, we continued to follow our old fellowship in the other city online as much as we could. Honestly, I found it a bit ridiculous that we were actually in a situation where we couldn't find a church we both enjoyed in the city we were in. The only redeeming factor was that we were leaving in two months' time. Let me tell you, after the lockdown days and not connecting to a church in our current city, I will be beyond blessed to practice fellowship in person again. I will never again give an excuse to skip physical church again. Honestly, my heart can't bear it anymore.

Lord, forgive me when I took going to church for granted. Forgive me when I made lame excuses to miss church, or when I was just too lazy to go. Forgive me for not appreciating fellowship in person with my brothers and sisters in Christ. Help me to be more gracious and appreciate what I have, before I lose it. Help me to get plugged into a church again, one both my husband and I enjoy.

'Not forsaking the assembling of ourselves together.'
—HEBREWS 10:25

Is This What God Meant?

We've been having issues with our washing machine. It's been staining our white clothes, sheets, and towels red. Most of those items are pretty old and very worn and will be thrown out when we leave in two months' time, so it didn't bother me much. Still, I spoke to the compound manager about it on multiple occasions. His response was to take it away for servicing and cleaning. Then it stained one of my husband's blue work shirts, after which I got a bit more peeved, but luckily it was on an area that's not very noticeable, so it's still wearable. But then it stained one of my lovely white night dresses, which I ordered specifically from Australia, and I got super pissed! That was an expensive night dress and shipped all the way from Australia! Funny how if it's not your stuff, it's not that bad, but once it affects you directly, all bets are off. But then I

See the Good/God in Everything

realized God mentioned worrying about clothes in the Bible. And it's only a night dress. So, is this what He meant? I think so. In the scheme of my life, this night dress is actually very, very unimportant. Even though it was expensive and shipped from abroad, my life will go on unaffected. So, yup, I'm quite sure this is what He meant. Yes, of course, I still notified the compound manager, because it's his job to look after these things, but I put the anger to the side because it's really not worth my energy to get into a tizzy over it.

Thank You, Lord, that Your Word has all the answers for my life. Help me not to lose my peace over the unimportant things, and help me to manage my emotions.

> *'Now if God so clothes the grass of the field, which today is, and tomorrow is thrown into the oven, will He not much more clothe you, O you of little faith?'*
> —MATTHEW 6:30

After Fear Is Excitement— But You Need a Vision

Here's the thing about us moving back to Australia. It's a huge step for us, and especially for me. We met in the Middle East almost ten years ago. We've built a life and a family here, and though we always knew we wouldn't be settling here, I kind of got used to it. Knowing we'd be leaving meant I would be working again, something I haven't done since we got married, and that my dear husband would be retiring shortly. I was feeling pressured. The need to support my family, plus our desire to grow our family all at once, seemed so daunting, even crazy. I could barely handle the stress. On top of that, for me and our daughter, we would be moving to a totally new country, one we had never lived in before. The fear was real. So much change all at once, and the pressure to do well can give you major anxiety. Yup, that was definitely me. So, I did what I always do. I sat with God and I processed all my fear. I had to go deep and see where the fear came from and why it was there, and I had to replace it with faith and trust in God. Around this time, I also came across a ministry by Terri Savelle Foy that focuses on dreaming big and trusting God. My goodness me, where has this ministry been all my life?! I took her Vision Board course and it literally changed my life! She speaks about what I've always known but never verbalized, that what you see, you become, because what you see, you think about and dream about. So, I discussed it with my husband, who thought it was amazing and supported me a hundred percent, and made myself a vision board. It has all the things I'm dreaming about and desire to do. I can't tell you how just being proactive and visual has helped to make me so much more focused. It was the God connection, and the push I needed to seriously believe my dreams are possible. So now I'm excited. I'm excited for change, and I'm excited for new things. Because He is amazing, and He can and will do amazing things in my life.

Thank You, Lord, for God connections and finding ministries that speak to our spirit. Thank You, Lord, for Your word, and that You teach us all things. Help me to deal with the fear in my life, so that I can be all that You call me to be. Help me to be a person of vision, focus and hard work, and that You would be glorified in all that I do.

See the Good/God in Everything

'Now Jacob took for himself rods of green poplar and of the almond and chestnut trees, peeled white strips in them, and exposed the white which was in the rods. And the rods which he had peeled, he set before the flocks in the gutters, in the watering troughs where the flocks came to drink, so that they should conceive when they came to drink. So the flocks conceived before the rods, and the flocks brought forth streaked, speckled, and spotted.'

—GENESIS 30:37–39

Take Only the Important Things

So, we're leaving the Middle East in a few months and moving back to Australia where my husband's from. We've been here almost ten years, and we've accumulated a lot of stuff. And when our daughter was born, we started to accumulate even more kids' stuff! So now as we're getting ready to leave, we've been going through all our things. We're going through our wardrobes and cupboards, getting rid of the unused, the old, and the unnecessary. We've been going through all our clothes, baby gear, luggage, and furniture and deciding if it's worth taking or not. Is it too old to take? Do we need it? Do we even like it? Will it fit in our new house? One thing I've realized through this process is that we've accumulated a lot of things, but only the most important things really matter. The special plate we got in Italy, pictures from our wedding, a gift from a friend. Those things have meaning, value, and worth to us, and those things we'll definitely take with us. It reminds me a lot of life. How we accumulate ideas, emotions, and opinions, but a lot of it is junk, really. Only the things of value and worth, things that uplift us, are the things we should hold onto, and we should do a regular check to get rid of the unnecessary in our lives, mind, and hearts.

Thank You, Lord, that You look after all of our needs. Help me to regularly check my heart, mind, and life, to get rid of unnecessary emotions, rubbish ideas, bad thoughts, and pain. Help me to keep the things of worth in my life, but to get rid of the things that hold me down from being who I am called to be, in You.

'Do not lay up for yourselves treasures on earth, where moth and rust destroy and where thieves break in and steal; but lay up for yourselves treasures in heaven, where neither moth nor rust destroys and where thieves do not break in and steal. For where your treasure is, there your heart will be also.'
—MATTHEW 6:19–21

Wise Older Women in the Faith

I got saved when I was 27 years old. I was living, working, and studying abroad, and had gotten used to being a very independent person. The first few years of being a Christian, I had some amazing mentors and leaders in the faith. Older women; sometimes not much older than me, but those who had been Christians for a long time, and were wise in their walk with the Lord. You see, I'd grown up in a very non-Christian background. I knew religion, and I knew my family's cultural upbringing, but I definitely didn't grow up in a Christian household. There were a lot of things to learn, and a lot of things to unlearn. Wise women of faith are precious commodities, and I don't take them for granted. I felt especially in need of mentorship from godly wise women, mothers, and wives when I became a wife and mom myself. There were things about parenting, things about raising godly children in a godly home, things about being a wife of noble character, that I wanted to learn from women who had done it and were outstanding at it. There are a lot of things wise older

See the Good/God in Everything

women in the faith can teach you. They've lived life long enough, learnt some tough lessons, and been through experiences, but have come out still loving and trusting in the Lord, and still full of joy. There's a reason the Bible tells the older women to teach the younger ones. So, pray and ask the Lord to bring some amazing godly women into your life. These ladies are gems and we can all learn a lesson or two from them.

Thank You, Lord, that You do not want us to walk through life alone. Thank You that You bring about friends, mentors, and godly leaders to lead and guide us on our walk with You. Help us to be teachable and humble. Help us to learn how to be the mothers, wives, and sisters You call us to be.

'The older women likewise, that they be reverent in behavior, not slanderers, not given to much wine, teachers of good things—that they admonish the young women to love their husbands, to love their children, to be discreet, chaste, homemakers, good, obedient to their own husbands, that the word of God may not be blasphemed.'
—TITUS 2:3–5

INFERTILITY

Challenges of Getting Pregnant

I heard someone in my family once say, 'All the IVF kids I know are spoilt brats'. I was newly married and didn't have much of an opinion of IVF, so when I heard the above line, I didn't think much of it. Sometimes things like this happen to me; I hear something that doesn't make sense to me at the time, but it's indelible for some reason. This was one of those times. Fast forward eight years, where if I'd heard that line again, I'd have words to say. One of the most unspoken topics generally, not just in the church, is infertility. Irrelevant of which partner has a health issue, infertility is basically trying to have kids and it being complicated, hard, or simply not possible. It's a hot topic, and a tough topic to speak about to people who are going through it. When we were trying to have kids, I basically only spoke to two friends about the logistics of our infertility. It was a touchy topic because it was so close and dear to my heart. I purposefully didn't speak to a lot of people because I just needed to protect my heart. Those years of infertility were hard, and my heart goes out to those going through that now. But one thing I do know is that those hard years were the most defining of my life. When you walk through the fire, through the despair, and through the valley, you will come face to face with your Creator. It's a road really only you and He can go through together. The choice through it all is to either trust Him or not. If you choose the former, I guarantee you will come out joyful, and with every inch of your being determined that He is a good God, that He is for you, and that He loves you.

Thank You, Lord, that You are for us, and not against us. That You know the innermost part of our being, and the desire of our heart. Help us, Lord, when life is hard, to trust in You for Your best for us.

'He heals the brokenhearted and binds up their wounds.'
—PSALM 147:3

Sometimes You Need to Be
Open to Other Options

My husband first got married at 23 years old. By the time he was thirty, he'd had five kids. So, at thirty he had a vasectomy. I met him twenty years later. When we got married, we were praying for a miracle baby. We just prayed and hoped that God would give us a miracle baby without us having to do any work. This went on for years unsuccessfully. It wasn't until a close friend asked why John hadn't had a reversal did we think maybe we should be doing more to help God along on the baby-making front. So, we found the best urology specialist in Europe and booked him in. We had another year of failure to conceive. Then we had another divine appointment. One of our family members is an infertility specialist, and after a chance conversation where John hinted we were trying to get pregnant, she mentioned to us to consider IVF. We spoke with our pastor and prayerfully considered it. Sometimes as Christians we prefer the big miracle. Of course, God can do huge, amazing things. But sometimes God wants us to use medical science, innovations, and medical specialists. Be open to God working, even if it may not seem like the way you pictured it. God can and will use anyone, anything, and any means to get you to your promise. Don't let the fear of the unknown keep you from your promise. Follow His lead. He might take you places that may be new and unfamiliar, but He is always with you.

Thank You, Lord, that You are faithful to Your Word. Help us to trust in You, especially into the unknown areas of life. Help us to remember that You are always with us and never leave us.

See the Good/God in Everything

*'But Naaman became furious, and went away and said,
"Indeed, I said to myself, 'He will surely come out to me,
and stand and call on the name of the Lord his God, and
wave his hand over the place, and heal the leprosy.'"'*

—2 KINGS 5:11

God Is Still on the Throne

We're going through secondary infertility. Basically, it's when you already have one child, but you have (or still have) fertility issues and it's hard to get pregnant a second time. Miraculously, on our first round of IVF we got pregnant. So, I thought perhaps the second time would be just as lucky. Unfortunately, no. My good friend encouraged me and reminded me that *God is still on the throne!* What a reminder! Irrelevant of what we're going through, God remains on the throne. The things I'm going through don't surprise Him or worry Him; he is still Almighty God. What a thought! It puts things in perspective. It also gives me peace. The things in my life, in our world, don't change the sovereignty of our God.

Thank You, Lord, that You are the Alpha and Omega, the beginning and the end. That nothing I go through changes You, but You remain on the throne through it all.

'God reigns over the nations; God sits on His holy throne.'

—PSALM 47:8

The Waiting

If you're reading this entry, it could be because you know all about waiting. Maybe your waiting is over, or maybe you're still going through it. I was waiting for what seemed like an eternity, but in reality was six years. What can I say about waiting? Though you're waiting for a promise, God will use that time to work on you. He'll develop skills and talents in you and develop your character to be more like Jesus. I used to play piano when I was younger. I'm not amazing at it, but I had some key skills like reading music and singing. When I moved out of my parents' house, I stopped playing. Many years later, in our first year of marriage, in one of the very small complexes we lived in, we randomly found a new Yamaha piano in the social room that no one ever used. With my husband's encouragement I started taking up playing again. I was so bad and rusty but he encouraged me in the small steps, and I started playing worship songs. I followed the lead of one my favourite worship leaders, Misty Edwards. When she worships, she doesn't perform or entertain, she does it solely unto God. That's how I worship, unto Jesus, the author and finisher of my faith. I worshipped through my six years of waiting. I worshipped through tears. I worshipped when I didn't know why I was going through what I was going through. I worshipped when my heart broke. I worshipped when I was in pain. I worshipped through it all. I worshipped because no matter what my circumstances are, He is still good. I worshipped because even through the waiting, He remains God.

Thank You, Lord, that even in our season of waiting, You are still working. You never sleep or slumber and You know our heart's desire.

'Wait on the LORD; be of good courage, and He shall strengthen your heart; Wait, I say, on the LORD!'
—PSALM 27:14

See the Good/God in Everything

War for Your Breakthrough

Before my daughter was born, we were fighting for our promise. I'm a firm believer that if you're believing for a promise, you need to fight for it. You need to war for it, and you need to keep going until you get it. When I got pregnant and then had my baby, all warring stopped. I rested. I was, and still am, full of thankfulness, but I was no longer fighting, for my promise had come. A year later and we are in secondary infertility. A round of unsuccessful IVF later, and the realization has hit me that we'll need to get back on our face and war in the spirit for our promises once again. We were thinking getting pregnant again would, God willing, be easy for us this time around. We were kind of just casually praying for more babies. Unfortunately, it's not happening as easily as we thought it would. So, we're getting ready to war again for our promise. It seems like it won't be an easy win, but we're skilled soldiers and this isn't our first time to war.

Thank You, Lord, that You give us the weapons of our warfare. Thank You that You have taught us how to war in the spirit and that You give us the strength and faithfulness to contend for our promises.

'And from the days of John the Baptist until now the kingdom of heaven suffers violence, and the violent take it by force.'
—MATTHEW 11:12

Remembering How to War

So, we're still on the secondary infertility journey. I thought to myself how I've overcome the long struggle of persevering for the promise of our beautiful daughter, and I've seen the fulfilment of that promise.

I battled through, I persevered, and I was faithful not to lose hope! I was strong! I think I just assumed that strength would automatically continue on, even though I've been a bit out of practice. How easy once the promise is attained do we forget the struggle. It really is like John 16:21, below. For some reason, I thought trying to get pregnant a second time around would be easier for me emotionally and spiritually. But then again, 2020, the year of the pandemic, was hard for us all; and being a stay-at-home mom and wife, the social isolation has been extremely hard for me, so with IVF on top of that, it probably shouldn't come as a surprise. Still, maybe because I already have one child, I thought the dedication and focus for a second child would be effortless. But the infertility journey is not one to take lightly. Emotions, be as they may, won't dissuade me from my promise. So, here I am again, warming up my muscles, remembering my training, and mentally preparing myself to be deployed back into the battle. Reminding myself that this isn't my first time to war, that I will persevere, that I won't back down. I'll endure this mission to the end. I won't fail.

Thank You, Lord, that You are faithful to Your word. Help us to stay focused on You and not on our emotions.

> *'A woman, when she is in labor, has sorrow because her hour has come; but as soon as she has given birth to the child, she no longer remembers the anguish, for joy that a human being has been born into the world.'*
> —JOHN 16:21

See the Good/God in Everything

Friends for the Journey

The journey of trying to have a baby can be a lonely one. In Christian circles, different people have different views of IVF, so it isn't something I openly discuss, even with some of my closest Christian friends. As well, because the process of IVF takes about a month from start to finish, it's not something a lot of people know the details of, even those who know that we're trying for children this way. We were recently praying for new friends and by God-incidence, we've recently grown closer to a couple who are on a similar journey. These friends have actually been known to us for some time, but recently a mutual friend convinced them to reach out to us about starting IVF themselves. Sometimes you don't realize how much of an isolating journey infertility can be. To have friends on a similar path makes you a little bit less selfish. It's all of a sudden not all about you. Reaching out, praying, encouraging, and supporting someone else on the journey is commendable. It's so easy to get in a little infertility bubble and forget that other people are going through a similar struggle.

Thank You, Lord, that we are never alone on our life's journeys. Thank You that You are always with us, and that You bring us friends and companions. Help us to be prayerful advocates for our friends and to be the kind of friend we desire for ourselves.

'Perfume and incense bring joy to the heart, and the pleasantness of a friend springs from their heartfelt advice.'
—PROVERBS 27:9 (NIV)

Triggers

It's a fact. There will be people who will understand and be compassionate about your infertility journey. There will also be people who will not understand your decisions. They may even think you're making the wrong choices. Those who don't understand your choices can come from within your family and people you're close to, and that can be extremely hard. Our infertility journey is not something I discuss often. There are very few people who know the journey we've been through, and even fewer with whom we've opened our hearts, regarding trying to have children. So, when I'm faced with an unexpected comment or opinion, or someone who thinks I'm making bad choices, it can be very hard to be gracious. This happened to me recently. I had a close relation make a comment about how maybe God had another plan for us, that maybe having more children wasn't for us. Oh, my heart. My own doubts voiced out loud. I was hurt but also angry. Of all the people in the world, this close person had to make this comment. There were many things I really wanted to say, but thankfully I chose not to say anything. It seemed like the easiest thing for me to do was to harden my heart against them, and cut off all ties with them to make my life easier. Honesty, that's what I wanted to do. But that really wasn't the way God wanted me to handle the situation. So, I swallowed my pride, ego, and anger. I forgave them for their comments. I recognized that they'd triggered my own doubts about having more children, so I needed to show them more grace. Eventually I thanked them for their love and support, in spite of their misgivings and personal opinions.

Thank You, Lord, that even though we may not agree with everyone, You still call us to love and be dispensers of Your love and grace. Help us to be peacemakers and do all we can to live at peace with everyone.

See the Good/God in Everything

> *'When you are insulted, be quick to forgive and forget it,*
> *for you are virtuous when you overlook an offense.'*
> —PROVERBS 19:11B (TPT)

It Might Not Be How You Expect

I'll be totally honest with you. For a very long time, I was anti-IVF. I didn't think it was natural, and I had a lot of concerns about it. I used to think God is the God of miracles (which He is, don't get me wrong), and that I wouldn't need to engage medical science. That all we needed to do was pray, pray, pray and that would be enough. But God doesn't work like that. He doesn't always work the way we think He's going to work. And more often than not, He'll confront you at your most insecure place. I was insecure about IVF. I'd done a bit of research (not much, to be honest), and had an unknowledgeable opinion about it. And as a Christian I assumed the stance was to be anti-IVF. So, I just didn't think IVF would be the way forward for us. Yes, there are definitely things we were against, even while going through IVF, like foetal reduction (but that's for another entry). God's plan may look different than the plan you have. It may not be how you expect. And it may take longer than you thought. He may want you to go via a slightly different route. But, it's all about learning to trust Him through it all and remembering that, if not, He is still good.

Thank You, Lord, that You are the God of miracles. That You work in ways we will never fully understand. Help us to trust in You more and more. Help us to not be so set in our ways, or so fearful of the unknown, that we bypass Your plan.

> *'If that is the case, our God whom we serve is able to deliver
> us from the burning fiery furnace, and He will deliver
> us from your hand, O king. But if not, let it be known
> to you, O king, that we do not serve your gods, nor will
> we worship the gold image which you have set up.'*
>
> —DANIEL 3:17–18

No Longer Bitter

Thank God that God can, and will, change our hearts if we let him. During my infertility journey, things were tough. We used to live in a compound community with a really nice café, but it was right beside a kids' park. It was in our neighbourhood and it was the perfect distance for a nice evening stroll, so we often made our way to that café in the evenings. At the height of my infertility journey, when we would go there and see the kids playing with their parents, I'd cry. It would break my heart to see happy families and be barren. When someone came to church and announced they were pregnant, I'd avoid them like the plague. When a relative had a new baby and we went to see them in the hospital, I wouldn't hold the baby because it'd hurt too much. The minute we left their room, I ran to the restroom and cried my eyes out. During this time, I was dealing with insecurity, bitterness, and anger. Why them and not me?! I was pissed off with God. It was a very hard journey. One day a friend of a friend was having a baby shower and I was (randomly) invited last-minute. I wanted to go because my friends were going, but it was difficult because I'd have to be happy and celebrate the new mom-to-be. But after years of bitterness, I'd grown tired of being angry, upset, self-centred, and sad all the time. So, I made the decision to go, and to be happy that this friend of a friend was having a baby. I was going to rejoice for them! I wasn't going to focus on my lack in that area,

     See the Good/God in Everything

but on God's goodness and faithfulness. The baby shower was beautiful and I blessed her and prayed for her in my heart. As I was leaving, my pastor saw me. He stopped me and said, 'Well done for coming to the baby shower and showing her love. I'm proud of you'.

Thank You, Lord, that You give us the freedom to make our own choices. Help us to make the right, godly decisions so that we can be free and love generously. Help us not to focus on our lack or on the waiting of a promise, but to instead focus on Your continuing goodness and faithfulness.

> *'Shout for joy to the LORD, all the earth. Worship the LORD with gladness; come before him with joyful songs. Know that the LORD is God. It is He who made us, and we are his; we are his people, the sheep of his pasture. Enter His gates with thanksgiving and his courts with praise; give thanks to him and praise his name. For the LORD is good and His love endures forever; his faithfulness continues through all generations.'*
> —PSALM 100:1–5 (NIV)

Support System

The journey of infertility is not one many people are familiar with. I spoke once about online support groups, which to me wasn't helpful. What I preferred over online groups was having one or two friends I could confide in (as well as my husband and parents). When we started the IVF journey a few years ago, I confided in only one friend. I confided in her because I knew her personal opinion was in favour of IVF, whereas I didn't know about my other friends. Also, she's a very responsive friend, and with multiple doctor appointments, daily injections, ultrasounds, and other procedures, there's often a lot of waiting around in the hospital. So, it's good to have a friend who can support you through the boredom and the humdrum of it all. Having a support system is also about those who will pray with you and for you, uplift you, cry when you cry, and are joyous when you are joyous. You need friends and a partner who you can share your heart with. There are so many highs and lows with infertility and IVF, and you need friends who can go the long haul with you. If you have friends like that, you're lucky; and if you don't, pray for some.

Thank You, Lord, that You never leave us nor forsake us. Help us when we are going through hard times, like infertility, to have friends we can turn to. And help us to be the kind of friend we desire to others.

'A man who has friends must himself be friendly, but there is a friend who sticks closer than a brother.'
—PROVERBS 18:24

It's Different After You've Had One Kid

The Bible says a barren womb is never satisfied. This is so true. Before we had our daughter, the pain, agony, and desperation to get pregnant was real. It was extreme, how low my emotions would go to; simple things would cause me anguish. Watching parents and their kids at a park, holding a baby, seeing a pregnant woman. That was pure torture, and my heart could barely take it. The number of tears I cried in that season is unreal, and the anguish I felt was unfathomable. But after we had our miracle baby, trying for a second child doesn't feel the same, though I'm sure every woman is different. For me, this second time around, I don't

See the Good/God in Everything

have the desperation to get pregnant like I did the first time. I do want more kids, but the desperation and despair aren't as strong. Thank God for His answered prayers.

Thank You, Lord, that You are still the God of miracles. Thank You when things are good, and when things are tough. Help us to trust You when our faith is failing. Lord, bring more children into our lives, and help us to be the godly parents You call us to be.

> *'A father of the fatherless, a defender of widows, is God in His holy habitation. God sets the solitary in families; he brings out those who are bound into prosperity.'*
> —PSALM 68:5–6

Praying Like It's for Me

I have a dear friend going through IVF. It's been the most interesting experience to know someone who's going through this journey that very few people understand. But it's also interesting because her personality isn't like mine. She handles things differently than I do. But as a sister in Christ, one thing we do have in common is our faith, and the desire to pray for each other. She's a sister and friend, and I pray that the desires of her heart will be fulfilled. But the other day something changed in me. I was praying for her, and it was a bit of a mundane prayer. I was basically just fulfilling the requirement of being prayerful. But then Holy Spirit came upon me in a powerful way. And I just thought I should pray for her with resolute determination. I should pray like my prayers have power, because they do. I should pray like God hears my prayers, because He does. So, I prayed with the same desperation and deep desire as if I was praying for myself. Praying for my babies to come. Praying like Hannah, out of the depths of heartache to Him, the only one who matters.

Lord, help me to be a friend of significance. Help me to be the type of prayerful friend I desire my friends to be. Help me to be more prayerful and more in tune with You, Holy Spirit. Help me to pray always. And help me too, Lord, not to grow weary in doing good.

'So Hannah arose after they had finished eating and drinking in Shiloh. Now Eli the priest was sitting on the seat by the doorpost of the tabernacle of the Lord. And she was in bitterness of soul, and prayed to the Lord and wept in anguish. Then she made a vow and said, "O Lord of hosts, if You will indeed look on the affliction of Your maidservant and remember me, and not forget Your maidservant, but will give Your maidservant a male child, then I will give him to the Lord all the days of his life, and no razor shall come upon his head."'
—1 SAMUEL 1:9–11

Praying Not to Wee All Over My Doctor

One of the procedures in IVF is the embryo transfer. It's when they take the fertilised egg and transfer it into the uterus. It's a super easy and super quick procedure, literally a few minutes for the doctor to do. In most places you're not even medicated or anaesthetised because it's such an easy procedure, and you don't feel a thing. There's only one thing about this procedure that's highly aggravating, and for me the cause of major anxiety, which is that you have to go in with a full bladder. If you're lucky, your clinic will only want a half-bladder, but the norm is a full bladder. It's the most uncomfortable thing. If everything's

See the Good/God in Everything

perfect and goes to plan, you're normally only uncomfortable for a short period of time. They'll do the procedure and make you wait for a bit (maybe 10 minutes) before you can relieve yourself. The first time I had an embryo transfer, I didn't drink enough water. We were all in the operating room when the doctor came in and checked with the ultrasound technician how my uterus looked, and it wasn't good; not enough water. How embarrassing. I was told to drink three bottles of water and wait. If there's not enough water, they can't see where to place the embryo, and as well, a full bladder affects the way the uterus sits for optimal placement, so it's an integral part of the procedure. It took about thirty minutes, then I was desperately calling the nurse to tell her I was ready. My bladder was definitely full! But I was so uncomfortable! My prayer and mantra in that operating room was not to pee on the doctor! Seriously, in my head I was just repeating, 'I have a strong bladder! I have a strong bladder!' The things we go through to have babies.

Thank You, Lord, for medical science and technology. Thank You, Lord, that children are an inheritance from You. Let us always remember that children are a blessing, and worth the sacrifice.

'A woman, when she is in labor, has sorrow because her
hour has come; but as soon as she has given birth to
the child, she no longer remembers the anguish, for joy
that a human being has been born into the world.'
—JOHN 16:21

Waiting

There's a part in the book *Oh, The Things You Can Do* by Dr. Suess that's all about waiting. I've been waiting a long time for babies, and it's a hard wait. It's a wait that will develop your character, patience, love for the journey, a heart for people going through a similar journey, and a heart for those who experience the joy you desire. I used to get angry and upset when other women would get pregnant. I used to think it was the worst thing when people announced their pregnancy. I would get depressed and fall into a hole I didn't want to climb back out of. But part of the journey of waiting is a heart journey; learning to protect your heart, but also learning to step into your joy, even if you haven't seen the promise yet, because His plans are for good, and to give you a future and a hope. Waiting isn't passive. Though in some physical respect you're being stationary, waiting is all about the inner changes that need to take place. God's in the process of making us perfect and holy. Waiting for promises is really just to allow us to focus on the internal.

Thank You, Lord, that You love us and accept us as we are. Thank You that You desire us to be holy and perfect, as You are perfect. Help me, Lord, to see the changes You are working inside of me, as I wait for Your promises. Help me to be pliable and obedient, and to trust in You. Help me to see the joy, even in the waiting.

'You, therefore, will be perfect [growing into spiritual maturity both in mind and character, actively integrating godly values into your daily life], as your heavenly Father is perfect.'
—MATTHEW 5:48 (AMP)

See the Good/God in Everything

When Walking with a Friend, Take Their Burden as Your Own

I have a friend going through secondary infertility as well. Actually, we were both going through infertility at the same time and in the same church, but we weren't close. We were both going through our own problems and didn't connect. But after we both had babies, and were trying for babies again, a mutual friend connected us. So now we're walking with each other through the IVF journey. She's done IVF a bunch of times, and now, so have I. Our babies are miracle babies and we desire to be fruitful and have more babies. To truly be there for a friend during this journey, you literally need to take their burden as your own. When another IVF round fails, you mourn as they mourn. Their joy is your joy, their pain is your pain, their prayer is your prayer. This is the first time I've had a friend who truly understood what I was going through, physically, mentally, and spiritually, without me needing to explain all the processes, procedures, and feelings. It's answered a prayer I didn't know I was praying. To have someone walk with me on this journey who is a friend is truly remarkable. I can see why God thinks it's important to bear one another's burdens. It's love in action. It's the fulfilment of loving your neighbour as yourself.

Thank You, Lord, that You bring friends to walk with us on this journey of life. Thank You for those special people who bear our burdens as their own. Thank You, Lord, that You don't desire us to be alone, but for our brothers and sisters to partner with us, and love us as themselves. Bless them, Lord, for loving us so much that they choose to walk with us.

'Bear one another's burdens, and so fulfill the law of Christ.'
—GALATIANS 6:2

Baby Prophesies

When we moved to a new city, we went to a service there and were introduced to the pastor and a female elder, who turned out to be prophetic. We came up to them for prayer and she said, 'By the way, do you want to have children?' My eyes opened wide with fear, confusion, and hope. How did she know? The answer was yes, but it was complicated. I desired children, but my dear husband at the time didn't. Adamantly did not. So, we were at odds with each other, and it was kind of a topic we didn't discuss. We eventually settled at that church and enjoyed many years there. We've grown to love that church dearly, and our daughter is named after that prophetic friend who spoke those words many years ago. Here's the thing—I've had many prophetic words about us having babies. And though I really don't speak to many people about my desire to have babies, even to those closest to me, the prophetic words we've received have always been a candle of hope to my spirit. A reminder that God does hear my cries, and knows the inner depths of my heart. God's timing is perfect, and He alone knows exactly what we're going through.

Thank You, Lord, that prophetic words are to edify, exhort, and comfort. Thank You that they bring me hope when I feel hopeless about the promises I'm waiting for. Thank You, Lord, that You do hear my cries, and know exactly what I'm going through. Help me to continue to trust in You, and have faith to believe for the things I don't see.

> *'He who receives a prophet in the name of a prophet shall receive a prophet's reward.'*
> —MATTHEW 10:41

See the Good/God in Everything

Hope Deferred

Hope deferred makes the heart sick, the scripture says. I was there once. It was early in our marriage and I had fully realized my desire to have kids. It was a season of prophetic words. Churches we went to, conferences, everyone was prophesying babies over us. Many known respectable leaders and prophets were prophesying the same thing—babies. So, of course I assumed that meant our babies were imminent. Like any second now, we'd definitely get pregnant and have babies; like now! How wrong I was. The season came and the season left, and I was still there with all these prophesies of babies, and no baby to show for it. I remember being so confused. I was excited whenever I heard another prophetic word for babies, but the longer it took, the more discouraged I became. Eventually things turned very dark. I became straight-out angry with God. Why would all these people prophesy these words, and nothing come of it? Why would God show them babies, and then nothing? I was angry every time someone announced a pregnancy, and I cried whenever I'd see kids and their parents playing in the park. I was a victim of my unhappy circumstances and I was bitter inside. I knew I was suffering from hope deferred, but I tried to hide it from myself and my husband, tried to pretend I wasn't really angry with God. Then one day at another church while on holiday, the pastor was prophesying and came up to me and said, 'Hope deferred makes the heart sick, but when desire comes it is the tree of life'. I don't remember what else he said, but I knew at that moment when he said 'hope deferred makes the heart sick', that that was me. My heart was sick. God knew it and I knew it. I'd given up hope and could find no way out. So, I did the only thing I knew how. I fell on my face, cried my eyes out, and repented for losing hope. I repented for losing faith in Him and His word. I might not know how it'll work out, or when it'll happen, but He is faithful. In the end, all those prophetic words were true and correct, and our daughter was born many years later. But protect your heart. Choose to live in hope, with faith, that those things we don't yet see will come to pass.

Thank You, Lord, that You know all things. You know our heart's desire; You know our hopes and dreams. You know the inner depths of us that no one else can see. Thank You that You love me so much. Help me to be faithful and to have hope, that Your promises will come to pass.

> *'Hope deferred makes the heart sick, but when*
> *the desire comes, it is a tree of life.'*
> —PROVERBS 13:12

Blessing and Crying

Bless the Lord O my soul, O my soul, worship His Holy name, sing like never before, O my soul, I'll worship Your Holy name. These are lyrics from '10,000 Reasons (Bless the Lord)' by Matt Redman. A relative of mine announced they're pregnant again. No one knew, but the announcement came right in the middle of another IVF round. This is round number five. I'd thought I'd overcome all the emotions of infertility while trying for a second baby, but I guess not. When push comes to shove, I still greatly desire more babies, and hearing this announcement was tough for me. I wanted to just go into a room by myself and cry to the Lord. It wasn't jealousy per se, but more 'what about me, Lord?' I know the Lord hears my cries, and I know the Lord knows my heart, but that still doesn't make the journey any easier. It does give comfort, though, knowing that I'm not alone. Even if I may feel alone, I know I'm not. It used to take me a long time to get to a place mentally and spiritually where I could bless others who were having babies. That's gotten easier. So, as I read this announcement and the tears fell down my eyes, I blessed them. I desired their children to be a blessing, for them to be blessed in every area of their lives. I don't want to be bitter or hurt or jealous; I want to

See the Good/God in Everything

bless, be joyful and celebrate life, even if it's not for myself. So yes, I may cry and bless at the same time, but it's part of being human and having emotions. But, I trust in Him and His perfect plan. That all things will work together for my good, and that He loves me through it all.

Thank You, Lord, that You are with me though it all. You never leave me or forsake me, and You know every tear I cry. Thank You that even though I am waiting for a promise, I can bless those experiencing Your blessings. Help me to truly be one who rejoices with those who rejoice, and not to be so overcome with my own hardships and emotions that I cannot rejoice. Help me to be patient and to trust in You, and to trust that Your plan and timing is perfect.

'Then they cried out to the Lord in their trouble,
and He delivered them out of their distresses.'
—PSALM 107:6

The Two Week Wait

So, here we are again. I've finished another round of IVF, and am currently waiting the two weeks until I have the Beta hCG quantitative blood test. It's not a particularly challenging time, as there's a lot of resting involved. It's a time where I try really hard not to count down the days, one by one, until the test. I have strict instructions not to lift anything heavy and not to have sex. It's the last bit of the marathon that is IVF, to see if you've made it over the finish line to pregnancy or not. I find this last part of IVF the most defining. In this last leg where you wait two weeks and then take a blood test, it really defines you as a person. It's the culmination of the doctors' and nurses' hard work, days of timed daily injections and invasive procedures. How you handle this last leg will determine your outlook, and will directly impact your heart. There are so many ways to handle this time. I actively try not to think too much during this time. I don't think about the future and the what-ifs. I stay present on the here and now. I thank God for His constant goodness, and remind myself that no matter what happens and no matter what the results of the test are, He is still good, and He still loves me. My husband and I actively assume I'm pregnant until proven otherwise. We try to be positive, and don't have any negative talk. I can't rush the days along during this wait, or anything else in life for that matter, so worrying about it won't help me one bit. So, I practice patience and take it one day at a time. He is still good, no matter what happens.

Thank You, Lord, that You are good. Thank You that You know everything I go through. Thank You that I am not alone and Your Holy Spirit is always with me. Thank You that You desire good things for me. Help me to be patient during the waiting and to remember that no matter what happens, You are still good.

'Oh, give thanks to the Lord, for He is good!
For His mercy endures forever.'
—1 CHRONICLES 16:34

Graduating

We're pregnant!!! We're waiting to do a viability test (an ultrasound to hear heartbeats and see how many babies), but just the fact that we've made it to this point is a huge win, and a huge surprise! Every time you go through IVF you have a little bit of hope and a little bit of reality—at least, that's how it is for me. Part of you is hopeful through the journey, but part of you protects your heart because if it fails, it can be hard to

See the Good/God in Everything

not lose hope. I have a dear friend who's also going through secondary infertility and IVF, and she's been well aware of our infertility journey, so she wanted to know the result of our pregnancy test. It was positive and I was a little concerned about how she'd take the news. She took it so well and was crying tears of happiness. She was so happy for us, and so happy that we'd graduated to pregnancy. I was so proud of her because I know it took me a long time to be happy for other people. It was a huge issue I had to overcome—and thank God I have. I know this outcome is a huge blessing and we are so thankful to God.

Thank You, Lord, that You are with us through our life's journey. Thank You that You never leave us nor forsake us, and that You know every desire in our hearts. Thank You when we are in the waiting, and thank You when we graduate. Help us to be the type of people who are happy for those who are happy, and to bless them when good things happen to them, because You are good, all the time.

> *'Give thanks to the LORD, for he is good; his love endures forever.'*
> —PSALM 107:1 (NIV)

BLENDED
FAMILIES

Blended Families Are Interesting

Anyone part of a blended family will tell you it's interesting. I have five step-children. They were all adults when I married their father. I felt like an outsider for a very long time, and even now six years later, feeling like an outsider creeps in again at times. There are a few things to note about blended families:

By law I'm their stepmother, though none of them would ever call me that. But the government of Australia will tell you I am (I filled out the form, so trust me, I know).

In reality I'm probably an acquaintance, or just slightly more than an acquaintance, in terms of personal relationship. They're all adults and have their own lives. And building a relationship takes time.

Heart issues must be dealt with. What is my heart posture towards them? Do I have issues, is my heart clean towards them? I believe they were put into my life for a reason, and I believe though I'm not close to them personally, I should love them, pray for them, and do the best I can to be a good person and a blessing to them.

Lord, help me to love like You love, to pray like You pray, and to see people the way You see them. Help me to be the best person I can be, and to represent You well to everyone You put in my life.

> *'Love is patient, love is kind. It does not envy, it does not boast, it is not proud. It does not dishonour others, it is not self-seeking, it is not easily angered, it keeps no record of wrongs. Love does not delight in evil but rejoices with the truth. It always protects, always trusts, always hopes, always perseveres. Love never fails.'*
> —1 CORINTHIANS 13:4–8 (NIV)

Who Wants to Be a Stepmom?

If you had told me when I was in my twenties that I would end up marrying a man twenty years older than me, divorced, who had five adult children, I would've thought you were joking. Being a stepmom is not for the faint-hearted. You must ensure your heart is in the right place because it *will* be challenged. You must make sure you don't have issues of abandonment, jealousy, bitterness, anxiety, or low confidence, or issues about divorce, because you'll be tested in all these areas, whether you like it or not. It's all a mind game, and the battle of the mind is a real one. One thing I've learnt over the years as a stepmom is to forgive quickly, don't take things too seriously, and focus on your marriage. Be generous, do good, and protect your heart above all else. When I first got married, I often thought about Joseph, Mary's husband and Jesus's stepfather. How did he feel raising God's son here on earth? Or about Israel, who had twelve sons from four different women? It's not a fairytale, it's real, and God used that blended mix of a family for His glory. Judah sinned with Tamar (his daughter-in-law) which resulted in Perez, through which Jesus eventually comes. It's really not the sort of family line one would expect the Saviour of the World to come through, but it's the one He does. God is a God of redemption. I love the Jesus Storybook Bible where it says 'every story whispers His name'. God is in every story, even mine and even yours. He takes the weak, seemingly unusable, and maybe even shameful and turns it for His glory. My life may not be a fairytale, but God is in my story and in my family, and He will use it for His glory. And He can, and will, use yours too, if you let Him.

Thank You, Lord, that You are in every story. Thank You for Your son Jesus and that He came for me and my sin. Let my life, and all aspects of my life, bring You glory, and let me shine Your light of love to all those around me.

See the Good/God in Everything

'For you see your calling, brethren, that not many wise according to the flesh, not many mighty, not many noble, are called. But God has chosen the foolish things of the world to put to shame the wise, and God has chosen the weak things of the world to put to shame the things which are mighty; and the base things of the world and the things which are despised God has chosen, and the things which are not, to bring to nothing the things that are, that no flesh should glory in His presence.'
—1 CORINTHIANS 1:26–30

Pray Like They're Yours

Probably one of my top five favourite scriptures is Matthew 6:6: 'But you, when you pray, go into your room, and when you have shut your door, pray to your Father who is in the secret place; and your Father who sees in secret will reward you openly'. What I appreciate is that God isn't so concerned with outward appearances, but instead values what we do when no one is looking (but Him). Quite a few years ago, we got a text message about one of my stepkids having some event. I honestly can't even remember now if it was an exam or a surgery, but it was something important. I replied my usual answer, 'Praying for you'. I remember going to bed that night and right before falling asleep remembering I'd forgotten to pray for the mentioned stepchild. So, I haphazardly prayed a 'God bless so and so in the thing, amen'. Then I started to doze off. What happened next was my correction. I remember a knock in my spirit. It literally felt like I could hear a door knock on my heart, and I was startled awake. I felt God say, 'If this was your biological child, would you pray for them like you just did?' He was right, and I repented. I know if I had a child and they were going through whatever the situation was, I'd probably be on my knees interceding and wholeheartedly praying for them, constantly. It was a stark wake-up call. No matter what my stepchildren may think of me as a stepmom is irrelevant. They'll never know my prayers for them and their families, and that's okay, because God does. God sees my heart, and He also sees them as part of my family, and as such I should pray and intercede without discrimination or favouritism.

Thank You, Lord, that You hear our prayers. Thank You, Lord, that Your ear is attentive to our cry. Help us in faithfully praying and interceding for those You have put in our lives.

> *'Rejoice always, pray without ceasing, in everything give thanks; for this is the will of God in Christ Jesus for you.'*
> —1 THESSALONIANS 5:16–18

The State Sees Me as a Stepmother

We went out once with one of my stepsons and his wife and kids. We were discussing what I should be called, as they had a new child. Let's be honest—who's ever heard of a step-grandmother? No one. But that's technically what I am. My husband will always say he wants me to be called 'grandmother'. (But most family members don't agree, and that's fair enough.) To my husband, though, I'm his wife, and therefore he wants me to share in the grandparenting title. So, I said to them I want to be called Grandma Gina, because that's what my husband wants. The reply was that I'm too young to be a grandma. I told them that according to the state, I'm a stepmother with five children. I explained that when I recently applied for my Permanent Resident visa, one of the questions was, 'Do you have children? Children includes biological or adopted, from a current or previous marriage, all stepchildren and deceased children'. I had to add all five names of my stepchildren, their dates of birth and places of birth, to my application. They were surprised. Shortly after that discussion, a friend of theirs came up to say hello, and I was introduced as 'so and so's stepmom'. It warmed my heart. Honestly, I don't need the title or the recognition as a stepmom, but just to be valued as a person in their lives meant a lot, and to be introduced and not ignored was very gracious of them. What's my point? My point is that sometimes, due to life, we may end up in places we didn't expect. I'm called Grandma Gina to some, and just Gina to others, and I'm grateful and gracious for the thoughtfulness and inclusion in both. Regardless of what I'm called, whether I'm a stepmom, Grandma Gina or just Gina, I am above all a child of God. Representing Him well where I am, loving others, and being a light and a blessing is always my first priority.

Thank You, Lord, that You know exactly where we are. Our circumstances and situations don't surprise You. Help us to be a light where we are.

'And we know that all things work together for good to those who love God, to those who are the called according to His purpose.'
—ROMANS 8:28

Be Prepared to Face Your Insecurities

If you want to face all the insecurities in your life, marry a divorcee who has adult children who are close in age to you. *Enough said.* There are very few circumstances in life that will make you come face-to-face with your insecurities, but this is one of them. Honestly, no one said anything or did anything to make me insecure, but there were a lot of conversations in my head, and a lot of heart-to-hearts with my husband. At the time I was young, and used to spend too much time thinking about how I was perceived by others. Do people think I'm a gold-digger because I married an older man? How do I compare to the stepkids? How do I compare to the ex-wife? Will the same problems that happened in his first marriage happen in our marriage? Will he easily divorce me if I do, say, or act in a certain way, or do something he doesn't like? Do we look like a freak couple? Do his kids even like me? Will I ever be accepted in the family? Some of these questions I have answers to, but mostly they're the musings of an over-active mind, with too much concern for others. I've learnt a few things. Firstly, people will think whatever they want, and you can't control that, you can only control yourself. I've also learnt that some insecurities are signs of root issues that need to be addressed, like your self-worth. Is your value coming from how others think of you, or from who you are in God?

Thank You, Lord, that You know everything we go through. Thank You that You know what is going on in the inner depths of our heart. When we are anxious or insecure, help us to turn to You first and address the issues of our heart. And help us to control our thoughts, as not all thoughts are profitable or worthy of meditation. And help us, Lord, to be confident in You and trust You with our lives. Help us to see ourselves the way You see us.

'But the Lord said to Samuel, "Do not look at his appearance or at his physical stature, because I have refused him. For the Lord does not see as man sees; for man looks at the outward appearance, but the Lord looks at the heart."'

—1 SAMUEL 16:7

See the Good/God in Everything

FRIENDS

You Do Not Have to Solve Your Friends' Problems

I had a friend who was going through some issues in her life, which were crazily similar to something I had gone through in my life. It was uncanny. Because of this, she'd often tell me long stories about what was going on in her situation. She told me all the details, the history, and how this was affecting all the different people in her family. Things were raw for her as she was going through it at the present moment, so I'd get messages late at night after she'd spent a lot of time crying or praying, not knowing why she was going through all of this. In reflecting on my own situation, I knew that while it was hard, and may last a fairly long time, she'd come out stronger and wiser. I could see where she needed to change, have boundaries, and forgive. But though I love my friend, and want to support her through her hard times, I am not her counsellor. We have to have wisdom to know the balance of how much information to share, when to help, and when to back away a bit to let them grow and forge their own way forward.

Lord, thank You for our friends. Help us to have wisdom in our friendships to know how to support and show Your love.

'A man who has friends must himself be friendly, but there is a friend who sticks closer than a brother.'
—PROVERBS 18:24

Something to Teach You

I've had a lot of different friends in a lot of different places over the years. Some friendships lasted longer than others, and some were more meaningful than others. But what I've learnt over the years is that though these people are in my life for friendship, companionship, shared interests, or whatever else, they're also in my life to teach me something. I don't mean that they're actively teaching me a skill, but that there's something to be learnt from them as people. They may be extremely loving and compel us to be more like that, or they may show us how to honour others, how to be inclusive, how to be resilient, or maybe even how not to act, or how not to do life. We love our friends for who they are, but let's not forget that we're constantly striving to be more like Jesus, and our character should be changing to have more fruit of the Spirit, and to exemplify Jesus more and more every day.

Lord, thank You that there is a friend closer than a brother. Thank You that You put these people in our lives for a purpose. Help us to learn and grow as people and display Jesus well in our lives.

'But the fruit of the Spirit is love, joy, peace, longsuffering, kindness, goodness, faithfulness, gentleness, self-control.'
—GALATIANS 5:22–23

Always Something to Learn

I've gone through many different seasons, trials, highs, and lows in my life in the last decade. Over those ten years I've gone through my fair share of friends. These friends have spanned many different cities, countries, universities, jobs, hobbies, and churches. Some have lasted,

See the Good/God in Everything

and some haven't. Some were only for a season, and some I hope will be lifelong. There have been friends I've learnt from, and friends who have learnt from me and my experience. One thing I've realized is that, no matter how or where the friendship comes from, there's always something to learn. Some friendships are easy and some are harder. I have a friend with cancer, for example, which recently came back after a time of remission. When her cancer came back, I had just had my daughter and was living on a high of answered prayer. She was in the valley and battling a very hard battle. She was on my mind constantly but I didn't know how to reach out, because I was very conscious that we were in two very different places. I had to learn that my love and friendship still matters, even if we were in two very different places. I had to put my ego aside and be the friend I was meant to be, and show the love God wanted me to.

Thank You, Lord, for our friends. Thank You that You put people in our life to go through life's highs and lows with us. Help us to be the kind of godly friend You call us to be, and to show Your love.

'Ointment and perfume delight the heart, and the sweetness of a man's friend gives delight by hearty counsel.'
—PROVERBS 27:9

Don't Be an Enabler

Many years ago, when my husband was single, he became friends with a single mom from church. He soon learned that she was very much in need, and though she received government assistance and child support from her ex-husband, it didn't cover all her needs for her and her two boys. My husband had the financial means, so thinking he was being a good friend, he offered to pay for a substantial amount of her monthly housing. He intended for this to be short-term assistance, but it ended up dragging on for years. When we got married and started to look at our long-term future, we finally realized the gravity of the situation. My husband had been helping to support his friend without realizing the need for an exit strategy, nor had he been really helping her, but enabling her in her circumstances. After much prayer, we resolved to end the financial support. We gave much advanced notice to his friend, and made sure she had financial counselling and support, and a budget in place before we ended support. We learnt from this that even those with good intentions can inadvertently become an enabler. It's the 'give a man a fish, feed him for a day; teach a man to fish, feed him for a lifetime' type of scenario. My husband wanted to help his friend, but by just giving her money every month he really just enabled her in her situation, and didn't help in making her financially independent.

Thank You, Lord, for Your discernment and wisdom. Help us to be sensitive to You in all aspects of our lives. Help us when we want to help others, to ensure we are walking in Your will, and that we are truly helping and not enabling.

> *'For you yourselves know how you ought to follow us,*
> *for we were not disorderly among you; nor did we eat*
> *anyone's bread free of charge, but worked with labor and*
> *toil night and day, that we might not be a burden to any*
> *of you, not because we do not have authority, but to make*
> *ourselves an example of how you should follow us.'*
> —2 THESSALONIANS 3:7–9

See the Good/God in Everything

I Am Not a Rubbish Bin!

I've been through a lot of stuff in my life. I've had major family disputes and drama and came out the other side, fairly unscathed. It took a lot of forgiving, prayer, and time, but things have gotten a whole lot better with my family. I've had seven years of reflection, hindsight, and a lot of humbling. I once had a close acquaintance who was going through some family disputes. It wasn't exactly the same, but our family issues had a lot of similarities. When this friend would tell me her problems, I could easily see the areas she needed to address, people she should forgive, and people she should pray for and bless, though difficult. At first, I didn't mind the unloading of problems. I would listen, then provide some insight, advice, and prayer. I felt I was helping her on her journey. But after a while she became less interested in what I had to say, and just wanted my support and vocal agreement that her family was crazy. Here's the thing—I've never met them, have heard only one side of the story, and am conscious of the power of my words, so I refused to say they were crazy. She wasn't pleased that I wouldn't just badmouth them like she was. There are actual friendships, and then there's being a rubbish bin. I realized I'd been allowing myself to be a rubbish bin to her family problems. When it got too much for her, she'd bring it to me and dump all the drama, hearsays, accusations, and conspiracy theories onto me. I am not a rubbish bin! This realization made me decide it was time to put up some boundaries in that friendship. Though I wish her well, pray for her, and bless her, I choose to have boundaries and stepped away from that relationship.

Lord, thank You for friends. Help us to have wisdom in our relationships and to know when our relationships are healthy and unhealthy.

*'He who walks with wise men will be wise, but
the companion of fools will be destroyed.'*
—PROVERBS 13:20

Two Sides of the Story

In the previous entry I spoke about a friend I used to have. She used to tell me about her family problems. In some aspects our family problems were similar, but in others they were totally different. I used to give her godly advice, but over time I felt she wasn't at all interested in what I had to say, and only wanted me to support her in her thoughts that her family was crazy, demonic, and public enemy number one. I used to agree. I mean, from what she told me, these people were the worst of the worst and irreparable. Then one day I was reading the Bible and came across this: 'There are two sides to every story. The first one to speak sounds true until you hear the other side and they set the record straight' (Proverbs 18:17, from The Passion Translation). I had to repent to the Lord. I had been believing and agreeing with one side of the story and demonizing the other parties, but I only knew one side of the story. It was after this that I realized I couldn't blindly agree with my friend about her views of her family. I don't know them, and I don't know their side of the story.

Thank You, Lord, for wisdom. Help us to be wiser! Help us to implement wisdom in all areas of our lives and relationships.

*'All Scripture is breathed out by God and
profitable for teaching, for reproof, for correction,
and for training in righteousness.'*
—2 TIMOTHY 3:16 (ESV)

See the Good/God in Everything

Emotional Manipulators

We know some people who I like to call emotional manipulators. I'm not sure if they actively know what they're doing or not, but they're pretty good at it. What they do is get you emotionally hooked to their lives. When you see them, they tell you all their problems, and try to get you hooked onto their issues. We have one friend who at one of our first meetings started to tell us his problems with his wife. He told us all her problems—how she was a gambler, how she lied to him, how she used up a lot of money without him knowing, and how she was now on an allowance and had no access to their funds. Firstly, what was the point of him telling us this? Secondly, speaking about your spouse and your affairs like this is dodgy, period. And on one of our first meetings as well? Really, your counsellor, pastor, or extremely close family and friends should be the only ones you disclose this kind of information to. It shouldn't be open knowledge, and it definitely shouldn't be something you share with new people you've just met. What I realized about this friend was that he would tell you these kinds of stories to get you hooked in, and to support him. He was drawing you in with an emotional tie to him and his family, so that you felt connected and part of his inner circle when really you weren't at all. But it'd be just enough to keep you hooked in and feel like you'd connected with that person. Why do people do things like this? I'm not totally sure, but probably for power, information, and maybe so you'll support their ministry.

Lord, we thank You that Your Holy Spirit guides us in all things. Guide us in our relationships. Help us to know when our relationships are good and healthy and when we are being manipulated and coerced through emotional manipulation. Lord, help us to be discerning and to have more wisdom.

*'And this I pray, that your love may abound still more
and more in knowledge and all discernment.'*
—PHILIPPIANS 1:9

Some People Just Don't Want
to Be Your Friends

Some people just don't want to be your friends, and that's okay—you're still amazing, just that they don't know it! Having lived abroad in many different places over the years, I've had to make new friends many times. I tend to lean towards being an introvert, so making new friends is something I personally don't like to do. But, it must be done. I've made some amazing friends over the years, but I've also met some people who just don't want to be my friend. I have one acquaintance who lives in the same city as me, but always seems to have an excuse not to see me. We used to reciprocally message each other, but now even that has stopped and my messages go unanswered. I hated to admit it to myself, but I realized she just didn't want to be my friend. As unpleasant as that may be, it was the hard truth. It can be easy to feel dejected when someone you're trying to befriend doesn't want to be friends with you. But we need to remember that that's not because of us. We're still amazing!

Thank You, Lord, that You know the desires of our hearts. You know that we desire to have more friends who will love and appreciate us, and value us as we are. Help us not to let resentment or bitterness in when acquaintances choose not to become our friends. We bless them, Lord.

'Bearing with one another, and forgiving one another,
if anyone has a complaint against another; even
as Christ forgave you, so you also must do.'
—COLOSSIANS 3:13

Friends for a Time

When I was living in London, I had one of the most wonderful friends. She was a beautiful soul, and I always thoroughly enjoyed seeing her. We were very close and even after I left, we continued to keep in touch as much as possible. I don't FaceTime many people, but she was one of the few I would. When I met my future husband for the first time, she was the first person I told. My seasons as a single person, and then a married woman without kids, was easy to share with her. She was my sister in the faith and one of those friends you think will always be there. But one unfortunate day she FaceTimed me with bad news. She had cancer. We cried together and prayed. She had battles to face. During that time, I was also dealing with infertility, but was near the end of the journey. When my daughter was born I was hesitant to share the joy with her, knowing she was dealing with a lot and not wanting to be insensitive. But I did nonetheless. Months went by and I wanted to share more and more of my young daughter's life with her. I did, hesitantly, but anticipating that maybe our season of friendship may be at an end. I was right, and I never heard back from her again. With our journeys going in vastly different directions, it was difficult to reconcile. I miss her and love her a lot and pray for her.

Thank You, Lord, for all those special friends who You've given us. Whether for a season or a lifetime, we are so thankful for their love, companionship, and friendship. Lord, help us to pray for them and

their journey. And Lord, we bless them, and pray You would bless them so abundantly in all aspects of their life.

*'As iron sharpens iron, so a man sharpens
the countenance of his friend.'*

—PROVERBS 27:17

Leaving Is Hard

The one thing about living abroad that I don't hear or read about often is that leaving is hard. It just is. You've got friends and a community of people who you've been doing life with for however long, then it's time to leave, probably for good. It can truly be heartbreaking. I've been thankful that in the past when I've left, I wasn't so attached to my friends, and/or I thought I was returning, so I said 'see you later' in the hopes of returning, which I never did. But in hindsight it was better that way. Being familiar with people coming and going, I would normally distance myself a little bit if I knew someone was leaving. It was just my way of protecting my heart. Now I'm actually faced with the same thing. I unintentionally mentioned to our closest friend that we're leaving in a few months and she's started to distance herself from us. I get it. I know exactly what it's like. But it still hurts. This is the reality of living abroad. But I wouldn't have changed this experience and these past years for anything. These wonderful brothers and sisters in Christ who have been family, when biological family was scarce, have enriched our lives and given us a glimpse of the beauty of the Body of Christ and how we're all interconnected. I'm just thankful that God has been so gracious to us by putting us in such a loving and wonderful community. I remember when we were like nomads many years ago, moving from various cities and without friends, our desperate prayer was for friends. And He's

See the Good/God in Everything

been so faithful to answer that prayer. So, though it's hard to leave, we're extremely thankful for the friends we've made.

Thank You, Lord, that You know the desires of our hearts. Thank You for the friends that You have brought into our lives, and the friends You will bring in the future. Help us to always be the type of friends to others that we want for ourselves.

> *'Every good gift and every perfect gift is from above,*
> *and comes down from the Father of lights, with whom*
> *there is no variation or shadow of turning.'*
> —JAMES 1:17

Just Ask Them Straight

I have a dear friend who our family loves. But we often go through seasons of closeness with her. There are seasons when I'll hear from her multiple times a day. She knows what I'm doing throughout the day, and as well, updates me on her work and family. Sometimes I get a running commentary of the day, which is fun. But then there are seasons where we aren't so close. We're currently in that season. I thought I'd offended or upset her. I mentioned this to another friend, who suggested I just ask her straight if she was upset with me or not. It wasn't what I wanted to do. I don't always like to be so frank and straightforward, but decided it was probably better to just find out if I'd offended her or not. Well, it came back that, no, I hadn't offended or upset her; she was just busy and stressed at work, so was being a bit quiet. Fair enough. The reason it's good to be straightforward is that our minds can do crazy things. I was literally going though past conversations in my head, trying to figure out if I'd said something or done something to offend her. Whereas we could save all that time, energy, and anxiety and just ask straight up.

Thank You, Lord, that You are not the God of confusion, but of peace. Help me to keep the peace in my friendships and relationships. Help me to have wisdom and to be open and honest with my friends.

'For God has not given us a spirit of fear, but of power and of love and of a sound mind.'
—2 TIMOTHY 1:7

Be There for You

I've had some friends go through some absolutely devastating and terrible things; stillbirth, infertility struggles, and unexpected deaths. For most of these things I was usually living in another city or country, and it makes it so hard to be there for them, since I'm not there physically. As my first mentor always said, 'If you can't go, pray', which is my mantra in these times. Though I can't be there physically, I do what I can by praying for them. I pray for their hearts, for God to give them peace and comfort, for healing for their bodies, for wisdom in their relationships; I pray for it all. On the rare occasion when I'm able to be a bit more present, I constantly ask the Lord how I can support. Some friends want constant input and support, and others want time and space. I don't know these things, so I ask the Holy Spirit to guide me on how best to support them, when I should ring or visit or call, or maybe send a little gift or something to cheer them up, or maybe just pray. I also think about if I were in that situation, how I would want my friends to respond and support me, and I do that.

See the Good/God in Everything

Thank You, Lord, for the wonderful friends You bring into our lives. Help me to love and support them when they're going through trying times.

'Do to others whatever you would like them to do to you. This is the essence of all that is taught in the law and the prophets.'
—MATTHEW 7:12 (NLT)

Sometimes You Just Need to Listen and Be There

One of our friends has gone through a lot of hardships in life recently. I didn't really know what to do to help her, as it's a complicated situation. So, I prayed about it, and felt I should just be there for her. That she just needed someone to listen with an open heart, and to be a friend. To not close the door to her, and let her sort out her problems on her own—but to be there physically, emotionally, and spiritually. I've been through my fair share of hardships. During those times I've always had someone there for me just to listen and be a friend. Often the burden is lessened just by having another ear to listen, and by feeling that you're not alone.

Thank You, Lord, that You put the lonely in families and that You never leave us or forsake us, no matter what we are dealing with in our lives. Thank You, Holy Spirit, for Your comfort. Thank You, Lord, that even when we walk through the valley of the shadow of death, we should not fear any evil, for You are with us.

*'Carry one another's burdens and in this way
you will fulfil the requirements of the law of
Christ [that is, the law of Christian love].'*

—GALATIANS 6:2 (AMP)

There When They Need You,
Then They Disappear

Keeping your heart clean is so important. It means making sure you're not holding unforgiveness in your heart, and that you don't have bitterness or offence towards others. I have a friend who went through some tough circumstances recently. She had no one else to turn to, so she came and stayed with us for a while. I was glad we could be of help and support. We comforted, prayed, and mentored her, letting her into our lives and family, no questions asked. She left and shortly after leaving, we didn't hear from her again. I was a little peeved and slightly perplexed. I didn't know if I should hound her or let her be. After trying to contact her a few times, to follow up and check up on her, I was totally ignored, so I had to let it be. So, I bless her and pray for her, and make sure I'm not offended by her or her behaviour towards us. We helped when she needed it, and maybe that's all we needed to do.

Thank You, Lord, that it is more blessed to give than to receive. Help us to know how to help our friends in need. Guide us, Holy Spirit, and give us wisdom and discernment to help in the way You want us to help, not in the way we think we should help.

See the Good/God in Everything

'And I have been a constant example of how you can help those in need by working hard. You should remember the words of the Lord Jesus: "It is more blessed to give than to receive."'

—ACTS 20:35 (NLT)

I Need to Be a Better Friend, But Still Learn the Lesson

As you know, I've lived abroad for over fifteen years now. I left home at 25 and only went back to my parents' house for holidays or for short intervals of unemployment. I've lived in multiple countries, wherever there was work in my industry. As such, I've had a lot of friends in a lot of different places. But I don't think I'm a great friend. One of my main downfalls—and I believe this is mostly due to living in various countries—is that once I know I'm leaving, I kind of disconnect from my friends. Let's be honest; unless you're the bestest of friends, keeping in contact with people once you leave is quite hard. You don't get the face-to-face interaction, and you lose the daily life commonalities you used to share with friends in the same location. But nevertheless, there have been some amazing friends I wish I would've been better at keeping in touch with. Yet, even though I haven't always been the best friend, one thing I'm good at is learning the lesson. Every person has something to teach us—how to be faithful, positive, a good listener, an encourager, a good parent, resilient. Sometimes, I even learn the lessons of mistakes my friends have made—don't manipulate kids, watch what you say about yourself, see the best in people and not the worst. So, let's work on our friendships now, to be better and longstanding friends, and let's learn the lessons that each friend brings to our lives.

Thank You, Lord, that there is a friend closer than a brother. Help us to be friendly to have friends. And help us to love our friends with the love of Christ. And help us especially to do to others as we would have them do to us.

'The righteous should choose his friends carefully,
for the way of the wicked leads them astray.'
—PROVERBS 12:26

Friends Who Ebb and Flow

I have a dear friend who ebbs and flows. We've known her for a handful of years now and I've noticed she goes through seasons. For some time, she'll be super close, and then it's like she'll take a break from speaking to you for a few weeks to a few months, and then she'll come back, totally normal, as if no time has passed, and be my best friend again. It's a bit of a hit to the heart, if I'm being honest. Part of the unpleasantness is she never tells you why she's taking a break from you, and it's always very sudden. Of the few times this has happened, I often wondered if I'd offended or upset her. I of course asked her, to which she said no. Usually she'll say she's just busy at work, she has family problems she's working through, or she just needs some time alone. At one point I thought it was just with me that she did this ebbing and flowing, until one day a mutual close friend told me she'd stopped speaking to her too for no obvious reason, and wanted to know if this had happened to me. So, I gave her the advice I wish someone had told me. Protect your heart, because this kind of ebbing and flowing for no obvious reason is hard on the heart. Reduce your expectations. She may not be there when you need her. If you think you've offended her, just ask. Don't see it as her

See the Good/God in Everything

rejection of you, but realize that she's working through issues, and this just happens to be the way she handles it.

Thank You, Lord, for our friends. Help us to love our friends through all seasons. Help us not to judge our friends but to be there for them and pray for them. And most especially, help us to learn life lessons and wisdom along the way.

'And the Lord restored Job's losses when he prayed for his friends. Indeed the Lord gave Job twice as much as he had before.'
—JOB 42:10

GROWING UP

Let Your Yes Be Yes, and Your No, No

At the very beginning of this devotional journey, my dear husband, the great support he is, suggested I start writing my ideas down, or I may forget them. I said, 'Yes, of course I'll do that'. But whenever a thought came, instead of writing it down straight away, I would put it off. But, as a new mom with a young baby, even though I liked to believe I'd remember, I definitely didn't! My dear husband called me out on it one day, asking if I was writing my thoughts and ideas down as he'd suggested. Long story short, he's wise for a reason. Saying yes or no and actually following through with it is so important. If you say yes, but don't follow through with it, then you lied. My husband thought I was writing my thoughts down, and he trusted me that I was doing that. So, when he found out I wasn't, it made him wonder what other things I may have said 'yes' to, but didn't actually follow through with, and that can lead to trust issues.

Lord, help me not to be wishy-washy, but to follow through on my yeses and to stick to my nos. Help me to protect my husband's heart, and to be a keeper of my word.

'Who can find a virtuous wife? For her worth is far above rubies. The heart of her husband safely trusts her; so he will have no lack of gain. She does him good and not evil all the days of her life.'
—PROVERBS 31:10–12

Control Your Thoughts (Golden Toilet)

Not all the thoughts you think are your own, let's get that straight. I have a vivid imagination and an active thought life. With that comes a lot of stuff going on in my head at once; it's creative (sometimes), but it can also be a nuisance. Scripture tells us to transform our minds and think about things that are true, honourable, lovely and commendable, etc. (Philippians 4:8). There are times when thoughts that aren't my own come, and it's important to have a way to deal with them. It's easy to say think about 'true honourable, lovely and commendable' things, but how do you get rid of unclean, plaguing or just bad thoughts? I use a Golden Toilet. Yes, you heard that right. I prophetically visualise a fairly large golden toilet, I take the awful, not-Gina thoughts, and I visualise them being put into the toilet. I then shut the lid and flush. If it's really bad thoughts, and I considered for a second that they were mine, I prophetically visualise two huge angels standing guard by the toilet to ensure that those bad thoughts go down!

Lord, help me to take every thought captive, and to be aware of what I am thinking about. Help me to think about good, true, honourable, and commen-dable things.

> *'For though we walk in the flesh, we do not war according to the flesh. For the weapons of our warfare are not carnal but mighty in God for pulling down strongholds, casting down arguments and every high thing that exalts itself against the knowledge of God, bringing every thought into captivity to the obedience of Christ.'*
> —2 CORINTHIANS 10:3–5

See the Good/God in Everything

Believe Prophets and Prophetic Words, Until Proven Otherwise

There were a few years where we were praying for a baby, and nothing much was happening. We have quite a few prophetic friends and pastors. During that time, they'd prophesy us having babies. When you first hear a prophetic word, it's usually met with great hope and enthusiasm. You're so glad to know that God really does know your heart, and your heart's desire. You're overwhelmed with love that Daddy God cares, and hears your prayers. Then time goes by. This is where many people sink or swim. Either they'll hold on with hope until the end, or not. I'm not saying it's easy. I know first-hand it's not. I've lost hope a few times, and cried an insane amount of tears. But I know that He is faithful. I know that because He came through for me, He'll come through for you. It may come about the way you envisioned, or not exactly, but He'll never let you down. Believe the prophetic words you get. Obviously, test them with a multitude of counsellors. But don't let time gone by make you lose sight of His promise for your life.

Lord, help me in the waiting to not lose hope, to not lose my joy, and to not get bitter. Help me to keep on blessing those whose answered prayers and promises come before mine. Help me to be joyful with those who are joyful. Help me to trust in You, every single day.

'He who receives a prophet in the name of a prophet shall receive a prophet's reward.'
—MATTHEW 10:41

Waiting for a Promise Is a Mind Game

Waiting for a promise is hard. You need to be tough and stubborn. The thing you must fight against, in the game of waiting for a promise, is yourself and your mind. The world, other people, close friends, family, your spouse; no one will really understand what you're going through. It really is just you and God. Waiting isn't for the faint-hearted, and you'll see that, because most people give up hope before reaching the promise. Waiting for a promise is a mind game because you'll have to fight against yourself. For me, I had to fight the doubt trying to creep in every month when I had my menstrual cycle. Or the doubt that maybe God isn't good. Or fight the bitterness when another person I knew got pregnant and not me. Fight the loneliness of knowing that, really, very few people know the struggle you're going through. Fight the anger that maybe it's your husband's fault. Fight the shame in thinking maybe you're not good enough to deserve the promise. Fight to keep your joy. Fight to go on. Fight to not let the promise consume you. So, prepare yourself; to wait for a promise isn't easy, you have to fight a lot of things, but you can persevere.

Lord, help us while we wait for Your promises. Help us to trust in You every day and with every area of our lives. Let us not lose hope, but continue to trust in You.

> *'Fight the good fight of faith, lay hold on eternal life, to which you were also called and have confessed the good confession in the presence of many witnesses.'*
> —1 TIMOTHY 6:12

See the Good/God in Everything

Keep Your Joy While Waiting for the Promise

The easiest thing to lose while waiting for a promise is your joy. Promises don't usually come easily. In the process of waiting, you're usually building your faith, building your trust in God, and strengthening your inner man. It's easy for me to preach now, after waiting seven years for our daughter. But during the wait, I'll tell you, that was the hardest thing I've ever had to do. It was emotionally draining, and lonely, and you'll come face to face with what you really think about God. Even if you think God is good, and really, really, really believe it, even that will be tested. After a few years of waiting, I started to question everything. Did I hear God right? Maybe it'll never happen. Maybe God doesn't love me. Maybe He doesn't really hear my prayers. Maybe He actually isn't a good God. I could no longer go to the café in the park with my husband, because seeing the kids there would get me upset or sad, and make me cry. Social media was terrible. Don't get me started on how seeing the picture-perfect images of my friends and their babies made me feel. Even when my own relations had babies, it was a cut to the heart. Bitterness was there, joy was gone, and the root of it was that I was waiting for the promise and it had consumed me. Even while waiting for a promise, don't let it take over your whole life. Do other things, take up new hobbies, make friends, mentor others, give back to your community. Don't sit at home idly, pining for the promise. (But I'm not judging; I've been there too.) Live your life, focus on other things, and stubbornly refuse to be discouraged. Just before I got pregnant, a friend invited me to her close friend's baby shower. I barely knew the girl, but I bought a present, put makeup on, and went and celebrated her and her baby, and in my heart blessed them. No matter the outcome, He is good, and He will fulfil His promise in His time. I can grow and be joyful and productive during my waiting time, or not. The choice is up to me.

Thank You, Lord, that You are faithful to Your Word. Help me when my faith is waning, and help me to always choose joy, instead of allowing bitterness to take root.

'Hope deferred makes the heart sick, but when the desire comes, it is a tree of life.'
—PROVERBS 13:12

Don't Forget to Pray About the Little Things

Sometimes I think prayer is underrated. We often think we need free time and peace and quiet away from distractions to pray. Let's be real; sometimes you don't always get that kind of peace and quiet. I also think I don't pray about enough things in my life, or that sometimes I stick to the big prayer items—salvation for my family and neighbours, blessing over my husband and his work, or protection over my family—but I don't pray about things that seem small and insignificant. I like how Paul says 'pray about everything'. I had a friend who before trimming her bangs would pray, or another friend who when she had guests over for dinner would pray there'd be enough food for all.

Lord, thank You that You hear all of our prayers. Help me to get in a better habit of praying for everything, even those things that seem small or insignificant.

See the Good/God in Everything

'Be anxious for nothing, but in everything by prayer and supplication, with thanksgiving, let your requests be made known to God; and the peace of God, which surpasses all understanding, will guard your hearts and minds through Christ Jesus.'

—PHILIPPIANS 4:6–7

Pray for Your Pastor

I've recently had some amazing pastors. Pastors who make you strive to be better. Pastors who take you under their wing, and who genuinely care for you and what you're going through. Pastors who will visit you in the hospital. Pastors who make you think, *This must be how Jesus is like.* Pastors who do the church job and the real job. Pastors who love people really, really well. Pastors who look after the community. Pastors who give it everything they've got. I've had these kinds of amazing people in my life recently. But I've gone awry. I've forgotten to pray for my pastor. My pastor goes through so much, but very few if anyone see all he does and goes through. He fights battles only God knows, and he has to deal with the jealousy and treachery of others. He needs my prayers.

Lord, help me to be consistent in praying for my pastor. Help me to remember to pray for him, and those in authority over me.

'Therefore I exhort first of all that supplications, prayers, intercessions, and giving of thanks be made for all men, for kings and all who are in authority, that we may lead a quiet and peaceable life in all godliness and reverence.'

—1 TIMOTHY 2:1–2

Sometimes Go Against Your First Reaction

Firstly, for the record, I'm still a work in progress. I need Jesus each and every day! So, I'll admit, in hindsight I think I can be a bit of a warmonger. My first reaction can sometimes be one of defence, preparation, and alertness for battle; a 'to arms!' type of mentality, if you will. This is obviously not for everything, but for some issues, definitely. My mother once sent me a link to a video she wanted me to watch, because it had some relevance to our family. So I watched it, but then I got incensed. Did she send this to my other family members as well?! Why do I need to solve everyone's problems?! I am *not* the problem! Other people are the problem!! I was upset, and my first reaction wasn't good, to say the least. After an hour I thought, hmm, maybe I should just be a bit gracious instead of incensed. So, I called a close friend. Her response when I told her about the video my mother had sent was one of love, mercy, and grace. It helped to see my friends' reaction and see that my first reaction was terrible, to say the least. But also, it put in perspective for me the God view vs. the fleshly reaction.

Lord, help me to respond to people and situations the way You would. Help me to put on love in every situation, and to be a peacemaker.

'Therefore, as the elect of God, holy and beloved, put on tender mercies, kindness, humility, meekness, longsuffering; bearing with one another, and forgiving one another, if anyone has a complaint against another; even as Christ forgave you, so you also must do. But above all these things put on love, which is the bond of perfection.'
—COLOSSIANS 3:12–14

See the Good/God in Everything

Control Your Mouth

It's a fact that when you say something, or write something in an email or text message, you can never retract it. If what you said was uncomplimentary or unkind, or maybe even hurtful, you can never take it back. You can apologize for it afterwards, and maybe even attempt to fix the relationship if what you said was very unkind; but that may or may not happen, depending on the other party. The words you spoke or wrote, though, don't disappear. I learnt this the hard way. I was upset and angry that some family members didn't respond to an important event in my life the way I thought they should, and in turn I wrote some very unkind emails. I am not proud of it, that's for sure, and it took years to move past it. But I lean into His grace and am so thankful that He forgives all my sins. More self-control is needed, but even more importantly, I'm more aware now of how my words bring life or death. My words can heal relationships or break them. They can heal hearts or break hearts. They can bring people together, or divide them.

Lord, help me to be aware of what I speak and write. Help me to show grace and mercy and not to speak hastily or willy-nilly. Help me to represent You well in my words and actions.

'Set a guard, O LORD, over my mouth; keep
watch over the door of my lips!'
—PSALM 141:3

Vulnerability Takes Courage

A few years ago, I went through a difficult time with my family. There were a lot of mistakes, regret, forgiving, and healing that had to be done.

It was an uphill road to reconciliation, and I wasn't even sure we'd get there one day. For the first few years post-argument I'd tried to repair the relationship a few times, all to no response, or even recognition I existed. I'd probably almost been wiped clean from the family. So, I double-downed my efforts and once again prayed for them, blessed them, and gave it to God. There was only so much I could do. I had no resentment towards them, and no ill feelings. During the pandemic, a close prophetic friend said that it was time to try reaching out again to my estranged family. To be honest, I had learnt the hard way about the consequences of not taking her words seriously, so I took it seriously, though not immediately. After a month or two of her suggesting that to me, my mother sent me a YouTube video of a church homily about arguments and family, and how we shouldn't split up the family over arguments, but still learn to love and be family, even if we don't agree. So, I decided to reach out again and sent two messages—one directly to her, and one to a family group chat that had remained untouched for a long time. Many hours later, there were still no responses, when suddenly on the family chat a member left the conversation. I burst out crying. I felt instantly transported back to when our family first stopped speaking to each other. The pain was so real again, and the longing to be accepted and loved by my family hurt. Who said being vulnerable is easy? Even to send a text message can take vulnerability. It takes a courageous person to put themselves out there, to reach out again after being ignored, to show love and humility. Another day went by, and then I received a message. It was a short message, and very simple, but it was enough. I hadn't been ignored and there was a bit of room for God to move.

Lord, thank You that You work all things for good. Thank You that You are the God of forgiveness and reconciliation. Help us to be peacemakers with everyone.

See the Good/God in Everything

*'Then he fell on his brother Benjamin's neck and
wept, and Benjamin wept on his neck. Moreover,
he kissed all his brothers and wept over them, and
after that his brothers talked with him.'*

—GENESIS 45:14

Faithfulness Is Stubbornness

There's a level of stubbornness found in faithfulness, especially while
waiting for a promise. Stubbornness usually has a negative connotation,
but in waiting for promises it doesn't. Some synonyms for stubborn
include adamant, determined, headstrong, persistent, relentless,
steadfast, tenacious, tough, and unshakable. While waiting for a
promise, you must be so stubborn/determined/persistent/relentless in
your belief that your promise will come. Everything and almost everyone
will try to sway you in this belief; maybe not intentionally, but the doubt
will come in many forms and through many people. The enemy would
love to steal your hope, steal your joy, and steal your breakthrough by
doubting it will ever come. You must be so stubborn in your belief that
He is a good God, and He desires to give you good things. So, let your
inner stubbornness come out and hold onto your promise! Don't let
anything sway you!

**Thank You, Lord, that You desire to give us good gifts. Thank You
that all Your promises are yes and amen. Let us hold fast to the faith,
looking onto the author and finisher of our faith.**

*'Let us hold fast the confession of our hope without
wavering, for He who promised is faithful.'*

—HEBREWS 10:23

How Not to Get Easily Offended

Stop being so serious! Grow a funny bone! And be grateful! I'm not totally sure that's the answer to not getting easily offended, but that's my response for now. When I get more revelation, I'll update you. The other day I was telling my husband about how my writing was going. I had told him that before I'd started writing, I had prayed and then the writing had come easily. His response was, 'You should do that praying thing more often'. If I'm being honest, I got really peeved off. In hindsight, I could have reacted in a few different ways. I could've impassively just agreed. Or, I could've playfully laughed it off. I could've just taken it lightly—'I'm not perfect, ha ha ha, yes, I should pray more'. Sometimes I think I can be too serious for my own good. Also, I need to be more grateful. Really, life is pretty good. We're healthy, our baby's happy, my husband gets a salary every month, thank God, and we don't lack anything. If you do get offended easily like me, move on quickly. As my husband says, 'Don't get on the disaster bus'. We're all works in progress, after all, but don't get stuck there! Apologize, repent, acknowledge you need to improve, and move on.

Thank You, Lord, that You are always teaching us how to be more like You. Help me to be teachable, humble, and open to improvement. We want to be more like You in all areas of our life.

'All Scripture is given by inspiration of God, and is profitable for doctrine, for reproof, for correction, for instruction in righteousness, that the man of God may be complete, thoroughly equipped for every good work.'
—2 TIMOTHY 3:16–17

See the Good/God in Everything

Change Is Change

Change is change. I heard this in a sermon many years ago, and it was a powerful reminder that to change, you actually need to do something different. I don't know about you, but at times I have ideas of things I want to change in my life. I want to get into the Word more, I want to eat healthier, I want to get off social media, and I want to be more productive with my time. I've actually achieved some of the things mentioned above, but it required action, and an actual change of some sort. Some were easier to implement than others. To get into the Word more, I ensure that the last thing I do before going to sleep is read my Bible. It's the perfect time of day—my baby is asleep, I have no other commitments, and if my husband wants to listen we may even read it together. The change for this was small; I just had to alter my routine a bit. Instead of scrolling through social media before bed, I just had to put down my phone and pick up my Bible. What do you want to change? You'll need to change something in your life to get the results you want. It's as simple as that. Change is change.

Thank You, Lord, that You help us in all things. Help us to better ourselves, to let go of habits that aren't profitable, and to become all we can be. Help us to make changes where we need to in our lives.

'Be strong and of good courage, do not fear nor be afraid of them; for the LORD your God, He is the One who goes with you. He will not leave you nor forsake you.'
—DEUTERONOMY 31:6

You Can Learn It the Hard Way, or by Wisdom

There are two ways to learn something: by wisdom, or the hard way. Wisdom can mean many things. It can mean listening to your parents or other knowledgeable, wise people. It can mean getting the knowledge from a book or the internet, and deciding to follow it. It can mean thinking through an issue and deciding on a specific course of action. Learning it the hard way means, irrelevant of the common advice or even warnings of others, you decide to go ahead with something. Sometimes learning it the hard way just means you made a choice and it was the wrong one. Hello, that's me! I've learnt that when you learn something the hard way, it'll hurt. You're forced to be humble and have a teachable spirit. You made the wrong decision, okay; it's not the end of the world. Pick yourself up, dust yourself off, and move on. It was a learning experience and now you know better. (Still speaking to myself.)

Thank You, Lord, that You say if we lack wisdom to pray for wisdom and it will be given to us. Lord, please give us more wisdom! Help us to be wise and make good decisions. Help us to be teachable and willing to learn. Thank You for moulding us into the image of Your son Jesus, each and every day. Amen.

'If any of you lacks wisdom, let him ask of God, who gives to all liberally and without reproach, and it will be given to him.'
—JAMES 1:5

See the Good/God in Everything

Don't Get So Stuck in the Tough Times

When we go through tough times, difficult times, or times of testing, sometimes we can get so attached to that way of life that we find it hard to move forward when things get better again. I had a huge falling-out with some people in my family a few years ago. It was very difficult for me. I had to constantly forgive, and make sure I didn't have resentment or bitterness towards them. I spent years praying for restoration and reconciliation, and for their hearts to be softened. I spent years in that place of estrangement. I may have even started to build a house there, I was getting so used to it. But literally one day I sent a message and I got a response. After years of no response, it was a miracle. Then quickly I got more messages and more communication; I was dumbfounded. I actually got a message that said we should all work together to move our relationship forward. I was absolutely shocked. After years of estrangement and distance, in a very short time my family wanted to be communicative with me again and move past our issues. I had to check my heart, though; because for a second, I was so used to being stuck in that tough, hard place that I almost forgot that this is what I'd been praying for, for many years. Don't get so used to the tough times that you forget to move forward and rejoice when the breakthrough comes.

Thank You, Lord, that You are faithful to Your Word. Help us not to get stuck in the past, but to move forward with You into the new.

'Do not remember the former things, nor consider the things of old. Behold, I will do a new thing, now it shall spring forth; shall you not know it? I will even make a road in the wilderness and rivers in the desert.'
—ISAIAH 43:18–19

Close the Door

We had plans to visit my parents for Christmas and my daughter's first birthday, which is a few days after Christmas. But only days away from November, and still in the middle of a global pandemic, those plans didn't look like they'd come to fruition. I was really, really hoping and praying that we'd be able to spend Christmas and my baby's first birthday with her grandparents. I was so expectant! When I realized those plans might not come to pass, I got very upset. I even got pissed off. Pissed off at the world, pissed off at the coronavirus, pissed off at God; just really, really pissed off. I got to the point of straight-up anger and bitterness. I laid in bed that night and had a dream. I was standing by my front door and it was ajar, just about an inch. But it was nighttime and it should've been closed and locked. I woke up with a start. My anger and bitterness had opened the door to the enemy, even if ever so slightly. I repented quickly of my anger and ungraciousness, and thanked the Lord for His faithfulness, provision, and goodness in my life.

Thank You, Lord, that Your Holy Spirit is constantly teaching us. Help us to be sensitive to the Holy Spirit and to not let the devil get a foothold into our lives.

'So the LORD said to Cain, "Why are you angry? And why has your countenance fallen? If you do well, will you not be accepted? And if you do not do well, sin lies at the door. And its desire is for you, but you should rule over it."'

—GENESIS 4:6–7

See the Good/God in Everything

Loan to the Lord

First, read the scripture at the bottom. I don't come from a particularly generous background. We did some things like donate old clothes to consignment or charity shops, give food to the food bank for Thanksgiving, and tithe regularly, even if maybe not ten percent. That was kind of the extent of my giving. When I was a baby Christian, one of my mentors regularly tithed twenty percent. That was news to me! I didn't really get why she was doing it at the time. I guess giving more to God was good? Then one of our pastors started a charity to give regular clothing and supplies, money, food, ministry support, and therapy to a local shelter. I was a bit taken aback. Was giving that much and that regularly normal? Then I met another pastor who regularly ministered to prisons, shelters, and people in terrible situations, and he brought supplies and donations to anyone he heard was in need. It was well-known that people in prison had this pastor's number written on their prison cell walls, because they knew he'd come and help them, and that he was always willing to help. After being in regular fellowship with both these pastors, I understood they were doing good, and I supported that. But I didn't realize how good the good they were doing was, until I realized that in giving to the poor, they were making a loan to the Lord, and the Lord would repay them! Let our hearts move with compassion to those in need, and do what we can to help them, as the good deed is seen by God and will be repaid in full.

Thank You, Lord, that You always provide for us. Help to keep our hearts soft and sensitive to You and compassionate to those in need. Help us to give generously of our belongings, time, energy, and money, knowing that You are our provider.

*'Every time you give to the poor you make a
loan to the Lord. Don't worry—you'll be repaid
in full for all the good you've done.'*

—PROVERBS 19:17 (TPT)

A Child of God Above All Else

I find it unusual that some believers associate being of a certain nationality, denomination, city, or even political party as more important than being a child of God. Let's be clear about who we are in God, and that we belong to His Kingdom above all else. There was a man who was visiting his daughter and came to our church one Sunday. At our church, normally newcomers introduce themselves with their name and nationality. This man was an elderly man from India but he whole heartedly declared 'My name is Philip and I was born in India, but I am a child of the Kingdom of Heaven!' What boldness!!! On the other end of the spectrum, I once knew someone who declared often that he was how he was because he was a New Yorker. I understand that we do often associate who we are with where we grew up, where we live(d), or the nation we're a citizen of, as it shapes and affects who we are as people. But let's allow the Holy Spirit to shape us even more than anything else. Let's be children of God above all else, and let's let our identity and character be His character, and remember our identity comes from Him.

Thank You, Lord, that as we are born again, we get born into the family of God. Help us to represent You well in all areas of our life. Help us to display Your character and love.

See the Good/God in Everything

'But as many as received Him, to them He gave the right to become children of God, to those who believe in His name.'

—JOHN 1:12

Get Community

We were lone Christians for a while, my husband and I. After we got married, his job meant we moved to a few different cities. We weren't plugged into a fellowship, we didn't have any mentors, and we didn't have any friends. That was a hard year. We prayed desperately for a fellowship, and we prayed desperately for friends. We went to church when we were able, and we followed church online as well, but it still wasn't enough. There's nothing like being plugged into the life of church and letting your roots grow deep. Eventually we settled into a new city and a new fellowship, and we've been flourishing ever since. I've always flourished more when I'm plugged into what God's doing, whether it be evangelism on the streets, prophetic training, ministry to the needy, or part of a worship team. When you're plugged in, you're in close contact with brothers and sisters, and you're able to really learn from others' godly examples. Find a community of strong, biblical, obedient worshippers of Jesus, and let your roots grow deep in Him.

Thank You, Lord, that we are one body in You. Guide us, Holy Spirit, to where You are calling us, and to be plugged into what You are doing. Let us not just be observers but participators and co-workers with what You are doing on the earth.

'Now all who believed were together, and had all things in common, and sold their possessions and goods, and divided them among all, as anyone had need. So continuing daily with one accord in the temple, and breaking bread from house to house, they ate their food with gladness and simplicity of heart, praising God and having favor with all the people. And the Lord added to the church daily those who were being saved.'

—ACTS 2:44–47

Don't Wait for a Vision

Change is not always easy and not always ideal. Some people handle it better than others. But there are believers who often expect God to give them a dream or a vision of what to do in a circumstance, and absolutely won't do anything until they get that dream or vision. Of course, God speaks via dreams and visions, but we can't wait for that alone. The Holy Spirit speaks to us in so many ways. My husband has an interesting way of handling opportunities that come his way. As a well-regarded engineer with ample experience, he's highly sought after and has recruiters calling him constantly. His way of handling these opportunities, especially when they're very good opportunities, is to pray for God's guidance to open and close the right doors of opportunity, then apply for said job, and then wait and see what happens. It shouldn't surprise you to know that God has always led him, and God often closes doors to where He doesn't want us to go. God once told our pastor, 'I will guide your steps, not your chair'. In other words, that God would guide him when he stepped out in a certain direction, but that He wouldn't guide him if he didn't make any move at all and stayed in his chair.

See the Good/God in Everything

Thank You, Lord, for Your Holy Spirit who is always guiding us. Help us to be bold and courageous, and to trust You in all things.

'Trust in the Lord with all your heart, and lean not on your own understanding; in all your ways acknowledge Him, and He shall direct your paths.'
—PROVERBS 3:5–6

He Is Always with Me

The last few months have been hard for me. With the pandemic still raging and not getting to socialize often, as well as going through two unsuccessful rounds of IVF, I'm dangerously close to the limit of what I can handle physically and emotionally. But God's always with me. While in the operating theatre, lying there waiting for the anaesthetist to put me to sleep, I said, 'Lord, where are You?' In the spirit I felt, I saw the Lord standing beside me with His hand on my shoulder. What a comforting picture, that the Lord is always with me and never leaves me. It can be easy to forget that Holy Spirit is with us and in us all the time, especially in non-church settings. But it's these non-church settings where it's most important to remember that we have the Holy Spirit with us and in us.

Thank You, Lord, that You have not forsaken us. Thank You for Your Holy Spirit, the comforter who is with us all the time. Help us to be sensitive to Him at all times, and in all situations every day.

'If you love Me, keep My commandments. And I will pray the Father, and He will give you another Helper, that He may abide with you forever—the Spirit of truth, whom the world cannot receive, because it neither sees Him nor knows Him; but you know Him, for He dwells with you and will be in you. I will not leave you orphans; I will come to you.'

—JOHN 14:15–18

Self-Control (Or: I Didn't Take His Chocolate!)

Chocolate is my nemesis. Depending on what kind and the brand, it can be gone in a ridiculously short amount of time. If we have two bars of chocolate, and my husband wants one and I want one, we'll allot it one bar each. So, the other day I had a moral dilemma. The baby and I had been up for almost three hours in the night, and I was in that female time of the month. I was sitting at my desk, craving chocolate, only to realize I'd finished all of mine. I went to my husband's treats box and found that he had an unopened Fruit and Nut bar. I could've eaten it and asked for forgiveness later from him, which is my norm. But, surprisingly, I thought to myself, 'I should ask Johnny first'. I actually went back three times and was about to eat it, but kept stopping and saying, 'I should ask Johnny first'. Thank You, Holy Spirit, for those few seconds of self-control. Eventually I sent him a text message asking if I could eat it, to which he replied yes. You probably think this is a ridiculous entry, but I don't. You see, in the past, resisting chocolate was extremely hard for me to do. I can't tell you how many times I'd just eat his chocolate and repent later. So, for me, this is a huge improvement in self-control. Self-control, I find, is one of the most overlooked fruits of the Spirit, for the reason that it involves determination, willpower, and for me in this situation, physical restraint.

Thank You, Lord, for Your Holy Spirit. Help us to always be sensitive and obedient to Your leading. Thank You, Lord, that as we stay connected to You, we will bear the fruits of the Spirit in our lives.

'But the fruit of the Spirit is love, joy, peace, longsuffering, kindness, goodness, faithfulness, gentleness, self-control. Against such there is no law.'
—GALATIANS 5:22–23

Decide Your Legacy and Then Work Backwards

I was dreaming and thinking with the Lord while on a walk recently. I was thinking about my legacy. I was thinking about the type of woman, wife, and mother I want to be for me, for my husband, and for my children. In fifteen years, how do I see myself? What does my professional life look like? What does my relationship with my kids look like? In fifteen years, what godly characteristics have grown and borne more fruit? I felt the Lord was telling me to dream and see the type of legacy I want to have and leave, and to move backwards from there. To see the end from the beginning. This was confirmed by a podcast by Daniel Kolenda I listened to recently. It was called 'How Leaders Fall' (on his YouTube channel) and on its own is a very enlightening listen. In his '4 Ways to Guard Yourself' his second point is, 'Mind in the beginning what matters in the end...living with the judgement seat of Christ in mind'. He said if the fallen leaders at the beginning of their ministry were given a time machine into the future where they were shown the damage, hurt, anger, and loss of legacy caused by their sin and compromise, many probably would've had a righteous anger and would've addressed the issues and sin in their lives immediately and resoundingly. It is so important to keep in mind the end, now. What kind of legacy do we want to have when we leave here? Then, let's work backwards. The things we do today will directly impact our future whether we think it will or not. So, let's work hand in hand with God and build a legacy that will bring Him glory, honour, and praise.

Thank You, Lord, for Your grace. Help us to stay focused on eternity and the legacy we leave behind. Help us to walk in a way that brings You glory, all the days of our life. Help us to instil godly habits now.

'For we must all appear before the judgment seat of Christ,
that each one may receive the things done in the body,
according to what he has done, whether good or bad.'
—2 CORINTHIANS 5:10

Bounce Back Quickly

We all have meltdowns and what I call 'woe is me' moments, but the most important point is not to get stuck in that place. Bounce back quickly. I've known a few people over the years who decided one day that life was too difficult, things were too hard, and their circumstances too overwhelming, and they figuratively and spiritually never got back up. They never tried to better their circumstances, they never sought help, and they couldn't even allow themselves to hope things could change. These people I speak of became victims of their circumstances. They allowed bad thinking, hopelessness, and depression to seep in. Thinking

See the Good/God in Everything

affects everything. We must be careful what we allow ourselves to think on and ponder. Gratitude changes everything. It sounds like such an easy fix, but if we watch what we think and have gratitude to God for all He's done in our lives, He becomes our anchor and focus, and our whole mental posture changes. We make the change from being a victim to being gracious.

Thank You, Lord, that there is no situation in our lives that is too big for You. You are not surprised by anything and You remain on the throne. Help us not to become victims of our circumstances. Help us to be gracious for everything You have done for us, and for Jesus' sacrifice.

> *'Always be joyful. Never stop praying. Be thankful in all circumstances, for this is God's will for you who belong to Christ Jesus.'*
> —1 THESSALONIANS 5:16–18 (NLT)

Life's Not That Bad—Think on the Good

During this pandemic, things have been hard. I've gone through my share of ups and downs. Over time I've realized that my thinking directly affects my attitude and demeanour. If I sit and dwell on the thought that I can't go visit my parents in Canada, that we can't go to church because group meetings are cancelled, and that we can't even go out to eat in a restaurant because we're in lockdown, things will go downhill fast. The same thing goes for my thoughts about people. If I think about how my husband gets everything wrong, how after all these years he still doesn't understand my needs, and how after I've told him multiple times he still forgets some things, my ability to even smile and be happy when I see him becomes non-existent. When I think like that about my husband, he becomes like a dreaded roommate you don't want to bump into in the kitchen. When we change what we're thinking about, we change how we feel. If we think about how things in our life are good, how our spouses are loving and helpful, and how God is gracious to us, our emotions will change. We'll be loving, affectionate and happy. We need to get into the habit of focusing on the positive and being grateful to God for His provision, love, and blessings. As my husband likes to remind me, 'Life's not that bad'. It's a simple statement, but a good reminder that no matter what we're going through, it's probably not that bad, and either way we are overcomers.

Thank You, Lord, for Your Word. Thank You that as we change the way we think, we are transformed into a new person. Help us every day to focus our thoughts on the good, pure, loving, and righteous.

'Don't copy the behavior and customs of this world, but let God transform you into a new person by changing the way you think. Then you will learn to know God's will for you, which is good and pleasing and perfect.'
—ROMANS 12:2 (NLT)

Bearing Fruit of the Spirit Takes Time

I love the fruit of the Spirit. It's such an inspiring reminder to me of what to strive for in my journey of being a godly women, wife, and mother. I've had it printed and framed on my wall for many years now. It always encourages me. One thing about the fruit of the Spirit is that it doesn't just appear one day as fruit. Fruit starts as a seed. It takes time. It needs water and sunlight for it to grow. The same with growing the fruit of the Spirit in our lives. We have to plant the seeds of the fruit. If we want to see self-control in our lives, we have to start somewhere. We have to start with the little things, like asking your husband before eating all his chocolate. Our little seeds start to develop into regular habits, which with time and constant nourishment will grow into fully ripe and developed fruits.

Thank You, Lord, that You guide us with Your word. Help us to develop and grow the fruit of the Spirit in our lives. Help us start with the little things, and to establish good, godly habits that lead to the flourishing of Your Spirit in our lives.

'But the fruit of the Spirit is love, joy, peace, longsuffering, kindness, goodness, faithfulness, gentleness, self-control. Against such there is no law.'
—GALATIANS 5:22–23

Crap Dreams

I see my dreams in distinct categories: crap dreams, God dreams, enemy dreams, and not-sure-what dreams. God dreams I write down and pray for the revelation. Enemy dreams I pray about, plead the blood of Jesus, then flush. Not-sure-what dreams I just ignore. I may ponder them for a day, to decide if they're God dreams, but by then I've usually forgotten what the dream was about. These are probably my brain-processing dreams. Then there are crap dreams. Crap dreams are on the enemy spectrum of dreams. They're not demonic, invasive, or scary, but they're unpleasant and definitely from the enemy. They're negative dreams that make you feel like there's something wrong with you, or that you're incompetent, unlikeable, unloved. They bring up insecurities and maybe even old sin. They're dreams that try to make you believe a lie. I had a crap dream recently. It made me doubt myself and question stepping out in faith. It made me fear judgement from my peers. It was an awful dream that made me doubt myself and instilled fear and judgement from others; that's obviously not from God. So, we say goodbye to those dreams and flush them. We meditate on what God has said about us and who we are in Him.

Thank You, Lord, that we know who we are in You. Help us to be reminded and meditate on the fact that we were bought by Jesus' blood and are now children of the King, and co-heirs with Christ. Help us to be wise, to recognize lies quickly, and to choose not to believe them but to trust on Your word.

'And you shall know the truth, and the truth shall make you free.'
—JOHN 8:32

The Log in My Eye Is Huge

Since we're trying to get pregnant, dieting is off-limits for me. My preferred diet of choice is intermittent fasting and keto. But because my main goal is to be healthy for IVF, for development of good eggs, and to support a baby should I get pregnant, I'm eating a well-rounded diet right now, three meals a day and not restricting my carbs...much. I've recently starting exercising lightly again as well. Well, the other day I was judging my husband. I was noticing that he's put on a few pounds. That he's too busy and stressed with work to exercise. I was about to make a rude and pointed comment about how he's put on a few pounds, when I stopped. I literally had a moment's pause where I thought, *Wait, I'm*

See the Good/God in Everything

not exactly in shape as well. So, I refrained from saying anything. Then I examined myself. Up until very recently, looking after the baby had been my excuse for not exercising, and so I'm still carrying extra baby weight to my dismay. So, really, my position isn't much better than my husband's, yet my excuses were in my mind pretty valid and reasonable. It is so, so, so much easier to look at other people and judge them for their failings and shortcomings. It's actually much harder to stop before speaking, look at ourselves, and judge our own shortcomings, failings, and areas for improvement.

Lord, help us not to judge others. Help us to examine ourselves and remove the log from our own eye so we can clearly see.

'Judge not, that you be not judged. For with what judgment you judge, you will be judged; and with the measure you use, it will be measured back to you. And why do you look at the speck in your brother's eye, but do not consider the plank in your own eye? Or how can you say to your brother, "Let me remove the speck from your eye"; and look, a plank is in your own eye? Hypocrite! First remove the plank from your own eye, and then you will see clearly to remove the speck from your brother's eye.'

—MATTHEW 7:1–5

Hoping and Dreaming with the Lord

My husband mentioned recently that I've been more pleasant, laid-back, purposeful, and happy than I've been in a long time. It took me a second but then I remembered that I'd been exercising again. We have a treadmill at home, and I like to take long brisk walks or do a light jog. I'd stopped for a few months, but after two unsuccessful IVFs I was feeling like I needed to get strong again. The exercising is doing wonders—love those endorphins and slight changes to the mommy body. But actually what I love about the exercising, and walking in particular, is the time to hope and dream with the Lord. When I was a young Christian living in London, I lived very close to Kensington Gardens and Hyde Park. It was my daily routine to put some headphones on, turn on some good godly music, and walk around the park. If you take a walk around the perimeter of the parks it'll take you around an hour and a bit, give or take, based on your speed. But the best part of the walk was dreaming. There wasn't anything particular I was dreaming about, but I was dreaming and hoping about the good future the Lord had for me. I had forgotten how much I loved that. There's something uplifting about hoping in the Lord, thinking upon His promises for us, and dreaming of a bright future. It's easy to get caught up in newsfeeds and the media, where things are generally bad or getting worse. But He desires good things for us, and it's good to focus and think upon that.

Thank You, Lord, that You have a purpose and a plan for us, plans for us to prosper and to give us a future and a hope. Help us to hope in You. Help us to prioritise our lives around You, and to trust You in all things.

'For I know the thoughts that I think toward you, says the Lord, thoughts of peace and not of evil, to give you a future and a hope.'
—JEREMIAH 29:11

See the Good/God in Everything

Self-Control and YouTube

Self-control is one of my least favourite but probably most useful fruits of the Spirit. One of my faults is that I tend to waste too much time doing useless things. I don't always regulate myself; I just go all out. Watching YouTube is one place I don't normally practice self-control. Now, don't get me wrong, generally I love YouTube. I'm a dedicated fan of a few channels, which I watch fairly regularly. I also watch our Australian church's services on YouTube. My problem is that after I've watched those channels, I start to look for other things. I spend too much time scrolling random videos, watching cute animal videos that are slightly entertaining but mostly kind of mindless drivel. Next thing I know, it's a few hours later, and I'm wondering where the time went. Anyone else have this problem? It got so bad that at one point my husband and I would both be in bed watching YouTube for hours, separately on our phones, and not speaking to each other, only giving each other the perfunctory goodnight kiss before bed. That isn't the way to live, people! So, I had to set limits for being on YouTube. Self-control is a hard one to master, but so useful for life.

Thank You, Lord, for Your Holy Spirit that guides me and empowers me in all things. Help me to have self-control in all areas of my life. Help me to make good choices each and every day, to grow the fruit of self-control in my life.

'For this very reason, make every effort to add to your faith goodness; and to goodness, knowledge; and to knowledge, self-control; and to self-control, perseverance; and to perseverance, godliness; and to godliness, mutual affection; and to mutual affection, love. For if you possess these qualities in increasing measure, they will keep you from being ineffective and unproductive in your knowledge of our Lord Jesus Christ.'
—2 PETER 1:5–8 (NIV)

You Can *Never* Take It Back

One of our dear friends and elders in church once said to me that the greatest thing she'd ever been taught was to watch the words that leave her mouth. Because once they leave your mouth, you can never take them back. This is so true, and I've learnt it the hard way. When we were engaged and about to get married, the drama that ensued was epic. And I didn't handle it well. Instead of keeping the peace, instead of watching what words were coming out of my mouth, I was vulgar, angry, and foolish. I ended up regretting so many things spoken and written during that time, and wish I could go back and erase all those words. When things are right and well in our world, of course we think we're perfect and amazing and not foolish with our words. But when we're in a tight spot, when we're offended, when we're angry, when we're not getting our way, when people aren't listening to you, that's when you need to be even more careful, because that's the time unpleasant and vile words will want to come out of your mouth. You aren't wise when you're angry, you aren't strong when you're angrier than everyone else, and you aren't smart when you make the problem worse. It's a simple lesson but one of the most important ones. Watch what you say, because you can never take those words back.

Thank You, Lord, that You give us the words to live our life by. Help us to watch what we say, and to learn to keep our mouth shut to save us grief.

'Watch your tongue and keep your mouth
shut, and you will stay out of trouble.'
—PROVERBS 21:23 (NLT)

See the Good/God in Everything

Regret

Are there things I regret? Yes, definitely. Just off the top of my head, there are two occasions I definitely regret my words and actions. Why do I regret those times? Mostly because I hurt family. I was brash and insecure and took a hit at anything that would come my way. It wasn't pretty. I hurt a lot of people. It ended up hurting me too, because relationships I held dear were fractured and broken. They took many years to rebuild, and even though they're now better, the relationships definitely aren't like they were. So, what do I do when I have regret? First thing, if there are people to apologize to, I apologize. That's just basic. But the next big thing I do is to repent to God and forgive myself. I repent to God because I sinned and I hurt a lot of people. My actions and words were terrible, and I wasn't a peacekeeper at all. I had no self-control and no patience, kindness, or goodness. Then I forgive myself, because I know I'm not perfect and that I failed big time. Then I give my regret to God. I wish I did things differently but I just can't change anything, so I give it to God. Then I need to spend time with Him to heal me from messing things up. I don't know about you, but after all the dust settles, and I realize what a mess I've made, it's the worst thing. My heart needs healing, and I need Him to tell me He still loves me, even though I royally botched things up. I don't dwell on my mistakes, but I do learn from them. Maybe I need to control myself and not get angry so easily. Maybe I need to hold my tongue and keep myself from saying stupid things. Whatever it is, I make sure I learn the lesson and don't make the same mistake twice. And I pray. I pray for more wisdom and for better control of my tongue in the future.

Thank You, Lord, that You forgive all our sins. Help me when I fail. Help me not to live in regret, but to forgive myself and to not make the same mistake twice. Lord, help me to have more wisdom and more self-control. Help me to keep the peace in my relationships and not be a wrecking ball.

'Do not remember the former things, nor consider the things of old. Behold, I will do a new thing, now it shall spring forth; shall you not know it? I will even make a road in the wilderness and rivers in the desert.'

—ISAIAH 43:18–19

Wisdom, or The Hard Way 2.0

You can learn a lesson one of two ways; through wisdom or The Hard Way. I used to think I was pretty smart, maybe even wise. And then I botched up a bunch of relationships in a really bad way, and now I can definitely say I'm not smart. I learnt those lessons the hard way, and the hard way isn't fun. It was painful to the point where the muscle memory is legit. Like when I almost chopped my thumb knuckle off with a knife. Now, I'm super careful when cutting. I never rush, and I don't try to be Jamie Oliver. Learning lessons the hard way is like that. The relationship lessons I learnt are: keeping the peace is more important than being right; don't speak out of anger or offence; and hold my tongue, because once it leaves my mouth, I can never take it back. And once you offend someone, or damage a relationship, it's very hard to mend. You may ask for forgiveness and be apologetic, and you may even change your ways, but the other person may not, and they may hold a grudge until they die. It's not a nice thought, but it is real life. So, read Proverbs and gain wisdom and discernment. Don't be like me and think being 'good' is being wise. It is not.

Thank You, Lord, that if we lack wisdom we should ask You for some, and You give us wisdom generously. Lord, we pray for more wisdom! Help us not to be unwise. Help us to represent You well. Help us to have wisdom so that we don't learn lessons the hard way. And for those

See the Good/God in Everything

lessons we have learnt the hard way, help it to be so ingrained in us that we don't make the same mistake again.

> *'Therefore see that you walk carefully [living life with honor, purpose, and courage; shunning those who tolerate and enable evil], not as the unwise, but as wise [sensible, intelligent, discerning people], making the very most of your time [on earth, recognizing and taking advantage of each opportunity and using it with wisdom and diligence], because the days are [filled with] evil. Therefore do not be foolish and thoughtless, but understand and firmly grasp what the will of the Lord is.'*
> —EPHESIANS 5:15–17 (AMP)

Give It to God

Here's the thing—right now we're planning on returning to Australia in a few months. We'll be repatriating to Australia and officially leaving the Middle East, in what's known around here as Final Exit. Final Exit because you won't be returning to this country. It's a complicated move, which consists of closing bank accounts, paying credit cards, getting police checks, getting movers, getting a new job, getting your end bonus payout, organizing flights, selling cars, and saying goodbye. As well, we need to factor in having more babies via another IVF round and arrange to go to my brother's wedding. It's complicated, and I honestly don't know how it'll all work out. There are so many factors to consider, and we spend our time and energy discussing the different aspects of leaving. Because of all the factors, scenarios, and details, giving it to God is the only thing that gives us peace. We give it to God constantly and He gives us wisdom in the planning, organizing, and preparation in the way only He can do.

Thank You, Lord, that even when I make my own plans, You always direct my steps. Help me to walk in step with You, Holy Spirit. Help me not to be anxious or worrisome about the future, knowing You are always with me.

'A man's heart plans his way, but the LORD directs his steps.'
—PROVERBS 16:9

Finish Well

I was thinking once about how my husband was married before. He was married for a long time, about twenty years or so before he got divorced. I started to feel insecurities rise up in me because of his past, but then clarity came. Though he was married previously, that marriage ended in divorce. I was reminded of Ecclesiastes 7:8 (NIV): 'The end of a matter is better than its beginning'. And it made me realise my fears were irrelevant. How we end is more important than how we start. The process of life, staying on a faithful path with the Lord, and ending well is so much more important than the beginning. Part of my desire now in my life is to be faithful until the end. I want to end life well. Yes, I'm only forty and I have many years ahead of me, but I want to be focused on the end goal. I don't just want to live a good life while I'm young and healthy, and then slowly waste away the end years of my life. Neither do I want to wait until I'm older, or I have more children, or I make more money, or I have more time, to do important, meaningful, good things. I want to be focused on the end now. I want to use every minute of my life for God's glory. And stay faithful in my life, and in my walk with God, to the very end.

See the Good/God in Everything

Thank You, Lord, that how we end is more important to You than how we begin. Help us to remain faithful in all aspects of our lives and walk with You. Help us to be steadfast, rooted, and grounded in love. Help us to end well, and keep eternity as our goal.

'The end of a matter is better than its beginning.'
—ECCLESIASTES 7:8 (NIV)

Mentally Preparing and Praying into the Next Thing

So, we're leaving this country in the Middle East that we have lived in for the last eight years. For my husband it's been almost ten years. It's a sad eventuality. We can't live abroad forever, and there will always be a time when we'll need to return home. In preparing for this big move, there are a lot of discussions, a lot of decisions, and a lot of plans to make. One thing we're making of extreme importance is mentally preparing to go, and praying into the next thing. Mentally preparing to go encompasses all the practical things to leave, and being aware that to get them done will take time, energy, and flexibility. It also means preparing yourself for change. To get it in your head that big change is coming, and to be ready for it. It's so important to be mentally prepared, but it's equally important to pray into the change, and the future. It was like when I delivered our baby girl. From around the middle of our pregnancy we started praying about the delivery. We prayed into every aspect of my body to do what it's supposed to do, that it would be quick and easy and smooth. Delivery ended up being three hours of unmedicated labour, and to be honest it didn't feel any longer than thirty minutes, everything went so perfectly. But honestly, I totally attribute that to all the prayers ahead of time. So, we're currently praying into the change, praying into the move, praying about the future, praying for every little thing we can think of, and to God be the glory.

Thank You, Lord, that You guide us and teach us of things to come. Help us to be prayerful and adaptable. Help us to be sensitive and obedient to You, Holy Spirit. Help us to move with You and Your timing.

> *'But when He, the Spirit of Truth, comes, He will guide you into all the truth [full and complete truth]. For He will not speak on His own initiative, but He will speak whatever He hears [from the Father—the message regarding the Son], and He will disclose to you what is to come [in the future].'*
> —JOHN 16:13 (AMP)

Wear Your Own Shoes

We had a friend stay with us recently. When she left, she left her slippers behind. My indoor shoes were in the wash, so I used her slippers around the house. At first it seemed to work out fine. It wasn't the most comfortable pair of slippers, and they definitely felt like someone else's shoes, but I made do. Shortly after wearing her slippers, though, I had a few very unlucky incidents where I slipped quite badly, and could've very well broken something. When that happened, I realised it was because I was wearing ill-fitting shoes which weren't the correct size for me. So often we try to conform to other people's standards, expectations, or even perceived purposes for our lives—we try to wear shoes that aren't our shoes, and they don't fit us correctly! When I was growing up, I thought I'd be a teacher. Both my grandmothers had been teachers and

I'd always heard that I'd make a great teacher, so I thought maybe that was for me. I spent a few years teaching, and it was fairly rewarding and fun, but it wasn't for me for the long term, nor was it something my soul was fulfilled doing. But I'd always journaled and can show you the dozens of journals I've filled over the years. My husband thought I was pretty good at it, and it was something I enjoyed immensely. It wasn't actually until many years later, after I had gone through and come out of some family issues, done a very uninteresting MBA, and then done a tedious coding course, that I finally realized writing is what I want to do, something that fulfils the inner core of my being. When I finally put it together that writing is what I enjoy and that I'm fairly good at it, I didn't need anyone to remind me to start writing, nor did I need my husband to check up on me that I was actually doing it; the purposefulness of it all just pushed me along. So, don't get stuck wearing other people's shoes. Wear your own shoes, do what you're called to do, do what inspires your spirit and soul, and don't be scared of being different. Everyone has different shoes.

Thank You, Lord, that You have a purpose and a plan for my life. Thank You that You work all things for my good. Help me to trust in You and the process, and to remember that You are always good.

'I cry out to God Most High, to God who fulfills his purpose for me.'
—PSALM 57:2 (ESV)

Keep Your Heart Clean

My sister-in-law once asked me why, even though I've been through a lot of stuff in my life, I'm not bitter. I told her it's because I keep my heart clean. For me, it's the most important thing in my life not to be bitter, resentful, jealous, or angry towards others or towards God over things that have happened to me. I've been ignored, treated badly, made enemies, and estranged from family. Yes, sometimes these things hurt, but I forgive often (even people who probably have no idea I've had to forgive them), and I often check how my heart is doing. Like water over a duck's back, I forgive and move on. And a lot of times, if you don't take things too seriously, it really makes things easier. Having a clear conscience and a clean heart is so freeing. When your heart is clean, you don't have anything weighing you down in your mind or your spirit. It's so freeing to keep your heart clean.

Lord, help to keep my heart clean. Help me to forgive easily and quickly, and not to hold onto issues that I should really just give to You.

'Create in me a clean heart, O God, and
renew a steadfast spirit within me.'
—PSALM 51:10

Words Are Powerful

When I finally graduated high school, after a few terrible years (it was a self-directed-learning high school—enough said), my grandmother said to me, 'You'll do better in university'. A few simple yet encouraging words to a struggling student; but words I'd hold on to and remember, which I still do to this day. Those words, spoken by my loving grandmother, are words that gave me hope and strength. That though I didn't do so well in high school, I was still capable, able, and smart. That my past wouldn't dictate my future. These words literally fuelled my soul, like putting gas into an empty car. It was encouragement and hope to my

See the Good/God in Everything

spirit. I never told her when she was alive how much those words meant to me, but wish I did. Sometimes the smallest, maybe even seemingly inconsequential words spoken can literally bring life to a situation.

Thank You, Lord, that You love us and have the best for us. Thank You for the people You put in our lives. Help us to speak words of life into situations, words of encouragement to weary souls, and words of hope to the hopeless.

> *'Death and life are in the power of the tongue,*
> *and those who love it will eat its fruit.'*
> —PROVERBS 18:21

The Heart

My background before I became a born-again Christian was Catholic. One thing I really didn't like about my experience growing up was that a lot of kids I knew did the whole 'church thing' on Sunday, but then lived totally different lives every other day. A large majority of my classmates were sleeping around, getting drunk often, and doing drugs. But they went to church on Sundays with their families. One of my classmates actually said I was like the virgin Mary, because I hadn't had sex and they all had. When I became a Christian, I loved how Jesus said that the inside of the cup was more important than the outside. It resonated so much with me. I was so tired of fake religiosity in the church; I wanted authentic heart to heart with Jesus.

Lord, thank You that You see the hidden depths of our heart. Help us to be authentic. Help us to love You more. Help us to be humble

and teachable, and to have a soft heart. Help us to always remember that You care about what is going on inside our hearts above all else.

'Woe to you, scribes and Pharisees, hypocrites! For you cleanse the outside of the cup and dish, but inside they are full of extortion and self-indulgence. Blind Pharisee, first cleanse the inside of the cup and dish, that the outside of them may be clean also. Woe to you, scribes and Pharisees, hypocrites! For you are like whitewashed tombs which indeed appear beautiful outwardly, but inside are full of dead men's bones and all uncleanness. Even so you also outwardly appear righteous to men, but inside you are full of hypocrisy and lawlessness.'
—MATTHEW 23:25–28

Think Wisely

I'm a bit of a thinker. I think about a lot of things. I process things, I evaluate, I dream. Now, in Ephesians 3:20, it says, 'Now to Him who is able to do exceedingly abundantly above all that we ask or think, according to the power that works in us'. One of my absolute favourite scriptures. Have you ever wondered why it mentions our thoughts? I sure have. My thought life is very important, and because I think so much, I've often noticed that what I think about will affect my attitude, my demeanour, and even my temperament towards others. My pastor is a key believer that our thoughts are extremely important. He says that 'thoughts are like words in the Spirit realm'. I wholeheartedly agree. So back to the scripture. Why does it say 'to Him who is able to do exceedingly abundantly above all that we can ask or think'? I believe it goes hand in hand with 'write the vision and make it plain' (Habakkuk 2:2). Before you can even write the vision down, you need to actually think about the vision. The steps being: think; write; pray/ask; believe. Hebrews 11:1 says 'faith is the substance of things hoped for, the evidence of things not seen'. We have to think and dream up the vision with God, then write it down, and pray, ask, and believe we've received it. So, dream big and think big, because God's able to do exceedingly above even that! Amen.

Thank You, Lord, that You are the giver of good things. Help us to think good thoughts, and to align our thinking with Yours. Help us to renew our mind daily.

'Therefore I say to you, whatever things you ask when you pray, believe that you receive them, and you will have them.'
—MARK 11:24

Attack on the Mind

I love my mind. I love thinking, praying, and dreaming. This is partially why I rarely drink, because I don't like when my mind isn't perfectly functional. I've had three very big attacks on my mind in the past few years, and I believe it's because I dream wild big things, and I pray even wilder bigger things. The attack starts with a few little thoughts. Now, these thoughts are related to something I may have seen or heard recently. But then it goes a step further. It connects what I've seen or heard to a thought. And without getting into the details, the thoughts are usually extremely bad, totally impure, and fully ungodly. You know they're not your thoughts, and you start flicking them off, but then the barrage starts. Seconds and milliseconds, one after another, you're bombarded with more and more and more things. Thoughts, images, remembering old bad thoughts or habits, or even sin. Bringing things up that are under the blood, and part of the old man. It's intense and very disturbing. All the while, you're still trying to go about your daily life, so you may not have even put it together that you're being attacked. You keep flicking the thoughts off but because you're also trying to live life, it may be that you've just ignored some and they're sitting there in the background, festering. Eventually when it hits you that you're being attacked, this should be your plan of action, in order of least important to most important. All must be completed to ensure total defence:

- Remember that these are not your thoughts
- Focus and think on good things
- Put a visual image of blood over the ungodly images
- Remind yourself this isn't your character, that you're a child of God and full of the Holy Spirit
- Remember that those old habits and sins are under the blood
- Repent and take communion
- Get your spouse or someone to lay hands on you and anoint you with oil
- Get prayer from other believers

Thank You, Lord, that Your Word and Holy Spirit guide us in all things. Thank You that the blood of Jesus is powerful to redeem, save, and deliver us, and that it covers us and protects us.

'Be sober, be vigilant; because your adversary the devil walks about like a roaring lion, seeking whom he may devour. Resist him, steadfast in the faith, knowing that the same sufferings are experienced by your brotherhood in the world. But may the God of all grace, who called us to His eternal glory by Christ Jesus, after you have suffered a while, perfect, establish, strengthen, and settle you.'
—1 PETER 5:8–10

Family Passing

My father-in-law and mother-in-law passed away recently. They were believers in the Lord and firm in their faith. I had only been in the family for six years when they died, and since we live abroad, I only saw them on a handful of trips back to Australia. My mother-in-law asked me on my first trip to Australia why I choose to marry her son. I said, 'He's a good Christian guy', and she was very pleased with that answer. I was so thankful to have a mother- and father-in-law who believed in God and valued putting Christ in the centre of their lives. At my mother-in-law's funeral, my brother-in-law told the story of how she prayed their father into the faith, and how her prayers are an inheritance for the family, many of whom are Christian. It was a powerful eulogy and a powerful testimony of answered prayers. It's sad when family dies, but of those who were of the family of God, we can put our trust in knowing that 'to be absent from the body is to be present to the Lord' (2 Corinthians 5:8).

Lord, You are the ultimate comforter. I trust in You to comfort my spirit when people I love leave this earthly realm. Help me to rise up and pray for my family who does not yet know You, and help me to be more aware of eternity.

'For God so loved the world that He gave His only begotten Son, that whoever believes in Him should not perish but have everlasting life.'
—JOHN 3:16

Building Gratitude and Character

I'm convinced that in every situation in life, we're either building character or gratitude in our lives. When things are hard, we're building character, and when things are going well, we should be building constant gratitude. When there are hard things in life, stress at work, lack of employment, difficult relationships, unanswered prayer, we're forced to build character in our lives. Character building is hard work. It can be building graciousness, humility, compassion, or love. It isn't easy. When we're in tough situations, it can be easy to fall into a 'woe is me' victim mentality. Been there, done that. Did it help? Not really. I realized I was being an idiot. I was never happy and all I did was complain and think about how terrible my life was. So instead I choose to force myself to stop being so self-centred and a drain to myself and those around me. So, what are you building? Are you building character and gratitude, or self-centeredness?

Thank You, Lord, that You are with us always, notably when we have troubles. Help us to grow in character in every step of our walk. Help us to keep the faith and trust in You, knowing that our tribulations are producing in us perseverance, character, and hope.

'These things I have spoken to you, that in Me you may have peace. In the world you will have tribulation; but be of good cheer, I have overcome the world.'
—JOHN 16:33

See the Good/God in Everything

Be Honest, Even If It Costs You Your Job

Proverbs 19:1 (TPT) says, 'It is better to be honest, even if it leads to poverty'. This happened to me when I was being honest at work. When I got married, I was working at a university. It was the school's summer holiday, so that was when we planned to go abroad, get married, and have a short honeymoon. I knew when I went on holiday that the university didn't allow any special treatment when it comes to return delays, and that there was no such thing as taking a leave of absence. The only reason allowed was 'family emergency'. My colleagues tried to convince me to just call my honeymoon a 'family emergency' to keep my job. I wasn't so sure about that. I had a very good job, and at a very respectable institution. But, nonetheless, when it was time to let the university know I'd be returning late, I told them the truth; I had gotten married and I was on my honeymoon. It boiled down to this—I could lie (or stretch the truth), or I could be honest. But getting married isn't an emergency, so I couldn't go down that path. Lying is one of the things the Lord hates; so, though it cost me my job, it's better to follow God's standard than anyone else's. Plus, it all worked out well in the end.

Thank You, Lord, for Your Word. Thank You that it is a lamp to our feet and a light onto our path. Help us to follow Your Word, even when it seems like the harder decision. Thank You that You know every decision we make and always provide for us.

'These six things the Lord hates, yes, seven are an abomination to Him: a proud look, a lying tongue, hands that shed innocent blood, a heart that devises wicked plans, feet that are swift in running to evil, a false witness who speaks lies, and one who sows discord among brethren.'
—PROVERBS 6:16–19

God Cares More About You
Than Your Ministry

We had a good friend and pastor recently go through a health issue out of the blue. It was a random heart issue and we and the community around him intensely interceded in prayer. It was a miraculous recovery and even the health professionals were surprised. When we saw him afterwards, he was absolutely convinced that the health scare was a wake-up call from God. That he'd been focussing too much on his ministry, and not enough on his personal relationship with God, and that God was calling him back to his first love. I couldn't have agreed more. We love this pastor dearly, but when your marriage is falling apart, with multiple attacks happening, accountability issues, and insinuations of relationships with your co-workers, you've got to realise maybe something's up. This tends to happen with people in ministry a lot. Especially people who are defined by their ministry, or who have been doing ministry a long time. They tend to confuse their ministry with their relationship with God. They may even start to see their ministry as works-based faith. This pastor is doing amazing work in his ministry, but if it's taking away from his time with God, and hindering his walk with the Lord, it definitely needs to be reassessed. We need to minister out of the overflow of our intimacy with God.

Thank You, Lord, for the way You guide us and speak to us. Help us to be receptive to hearing from You; and more importantly, help us to be obedient to You. Help us to constantly be in contact with You, and to spend time with You daily. Help us not to be so busy with life, work, or ministry that we put You on the back burner. Help us to focus on the important and to seek You more and more. Help us to get back to our first love with You.

See the Good/God in Everything

'Not everyone who says to Me, "Lord, Lord," shall enter the kingdom of heaven, but he who does the will of My Father in heaven. Many will say to Me in that day, "Lord, Lord, have we not prophesied in Your name, cast out demons in Your name, and done many wonders in Your name?" And then I will declare to them, "I never knew you; depart from Me, you who practice lawlessness!"'

—MATTHEW 7:21–23

The Little Prayers Matter

I used to think prayers needed to be something super spiritual. You needed to be in the right frame of mind, alone, in the quiet; and that it needed to be meaningful, have lots of scriptures, and be super long. Boy, was I wrong. I used to also say 'yes, I'll pray for you' and wait for an opportune time in the future, where all the above-mentioned requirements were met. This was futile. I've learnt that sometimes prayers come in the form of little prayers, short prayers, prayers said on the fly, in public, under my breath, or in my heart. Why do we limit praying to God as something that can only be done in certain situations and circumstances, and when we feel super spiritual or particularly Holy Spirit-led? God can and will use every prayer—long or short, alone or in public, said out loud or in our heart, prayed with a lot of conviction or a little, prayed in desperation or with faith. It doesn't matter; all of them count. We just need to pray them, and He'll do the rest.

Thank You, Lord, that You hear all our prayers. Thank You that You don't judge or rate our prayers. Help us to pray the big and the small prayers. Help us to be more prayerful, and to seek You in everything we do.

*'Do not be anxious about anything, but in everything
by prayer and supplication with thanksgiving
let your requests be made known to God.'*

—PHILIPPIANS 4:6 (ESV)

Taking Every Thought Captive; or,
Don't Think About Everything

You can control your thoughts. It's a fact. I used to think otherwise, but then I realized that some thoughts that came into my mind were definitely not my own. Some thoughts are dodgy, some inappropriate, some accusing, and some just plain lies. And any thoughts that fall under any of the aforementioned headings are things you shouldn't be thinking about. End of story. There's a second, after a thought comes, where you have a choice. Don't believe me? Try it out and see. In that second, you have a choice to continue thinking about it, or disregard it and chuck it in the trash. I know it sounds daunting to take every thought captive, but once you get into a habit of evaluating each thought, it becomes easier. I use the good-or-not-good method; it's the best and easiest standard. Good things are things that are lovely, pure, and praise-worthy, as said in Philippians 4:8. Things that don't fall into that category are thoughts to throw away. And if you let a not-good thought stay in your mind longer than a few seconds, it becomes harder to throw away, and you'll really start to believe it's your own. Think of the thought like a seed with super growing capabilities. If it stays in your mind, it starts to grow roots and get a foothold. Of course, you can still get rid of it, it's just not as easy as when it first lands. So, don't think about everything, because not everything is lovely and good.

See the Good/God in Everything

Thank You, Lord, that You give us the words of life. Help us to control our mind, and to think about good things. Help us to take every thought captive, and to not think about everything, because not everything is useful or good.

> 'Finally, brethren, whatever things are true, whatever things are noble, whatever things are just, whatever things are pure, whatever things are lovely, whatever things are of good report, if there is any virtue and if there is anything praiseworthy—meditate on these things.'
> —PHILIPPIANS 4:8

Watch What You Say About Yourself

As you know, I'm a big proponent of watching what you say and think. I have some Christian friends who say the worst things about themselves. The worst part is that they're very much unaware of it. I have one friend who literally calls herself crazy. She has a high standard of cleanliness and once when she was staying at a hotel, she called the manager to ensure the room would be very clean. I think that's a fairly reasonable request, but she repeatedly told me it's because she's crazy. That she's so crazy, she needed to make sure the room was really clean. That she's a crazy old lady and that's why she does crazy things like that. And this was far from the first time she's repeatedly called herself crazy. She doesn't say it seriously, but more in a demeaning, joking manner. I've tried mentioning this to her on many occasions, saying, 'No, you're not crazy—don't call yourself that', but it really has no effect. She's so used to that phrase, and belittling herself, it just always comes out. I love my friend dearly, but please don't be like her. Listen to what you're calling yourself. Even in jest, and even if you think it's untrue, your words still hold power.

Thank You, Lord, that You give us amazing power in the words we speak. Help us to speak life! Life over ourselves, life over our families, life over our work, life over our friends, and life over every aspect of our lives.

> *'A man's stomach shall be satisfied from the fruit*
> *of his mouth; from the produce of his lips he shall*
> *be filled. Death and life are in the power of the*
> *tongue, and those who love it will eat its fruit.'*
> —PROVERBS 18:20–21

Sometimes I Really Dislike the News

Since the pandemic started, I've been reading a lot more news. I've not been a news fan for years, due to the bias in some countries' news outlets, but only because of COVID have I started to read it again. I'm sure I'm not alone in this—updates on lockdowns, tracking infection numbers, info on international travel, etc. I just had to read the news again. I go to the website of three news outlets only, relevant to where we live and where we're from. Here's the thing—the news is sometimes very unpleasant. I was reading the news from one of those sites the other day, and there were these stories of missing persons. Full of mystery, intrigue, quite scary and very unpleasant stuff. It wasn't nice. I know I'm conservative, but there's just some information I don't need to know about. I don't need to know about murders, missing persons, or abuse. I'm fully aware that those things happen in this fallen world; but when I read some stories, or even just glance at the headlines, I feel a bit tainted.

See the Good/God in Everything

Then I read this scripture in James 1:27 about keeping ourselves from being polluted by the world. So, you can get polluted by the world?! Instead of 'polluted', The Amplified Bible instead says to keep yourself 'uncontaminated' by the secular world.

Thank You, Lord, that Your Word is full of wisdom and shows us how to live our lives. Help us to make decisions in our lives to keep us from being contaminated. Help us to be careful and wise about what we watch, see, read, hear, or listen to. Help us to keep ourselves clean from the world.

> *'Pure and undefiled religion before God and the Father*
> *is this: to visit orphans and widows in their trouble,*
> *and to keep oneself unspotted from the world.'*
> —JAMES 1:27

A Dream About Our Cleaner

We have a cleaner. He helps us tremendously to keep the house clean and to do the kind of deep clean that both my husband and I really don't have a desire or inclination to do. We have a 20-month-old daughter who can pretty much destroy our kitchen and living room, or whatever room of the house she's in, in just under two minutes. And even though all our cabinets, drawers, and shelves have locks on them, she'll get into everything she does have access to. It's a skill, really. Basically our house is a total mess most of the time. So, when we were looking for a cleaner, we asked one of our pastor friends who recommended someone to us. He's a nice person, reliable and very active in their church. He's quite short and slim, and I wouldn't particularly call him handsome, but he is friendly. We've had cleaners before, so I treated him the same as I normally do; I give them space to work, and try not to burden them with requests or constructive criticism. We give them a better-than-average wage, and treat them with respect as someone doing a professional job in our house. So, after a week of him cleaning our home, I had a dream with him in it. He walked into our kitchen, and I remember seeing his face, and he was extremely handsome, and I was so surprised! I had had a similar dream previously where I was looking at myself in the mirror and I was a beautiful, confident lady. I couldn't believe myself. I believe it represented the way God sees me. And so, this dream with our cleaner was a surprise. I believe it was a gentle reminder from the Lord that though he does the job of cleaning our house, which one may see as a lowly job, he's still a brother in Christ, and that we shouldn't forget that.

Thank You, Lord, that though we all have different roles and jobs, we are still all one body in Christ. Help me, Lord, to remember to treat my brothers and sisters in Christ well.

'Bondservants, be obedient to those who are your masters according to the flesh, with fear and trembling, in sincerity of heart, as to Christ; not with eyeservice, as men-pleasers, but as bondservants of Christ, doing the will of God from the heart, with goodwill doing service, as to the Lord, and not to men, knowing that whatever good anyone does, he will receive the same from the Lord, whether he is a slave or free.'
—EPHESIANS 6:5–8

Living Free Course

I got saved in Weymouth in the UK. It's a small seaside town where I worked one summer teaching English. But by God-incidence when I

See the Good/God in Everything

worked there, two of my co-workers were born-again Christians. One used to take me to church and small group, and the other one, with his wife, used to have very timely, godly conversations with me. I ended up getting saved, then moved to London. One of them had been to Bible school in London, so I ended up at that church in Notting Hill Gate. It was a Holy Spirit-filled, Bible-based Pentecostal church. I was there for years and had the most amazing time, connected with wonderful people, and grew as a Christian. One of the most integral things about my time at that church was their Living Free course. It's basically an intro to Christianity course where you get healed and delivered from past sins, soul ties, familial bondages, and lies. You're taught how to live as a Christian, how to walk with God, and how to develop good devotional habits. In conjunction, you're encouraged to get water baptised and filled with the Holy Spirit as evidenced by speaking in tongues. This course has been the core foundation of my Christian walk, and I can't tell you how many Christians I've met who don't have this basic training. So, if you're still hounded by lies about who you are in Christ, if you still have soul ties, or if you're still in bondage to sin, I encourage you to find a similar course, and get free.

Thank You, Lord, that You want us to be set free from the lies, past beliefs, and incorrect views of the world. Help us to recognize and address the areas where sin is still holding us down from living free in the fullness of who we are in Christ.

'For no other foundation can anyone lay than
that which is laid, which is Jesus Christ.'
—1 CORINTHIANS 3:11

Be Careful with Airplane TVs

Normally I'm very limited with what I see, watch, or read. I watch very limited YouTube, and no recommended channels. I don't have a TV, and I have no social media accounts. I'm even pretty careful about using iTunes, as some of the videos and movies on there are dodgy, even just while reading the title or looking at the poster image. You've got to keep yourself clean and pay attention to what you're looking at, watching, or reading. Anyways, one place where I've had some pretty terrible experiences has been on airplanes. Obviously, these were the days prior to COVID, when air travel was easy. In those days, you'd usually be crammed into the plane like sardines. Here's the thing with that, though—you can very easily see everyone else's screens. And if you go to the toilet, you'd see even more TVs. Can I just say, not everyone on the plane has the same sensibilities you do. I've more than once caught myself watching someone else's screen to see what kind of movie they were watching. Sometimes it was safe, but on numerous occasions it was pretty darn dodgy. And can I just say that on airplanes, they do cut out a lot of overt sexual scenes and the like, but there are a lot of things that aren't overt that can still be extremely dodgy. So, don't make the rookie mistake I've done—avert your eyes from airplane TVs! Fill your devices with safe movies and TV shows, or read a safe book.

Help us, Lord, to guard our eyes and to be mindful of what we see, watch, or read. Help us to make good choices about what we let into our eye gates. Help us to be strategic, careful, and wise, and to be prepared in advance for situations we cannot avoid.

See the Good/God in Everything

'You have heard that it was said to those of old, "You shall not commit adultery". But I say to you that whoever looks at a woman to lust for her has already committed adultery with her in his heart. If your right eye causes you to sin, pluck it out and cast it from you; for it is more profitable for you that one of your members perish, than for your whole body to be cast into hell.'

—MATTHEW 5:27–29

Sin Is Messy

I read an article recently about a pastor of a huge church who engaged in some indiscretions with women, and who stepped down from church leadership. The interim head of the church, in describing what had happened to their former pastor, said, 'Sin is messy'. Boy, is he right. Trust me, I'm not a perfect person, and I'm definitely still a work in progress. When I was a new Christian, I made some huge mistakes. I opened the door to sin; and trust me, when that door to sin is open, it's hard to shut, even if you want to. Part of why sin is messy is that it creeps in slowly, or it's hidden and away from accountability. I fell into sin when I was a new Christian working out my salvation, trying to make godly friends and moving away from bad ungodly relationship habits. And because at the time I was a very new Christian working out how life worked as a Christian, I just fell into the previous worldly habits I was used to, which were inconsistent with my new Christian faith. Sin is like an unending bad dream. It usually starts out as a miniscule sin, almost unnoticeable, but that makes you slightly morally compromised, then slowly gets worse and worse until you're definitely forced with a choice to do something to get rid of it, because it's taken over your life.

Help us Lord, in our weaknesses. Help us to keep far away from sin of all forms. Convict us, Holy Spirit, before we make bad decisions in our lives. Help us to have godly friends, accountable leaders, to work out our salvation quickly, and to live a life of righteousness that can only come from You, Jesus. Please, Lord, give us more wisdom. Help us to know good from evil, and to always choose the good.

> 'Do not enter the path of the wicked, and do not walk in the way of evil. Avoid it, do not travel on it; turn away from it and pass on. For they do not sleep unless they have done evil; and their sleep is taken away unless they make someone fall.'
>
> —PROVERBS 4:14–16

See the Good/God in Everything

Made in United States
Orlando, FL
28 March 2025

59928657R00177